GLOBALISM
THE GREAT WORLD CONSUMPTION

ONE WORLD GOVERNMENT, RELIGION, & ECONOMY

Church Age Global Chaos,
The Precursor to Antichrist's
Universal System

Richard R. Schmidt, D. Min., Ph.D.
Foreword By Jim Schneider

www.ProphecyFocusMinistries.com

Scripture taken from the New King James Version. Copyright © 1982 by Thomas Nelson, Inc. Used by permission. All rights reserved.

Editor in Chief: Mary Rebholtz
Cover Design By: Valori L. Schmidt

Globalism
One World Government, Religion, & Economy
Church Age Global Chaos - The Precursor to Antichrist's Universal System
ISBN-13: 9798800750959

P.O. Box 122
Hales, Corners, WI 53130
www.ProphecyFocusMinistries.com

All rights reserved. No part of this publication may be reproduced, stored in a retrieval system, or transmitted in any form or by any means—electronic, mechanical, digital, photocopy, recording, or any other—except for brief quotations in printed reviews, without the prior permission of the publisher. All internet sites that have cooperative share agreements for their content is also agreed to for reproduction and use of this content.

Prophecy Focus Ministries, Inc. is recognized by the Internal Revenue Service as a **501(c)(3)** corporation. This book is designed to advance transformational research in Biblical/theological education.
Printed in the **United States of America**

CONTENTS

INDEX OF CHARTS AND FIGURES	VII
ACKNOWLEDGEMENTS	IX
FOREWORD: Jim Schneider	XIII
PREFACE	XV

SECTION ONE:
CHURCH AGE CHAOS
THE PRECURSOR TO
ANTI-CHRIST'S GLOBAL SYSTEM

CHAPTER ONE:	1
ERILOUS/DANGEROUS TIMES:	1
SETTING THE CONDITIONS FOR GLOBALISM	
Perilous Current Events Summary:	1
Perilous Biblical Indicators:	5
2 Timothy 3:1-5	
Lovers of themselves	9
Lovers of money	11
Boasters	11
Proud	13
Blasphemers	14
Disobedient to parents	15
Unthankful	17
Unholy	18
Unloving	18
Unforgiving	20
Slanderers	20
Without self-control	22
Brutal	23
Despisers of good	24
Traitors	25
Headstrong	26
Haughty	28
Lovers of pleasure rather than lovers of God	29
Having a form of godliness but denying its power	31
And from such people turn away!	33
PREREQUISITES FOR THE	
ONE-WORLD SATANIC SYSTEM	
CHAPTER TWO:	35

DECEITFUL DOCTRINE:... 39
2 Timothy 4:1-5
    Five Biblical Commands for the Later Days
    Preach the word!.. 42
    Be ready in season and out of season........................ 43
    Convince.. 45
    Rebuke... 46
    Exhort..
    Four Additional Biblical Commands for the Later Days
    Watchful in all things.. 50
    Endure afflictions... 51
    Do the work of an evangelist....................................... 53
    Fulfill your ministry... 55

SECTION TWO:
THE PROPHETIC MANDATE FOR THE
SATANIC ONE-WORLD SYSTEM

CHAPTER THREE 59
GOD'S PROPHETIC TIMELINE
Summary of God's Prophetic Calendar............................ 60
Satan's Spiritual Fall... 64
The Great Tribulation... 65
    Satan's War in Heaven... 65
    Satan's Access to God Ends (Rev. 12:7-11)............... 67
    Satan's War on Earth (Rev. 13).................................... 68
        The Satanic Trinity.. 69
            Satan and the Antichrist.................................. 70
            Worship of the Antichrist and Satan.............. 74
                The Wound... 74
                The Period of Worship................................. 76
            Antichrist's Satanic Hatred of God.................. 77
            Antichrist's Satanic Hatred of God's Dwelling... 77
            Antichrist's Satanic Hatred of God's Saints...... 78
            Antichrist's Scope of Followers......................... 80
            Satan, Antichrist and the False Prophet........... 81
                The False Prophet's Deception.................. 81
                The False Prophet's Mission....................... 83
                The False Prophet's Methodology............. 84
                    Wonders and Miracles............................ 84
                    Mandatory Worship................................. 86
─────────────────────────────────────── 103

Mandatory Mark 87

SECTION THREE: ONE-WORLD GOVERNMENT

CHAPTER FOUR 91
COVID-19 / CORONAVIRUS PANDEMIC
Economic Impact from COVID-19 96
Historical Examination of Diseases and Plagues 99
Prophetic Guarantee of Diseases and Plagues 103
   One-Fourth of the World's Population Dies 103
   One-Half of the World's Population Dies 105
   Will Anyone Survive the Wrath of God? 107

CHAPTER FIVE 111
LAWLESSNESS
CRIME STATISTICS 112
CIVIL UNREST 119
BIBLICAL RESPONSE TO LAWLESSNESS 121
   Romans 13:1–7 121
   Titus 3:1-2 124
   2 Thessalonians 2:1–4 125
   2 Thessalonians 2:6–12 127

CHAPTER SIX 131
GENDER IDENTITY
Puberty Suppression 133
   Acronyms Associated With Gender Reassignment 133
   Definitions of Important Terminology 134
   Political & Social Pressure 135
Post-Pubescent 141
   Acronyms Associated With Gender Reassignment 141
   Definitions of Important Terminology 143
   Political & Social Pressure 144

CHAPTER SEVEN 153
CLIMATE CHANGE
A New Deception 153
Awakening Of Climate Change 157
   Position 1: 157
   Climate change is destroying the earth
   Position 2: 163
   Climate change is occurring but will not destroy the earth

ABSOLUTE PROPHETIC CLIMATE CHANGE.................................. 170

SECTION FIVE: ONE-WORLD ECONOMY

CHAPTER EIGHT.. 175
THE GREAT RESET
Economic Oversight.. 176
Government Control Implemented.. 186
    Canada's Trucker Boycott 186
    China's Social Credit Scores.. 187
The Federal Government and Digital Currency...................... 189
Conclusion... 192

APPENDIX A.. 195
Genesis 5 and 11 Genealogies
APPENDIX B.. 199
Worst Pandemics since the 1st Century
BIBLIOGRAPHY... 201
Internet Sources: No Authors Cited................................ 207

INDEX OF FIGURES

1.1	Characteristics of Perilous Times............................	8
2.1	New Testament Timeline..	38
2.2	Charge for God's Servants.....................................	39
3.1	Chronology of Gentiles, Jews, and Christians............	62
3.2	Chronology Creation to the Millennial Kingdom........	63
3.3	Chronology Crucifixion to the Millennial Kingdom.....	64
3.4	Chronology of Satan's War in Heaven.....................	66
3.5	World Empires in Daniel Two.................................	73
3.6	False Satanic Trinity...	82
5.1	Gun Violence Incidents 2014-2020..........................	113
5.2	Gun Violence by Types...	113
5.3	Active Shooter Incidents 2017-2021.......................	114
6.1	Generational Acceptance of LGBT..........................	148
7.1	USA Emissions of CO_2 by Fuel Types.....................	167
7.2	Prophetic Sets of Judgments.................................	170
7.3	Chronology Crucifixion through the Tribulation........	171
7.4	Chronology Crucifixion through Eternity Future.......	172

ACKNOWLEDGEMENTS

God placed an incredible group of people in my life whom He used to not only bring me to saving faith in the Lord Jesus Christ but to also develop my understanding of His most precious Word. When in high school, my oldest sister, Kathy (Schmidt) Papala invited me to a home Bible study, where I heard the Gospel for the first time. A few weeks later, I accepted God's free gift of salvation and gave my life to the Lord Jesus Christ.

My wonderful parents, Robert and Charlotte Schmidt, poured their lives into me, and encouraged me to serve and love the Lord. Both of them are enjoying the wonders of Heaven, because each of them accepted the Lord Jesus' gift of salvation in their teen years.

The list of my mentors covers many pastors, Bible college and seminary professors, godly Christians, and a plethora of outstanding theological authors. Dr. Sam Horn, who was my pastor for several years while he served in the Milwaukeeland area, encouraged me to start Prophecy Focus Ministries, traveling both nationally and internationally, teaching the prophetic Scriptures. Valori, my precious and talented wife and I began just that. Dr. Jimmy DeYoung encouraged me several years ago to commit my life to recording messages and writing books on the prophetic Word. He was a wonderful mentor, teacher, and encouragement in my ministry, and I love him dearly from afar, as He is now home in Heaven with His Savior, Jesus Christ. His wife Judy, and their adult children, Rick, Jody, and my very special friend Jimmy Jr., have had a great influence on our ministry, and I love these precious servants of God.

Dr. Les Lofquist, Dr. Henry Vosburgh and Pastor Chris Allen helped us get started with our first prophecy conferences. These men truly embrace helping others for the sake of the Gospel. I love these men and thank God for their ministries.

Six years ago, Valori and I made our first trip to the Pre-Tribulation Research Conference in Dallas, Texas, at the suggestion of Mary and Bernie Hertel. Mary and Bernie are two of God's choice servants who pour their lives into studying God's Word and encouraging people in ministry. Their suggestion to go to the Pre-Trib conference was extremely on target. I learned that the majority of the men who were the presenters at the conference were individuals whose many books I had read, which provided scholarly insights into the prophetic Scriptures.

Dr. Thomas Ice, Dr. Tim LaHaye, Dr. Ed Hindson, Dr. Randall Price, Dr. Arnold Fruchtenbaum, Dr. Mark Hitchcock, Dr. Andrew Woods, Dr. Michael Rydelnik and others were there in living color, and every last one was approachable, friendly, and supportive. I truly love these men and thank God for their willingness to share their wealth of knowledge with others.

My special thanks to Dr. Thomas Ice and his wonderful wife Janice. I was awestruck when first meeting this fine couple, but they treated me as a friend from the first moment we met. Dr. Ice, in my humble opinion, is the current most influential person in defending the pretribulation and premillennial interpretation of Scripture. His web site pre-trib.org carries a plethora of scholarly articles written by excellent theologians. The books he authored are some of the best available on eschatology. I highly encourage everyone to not only get and study his books and read his phenomenal articles, but to support his ministry in prayer and financially.

Several years ago, I attended a Prophecy Up Close conference in Milwaukee, sponsored by the Friends of Israel Gospel Ministry (FOI). David Levy was one of the speakers, and we immediately started a friendship. That morphed into me flying to New Jersey to meet the FOI director, Jim Showers and the director of the North America ministries, Steve Herzig. I had read many of the Friends of Israel published theological books and Bible study commentaries. The above-mentioned men, and many others in the organization, have had a very positive impact on my life. I loved traveling to Israel with FOI on their wonderful tours, to study the land of the Bible.

Dr. Randall Price and his wonderful wife Beverly, are another couple that mean the world to Valori and me. This couple serves the Lord day and night, and they have been a tremendous blessing to us. Dr. Price is one of the most intelligent men I know, and I have read his many books on prophecy, and the Temples in Jerusalem, past and prophetic. His influence in my life has grounded me in much of what I teach and preach. He is truly a scholar and a gentleman, and I thank God for this precious servant of God and his wife.

My extreme thanks to Mary Rebholz, the editor of this book. I greatly appreciate her many hours of work. If any errors are found in this book, it is strictly my failure to properly transfer her excellent detailed work.

My thanks also go to Jim Schneider, the Executive Director of VCY-America, VCY TV, and VCY-Radio. Jim has provided me the opportunity to speak on a weekly TV show Prophecy Focus, where we have aired over 100 programs on VCY-TV, and is available on the Internet at VCY.TV 24-hours a day 7-days a week. Jim Schneider also provided me the space on VCY-Radio for a 30-minute weekly show called Prophecy Unfolding. He also allowed me the wonderful opportunity to be a guest on his national radio program Crosstalk, and the local Milwaukeeland area TV program In-Focus, when I was the acting Sheriff of Milwaukee County, and now as a pastor with an eclectic background. What I appreciate most about Jim Schneider is his friendship, kindness, mentoring, his vibrant love for his family, his infectious love for Jesus Christ, the spreading of the gospel, and discipling believers in the Lord Jesus Christ.

My love and thanks to the wonderful, supportive, and loving people of Union Grove Baptist Church in Union Grove, Wisconsin, where I am humbled and thrilled to pastor. They have tirelessly worked to spread the gospel in multiple ways, and they are constantly bringing visitors virtually every Sunday. Their love for disciplining believers in the Lord Jesus is evident by the many Bible studies, adult gatherings and fellowships, youth groups, and many activities for all ages. Thank you to these dear, loving people who have a passion for serving the Lord, and a hunger to learn God's Word.

There are scores of others who have profoundly influenced my life and ministry, not the least of which are my adult children, Tabitha, Tiffany and Trevor. The one person who deserves my intense praise and thanks is Valori, my wife. It is common for an author to thank his family for their support, but this is a heartfelt commendation for the person who literally makes our ministry function. Valori is our graphic design artist, PowerPoint master, grammarian, business executive, financial planner, and she works tirelessly at every prophecy conference at our resource table. Her work is non-stop. Her love for the Lord and serving others with her robust skill set make her so much more than a business executive. She truly cares about producing for others what she and I jointly believe will help others find the Lord Jesus Christ as their Savior, and then help them learn the wonderful Word of God as He meant it to be literally understood. How blessed I am as an individual to have such a profoundly supportive wife who brings to our ministry talents and skills that God uses for His glory. Yes, I love her as my wife, and my ministry partner.

FOREWORD

As a Christian radio talk show host I have noticed a significant uptick in the intensity of the issues that are bombarding us. This intensity is only escalating with each passing day causing me to wonder, "What's next?" It is not a single battle being waged, but an all out war on numerous fronts. The attack on Biblical values, the demonizing of Christianity, the escalating lawlessness, the emerging secular agenda, and the growing control of the populace are all evidenced in this spiritual battle.

The unique aspect of these events is that the critical matters unfolding are coming from numerous sectors from all around the world. While to some they may seem incidental, accidental or disconnected, they all share a common thread. This common thread is the promotion of globalism by the powerful elite in order to have supremacy over the people, their land, government, commerce, energy and even religion.

In recent years II Timothy has become a Scriptural text I have referred to often due to its significant relevance to our times. Though written nearly 2000 years ago, the "perilous times" Paul warned of read like today's news feeds. And the solution to these perilous times is as critical as ever to "preach the Word."

What is most troubling are the churches which once stood upon the authority of God's Word are capitulating to this world's system. Doctrine has been weakened or discarded all together. Entertainment has become more important than evangelism and edification. Instead of proclaiming "Thus saith the Lord" many are mimicking the question the serpent posed to Eve in the garden, "Yea, hath God said?"

Dr. Richard Schmidt tackles these matters head on in the pages before you. Similar to the many times I have interviewed him, this book is documented fully with Scripture. He captures with great accuracy the perilous times in which we live, the crises (often manufactured) of our time which are used by desperate leaders for the purpose of gaining more power and more control. Such control mandates the surrender of individual freedom.

There is no doubt that this globalism is propelling us toward a one-world political system, a one-world economic system, and a one-world religious system. The speed by which this is all unfolding is remarkable and this book underscores its relevance to Biblical prophecy.

To believers in Christ who read this book, may it compel you to wake-up, to get serious about your faith and recognize the urgent need to share the Gospel while the opportunity is still present.

To non-believers, may this book compel you to recognize that Jesus Christ is your only hope and there is great necessity in placing your trust in Him alone for salvation, Who is "the Way, the Truth, and the Life."

PREFACE

What is truth? Pilate asked this important question when he conducted the hearing for Jesus Christ to determine is innocence or guilt of the charges the Jewish religious leadership had accused Him of committing (John 18:38). This probing question is still as valid today as it was 2,000 years ago. Citizens of countries around the world are constantly asking, "What is Truth?" Every day, the world's populace is inundated with alleged facts, delivered to them through various government sources and the media. Many people, Christians included, are in a state of panic and fear, as they digest the confusing and conflicting reports on COVID-19, public safety, climate change, global warming, economic challenges, inflation, digital currency, gender identity, and other challenging subjects.

This book will not allegorize, spiritualize, or sensationalize the sacred Scriptures. What is truth? God clearly states that His Word, the Scriptures are truth (Ps. 119:160). The following pages will examine multiple global issues from a strict Biblical perspective. Secular and Christian conspiracy theories, and speculation about the past, present, and future governmental controls continue to instill fear, panic, and at times unbiblical behavior. Truth, and only documented truth, provides understanding and the source of how one should react to what is currently taking place domestically and internationally.

The globalists who seek to implement a one-world system are very real, as documented throughout the pages of this book. However, getting their agenda to come to fruition is a massive undertaking, which involves disturbing strategic work that is taking place at this very moment. The fact that the globalists are implementing the beginning stages of the one-world system should not come as a surprise to those who embrace the pretribulation Rapture of the Church Age Christians. The stage is being set in the present, to prepare for the rising of the curtain and unveiling of the complete fulfillment of God's prophetic Word regarding the events of the seven-year Tribulation as revealed in Revelation 4:2-19:21 and many other passages in the Old and New Testament.

This book will guide the reader through the maze of current events and landmines that are leading to globalism. The pages examine relevant Biblical passages that mandate the one-world religion, government, and economy (Rev. 13), which comprise God's prophetic sovereign judgment for a world which has, is and will on a whole reject Jesus Christ. The reader is challenged to consider their response to the current and future guaranteed catastrophic conditions that will shock the conscience. This highly documented work provides factual, alarming truths, which synchronizes current events with impending Bible prophecy.

Despite the beginning stages of globalism that are absolutely in the formative stages, there is no need to fear the present or the future. There is a way to find peace and comfort in the midst of the chaos that is starting to unfold. The Scriptures provide the answer through starting and maintaining a personal relationship with the Lord Jesus Christ. The reader will find intermingled throughout this book how to start a relationship with Jesus Christ, and what He will do for all those who place their complete faith in Him. It all starts by receiving the gift of eternal life through faith lone in what Jesus accomplished through His death, burial, and resurrection. "For by grace *[God's free unmerited gift]* you have been saved *[saved from your sin and the eternal penalty of sin in the lake of fire]* through faith, and that not of yourselves; it is the gift of God, not of works *[as nothing you can do outside of exercising faith in what Jesus did for you can assure you will go to heaven]*, lest anyone should boast" (Ephesians 2:8–9).

SECTION ONE:
THE SCRIPTURAL MANDATE FOR CULTURAL DECLINE DURING THE CHURCH AGE THE PRECURSOR TO A ONE-WORLD SYSTEM

CHAPTER ONE
PERILOUS/DANGEROUS TIMES
SETTING THE CONDITIONS FOR GLOBALISM

But know this, that in the last days perilous times will come: For men will be lovers of themselves, lovers of money, boasters, proud, blasphemers, disobedient to parents, unthankful, unholy, unloving, unforgiving, slanderers, without self-control, brutal, despisers of good, traitors, headstrong, haughty, lovers of pleasure rather than lovers of God, having a form of godliness but denying its power. And from such people turn away! (2 Timothy 3:1–5)

Summary of Perilous Current Events

What constitutes "perilous times" in the last days? This book will point out many issues spoken of by the apostle Paul in 2 Timothy 3:1 that point directly to perilous times, which could also be translated "dangerous times".[1] Consider the following topics that continue to shock not only the Christian community but also conservatives who may or may not embrace a Biblical worldview. Does the worldwide reach of the COVID-19 pandemic, and the historic global changes that resulted from it, constitute the advent of perilous times? Are the volatile issues of gender identity and gender fluidity, including the propagation of lesbian, gay, bisexual, transgender, queer, intersex, and asexual (LGBTQIA) lifestyles, indicators of perilous times? The mainstream media, public schools, government officials, businesses, and activists across the U.S. and around the world aggressively promote the normalization of these constructs, which are antithetical to God's created order and design for marriage.

Is lawlessness a sign that we are in the last days? Consider the lawlessness that currently exists in the U.S. where the criminal justice system often fails to hold criminals accountable for their crimes

---

[1] Horst Robert Balz and Gerhard Schneider, *Exegetical Dictionary of the New Testament* (Grand Rapids, Mich.: Eerdmans, 1990), 452–453.

against people and property. Consider the following factors that contribute to the rise in lawlessness:
- Liberal judicial systems criminally charge a minimal number of actual offenders with a crime.
- District attorneys often defer prosecution, which means the judicial system will not, at the present time, hold the criminal accountable for the current offense, but the offender might be held accountable for the current crime if arrested again.
- Judges assign little or no bail, which expedites the release of serious offenders from jail and back to the streets.
- Courts impose minimum sentences for criminal activity. This action not only fails to deter criminal activity, it invites it.

Are the wars currently taking place around the world, conflicts discussed later in this book, evidence that the last days are upon us? Does the current war between Ukraine and Russia, and the positions of China, Iran, Syria, Turkey, and the United States point to the perilous and dangerous times referred to by the apostle Paul?

Many Christians around the world are suffering horrific persecution to the point of incarceration and torture; vigilantes burn their homes down, churches are destroyed, unconscionable crimes are committed against women and children, and thousands are literally murdered for their faith in Jesus Christ by brutal and degenerate people. The World Watch List tracks the fifty countries that have the highest rate of persecution against Christians. Though America does not fall into this category, the following worldwide persecution statistics should garner the attention of every believer in Jesus Christ.

While persecution against Christians takes many forms, it is defined as any hostility experienced as a result of identifying with Jesus Christ. From Sudan to Afghanistan, from Nigeria to North Korea, and from Colombia to India, followers of Christianity are targeted for their faith. They are attacked. They are discriminated against at work and at school. They risk sexual violence, torture, arrest, and much more.

In the first 9 months of the 2022 World Watch List reporting period, there have been:
- Over 360 million Christians living in places where they experience high levels of persecution and discrimination
- 5,898 Christians killed for their faith

- 5,110 churches and other Christian buildings attacked
- 6,175 believers detained without trial, arrested, sentenced, or imprisoned
- 3,829 Christians abducted[2]

Does this horrific treatment of Christians constitute perilous and dangerous times?

Is the globalists' alarming rhetoric regarding climate change, or global warming, and the changes implemented to address it a sign that we are in the last days? The United States stopped the Keystone pipeline that once provided the means for energy independence from other countries, but now America must once again rely on hostile countries to provide the resources necessary to supply its people with the fuel needed to function, with that fuel costing a significantly higher price than if produced at home. Does this lack of energy independence and the seeking of help from other nations point to the scenario of the last days?

Is the government and secular educational push for the critical race theory, and the once again heightened racial tensions in the United States of America, resulting in protests, riots, destruction of property, and even the loss of life, does that constitute the perilous times the apostle Paul referred to? Is the significant rise in socialism around the world, and now at an extremely accelerated pace for implementation in the United States of America, does that constitute perilous times? Is the rise of Marxism, which is the next fatal step after socialism, and the dictatorial outcomes that result pointing to the perilous times Paul warned about in 2 Timothy 3:1?

Is the abandonment of truth a sign that we are in the last days? Consider the rise in relativism, pluralism, syncretism, and dualism, and the downplaying and mockery of the Biblical worldview. The massive rise of secularism within the Christian community has resulted in a very confusing syncretism of the Scriptures with anti-Biblical doctrines and philosophies. Is this one more evidence that the perilous times of 2 Timothy 3:1 is present?

When considering that a former President of the United States made the statement that America is now in a post-Christian era, does that constitute that the world is now in perilous times? If yes, this points to the time when Jesus will return to take the Church

---

[2] 2022 World Watch List Booklet, Open Doors, https://www.opendoorsusa.org/2022-world-watch-list-report/, accessed September 20, 2022, found on page 2 of the downloaded booklet.

Age saints home with Him to heaven (1 Thess. 4:13-18; 1 Cor. 15:51-54). Is the government's initiative to implement a new digital clean currency, which gained significant traction during the COVID-19 pandemic, proof that the last days are upon us?

Is the considerable rise in executive orders from the President of the United States, which circumvents the checks and balances for which the constitution provided, a sign of the last days? Does the move towards unilateral authority to make massive policy changes, with catastrophic economic implications and consequences for the health and safety of the people, constitute perilous times?

Consider the broad use of what conservatives' term *fake news,* which is the deceptive spinning of the truth by the *liberal media*: does that constitute dangerous and perilous times? Does the significant change in technology and the massive increase in what is known as the information age constitute dangerous and perilous times? The massive increase of computers, the digitized world, social media, the internet, and the digital stronghold on power grids, industry, communication, the military, local, state, and federal security, and a plethora of other significant digital endeavors; do these things constitute perilous times?

Does the current move toward digital currencies in the United States and the potential for a global currency constitute dangerous times? Consider the significant uptick in implanting chips not only in animals but also in human beings. Digital implants, which a subsequent chapter analyzes, are rapidly increasing in popularity. The implanted chips provide access to buildings, vending machines, various personal records, and many other things where one no longer has to carry keys or cumbersome paperwork.

The Christian community must consider whether these and many other contemporary issues are setting the stage for Bible prophecy to be fulfilled, and determine the appropriate response to what I suggest are the last days of the Church Age. When you draw your conclusions regarding these issues, consider the necessity of placing yourself on a heightened state of spiritual alert, as you and your brothers and sisters in Christ carefully, and deliberately, don the appropriate spiritual armor as we daily, and hourly enter the battle to not only keep spiritually sharp but use our influence as ambassadors for the Lord Jesus Christ in the most effective manner (2 Cor. 5:20). As the war between good and evil escalates, the Christian community, during the final period of the last days, which are by Biblical definition perilous and dangerous times, must renew its spiritual vigor to accomplish the mission of the Lord Jesus Christ, "to seek and to save the lost" (Luke 19:10).

Biblical Indicators of Perilous Times

The student of the future needs only to understand the truths of God's prophetic Word contained in the Scriptures. Therefore, in the first three chapters of this book, we will examine three key Bible passages that provide the doctrinal truths and prophetic calendar of events that God's Word guarantees will take place in the future. Once we understand the chronological order of end times events, we will, in subsequent chapters, delve into current events, many of which will shock the conscience. The purpose is to accentuate the absolute necessity of God's people to take advantage of every opportunity to tell the greatest news ever given to mankind, that Christ Jesus came into the world to save sinners (1 Tim. 1:15). We also want to encourage Christians to keep serving the Lord with an unshakeable Biblical worldview, before the opportunity expires, and the one-world satanic system comes to fulfillment during the catastrophic seven-year Tribulation period.

> For the grace of God that brings salvation has appeared to all men, teaching us that, denying ungodliness and worldly lusts, we should live soberly, righteously, and godly in the present age, *looking for the blessed hope and glorious appearing of our great God and Savior Jesus Christ*, who gave Himself for us, that He might redeem us from every lawless deed and purify for Himself His own special people, zealous for good works. (Titus 2:11–14)

Second Timothy 3:1

But know this, that in the last days perilous *(dangerous)* times *(seasons)* will come.

The apostle Paul makes an emphatic statement regarding what must occur during the last days. *Know this*, is a straightforward phrase calling for the reader to pay close attention to what follows. Paul's letter carries the weight of God, as "All Scripture is given by inspiration of God, and is profitable for doctrine, for reproof, for instruction in righteousness, that the man of God may be complete, thoroughly equipped for every good work" (2 Tim. 3:16–17).

What are we to know? Paul states that in *the last days, perilous times will come.* The first question that requires an answer is, what are *the last days*? Dr. Andy Woods, a true scholar of the Scriptures and one who upholds the dispensational view, provides an interesting insight into the identity of the *last days* in an informative sermon he gave at Sugarland Bible Church in Texas, where he is the Senior Pastor.

> Now what are the last days? Many people think well, that is the seven-year tribulation period and the millennial kingdom that follows. But you see that the tribulation period is related to God's program with Israel. This is a Church Age letter written by Paul to a pastor. So he is not talking about the tribulation period and the millennial kingdom that follows. He is talking about what is going to happen as the Church Age reaches its conclusion.[3]

Dr. Woods explanation defines exactly what the apostle was writing about in 2 Timothy 3:1.[4]

Examine the indicators of the last days of the Church Age as listed in chart 1. Not one generation since the first century escaped the issues Paul presents. The historical facts show that there have always been issues with sinful humankind that bear witness to the nineteen characteristics of the last days as recorded by Paul. Why? The Scriptures make the sinful aptitude of humanity perfectly clear in a multitude of passages. Paul quotes Psalms, Proverbs, and Isaiah in Romans 3:10-18 to prove this fact.

> As it is written: "There is none righteous, no, not one; There is none who understands; There is none who seeks after God. They have all turned aside; They have together become unprofitable; There is none who does good, no, not one."
> "Their throat is an open tomb; With their tongues they have

---

[3] Andy Woods, 2 Timothy 021, The De-evolution of Man Part I, 2 Tim 3:1-2a, Sermon at Sugarland Bible Church, February 14, 2016, https://slbc.org/sermon/2-timothy-021-the-de-evolution-of-man-part-1/, accessed: Tue, Aug 16, 2022, 8:04 AM.

[4] Bible teachers who hold to a literal interpretation of Scripture, known as the dispensational interpretive model, with the caveat of parables and apocalyptic style writing where God uses stories and symbolism to illustrate literal Biblical truths, uniformly state that there is not one sign that needs to take place before the next major event on God's prophetic timeline, which is the Rapture, or snatching away of the Church Age saints (1 Thess. 4:13-18; 1 Cor. 15:51-54).

practiced deceit"; "The poison of asps is under their lips"; "Whose mouth is full of cursing and bitterness." "Their feet are swift to shed blood; Destruction and misery are in their ways; And the way of peace they have not known." "There is no fear of God before their eyes." (Rom. 3:10–18)

The apostle Paul provides a concluding statement that documents the sinful condition of every person ever born into this world except for Jesus Christ, "for all have sinned and fall short of the glory of God" (Rom. 3:23). God instructed Adam, the first person He created, to follow a specific command as recorded in Genesis 2:16-17.

And the LORD God commanded the man, saying, 'Of every tree of the garden you may freely eat; but of the tree of the knowledge of good and evil you shall not eat, for in the day that you eat of it you shall surely die.'" Adam chose to disobey God, and eat of the forbidden tree, resulting in the transmission of the sin nature down through the centuries by one's father. "Therefore, just as through one man [Adam] sin entered the world, and death through sin, and thus death spread to all men, because all sinned" (Rom. 5:12). This is the very reason Jesus Christ had to be virgin born (Isa. 7:14; Matt. 1:23), for if Jesus Christ had an earthly father, He would have inherited the sin nature, and He therefore, could not be regarded as the perfect sacrifice for sins, disqualifying Him from the ability to pay the sin debt through His crucifixion, burial, and resurrection.

It is helpful to examine the nineteen characteristics that men will exhibit in the last days. Dr. Andy Woods provides an excellent point regarding the certainty of this prophecy.

> Timothy is a pastor. Paul is describing a time when the spirit of the world will invade the church. And the church in essence will become just like the thinking and the value system of the world. Once that time hits, Timothy, and all those that are seeking to live a godly life in Christ Jesus, will encounter difficulty and danger. "But realize this, that in the last days difficult times", notice this last expression, *"will come"*. This is not something that you can opt out of.[5]

---

[5] Woods, The De-evolution of Man Part I.

> **CHARACTERISTICS OF PERILOUS TIMES**
>
> **2 TIMOTHY 3:1–5**
> But know this, that in the last days perilous times will come: for men will be:
> 1) Lovers of themselves
> 2) Lovers of money
> 3) Boasters
> 4) Proud
> 5) Blasphemers
> 6) Disobedient to parents
> 7) Unthankful
> 8) Unholy
> 9) Unloving
> 10) Unforgiving
> 11) Slanderers
> 12) Without self-control
> 13) Brutal
> 14) Despisers of good
> 15) Traitors
> 16) Headstrong
> 17) Haughty
> 18) Lovers of pleasure rather than lovers of God
> 19) Having a form of godliness but denying its power. And from such people turn away!

Figure 1.1

John MacArthur adds another important insight into this passage.

The most serious and lamentable aspect of such rejection of God and His Word is that the danger comes from *within* the church. As noted several times, near the end of his third missionary journey Paul sent for the Ephesian elders to meet with him at Miletus. Pouring out his heart to them, he warned, "I know that after my departure savage wolves will come in *among you*, not sparing the flock; and from *among your own selves* men will arise, speaking perverse things, to draw away the disciples after them" (Acts 20:29–30, emphasis added).[6]

The following definitions summarize each of the nineteen characteristics that are prevalent in the last days. Let it be a reminder of what every Christian should guard against as they seek to live a life pleasing to the Lord Jesus.

Lovers of Themselves

"Lovers of themselves" is a translation of the Greek word *philautos*, and means to love oneself or to be selfish. Human beings are self-centered by nature. However, this is antithetical to Christlike behavior, which highlights the age-old problem with human beings, that they are self-centered by nature. This is the antithesis of the attitude that is acceptable to the Lord, as documented in Matthew 20:28, "as the Son of Man did not come to be served, but to serve, and to give His life a ransom for many." The attitude of Jesus Christ was to serve, and every Christian should adopt the same attitude as the Lord. Every human being has an innate sinful nature so it is likely they will act in a selfish, all-about-me manner. Selfishness is a primary source of conflict at home, school, work, and in society. James sheds light on the results of selfish desires. "Where do wars and fights come from among you? Do they not come from your desires for pleasure that war in your members? You lust and do not have. You murder and covet and cannot obtain. You fight and war. Yet you do not have because you do not ask" (James 4:1–2).

The number one concern of many people who do not know Jesus Christ as their personal Savior, and unfortunately for many that do, is themselves. A self-absorbed lifestyle aggrandizes oneself and diminishes the value of others, and even God Himself. When one believes they are the epitome of success, or they have made themselves who they are without anyone else's help, they lose sight that God created them, and provided them with the ability to succeed (Col. 1:16). This leads to a major issue concerning how the average person attempts to go to heaven. Scripture teaches that the only way a person can go to heaven after death is through placing their faith alone in the death, burial, and resurrection of Jesus Christ to pay for their sins (John 3:16-17; Rom. 3:28; Eph. 2:8-9; Titus 3:5-

---

[6]John F. MacArthur Jr., *2 Timothy*, MacArthur New Testament Commentary (Chicago: Moody Press, 1995), 105.

6). All religions, except Biblical Christianity, teach that a person must do "good works," to have any possibility of going to heaven. The current narcissistic society has placed such a high value on self, that the majority believe they will in all likelihood go to Heaven when they die.

This writer has conducted and gone to many funerals, and has yet to go to a funeral and hear someone say that they are confident that a person did not go to heaven. The common conclusion at all funerals is that the person went to a better place. The very politically incorrect question to ask is, "How do you know they went to a better place?"

Dr. Andy Woods provides an analysis of why so many people embrace the false doctrine of works for salvation

> This is why the doctrine of works is so popular in Christianity, because it is an appeal to my pride. If I can do something to earn favor before God then I get part of the bragging rights. This is why the doctrine of grace falls into hard times in such an environment because grace means unmerited favor. If it is unmerited favor then I have nothing to boast in and that contradicts basic human pride. In fact, Paul in Romans three and verse 27, talks about the doctrine of grace and he says this, *Where then is boasting? It is excluded*. So as the church becomes like the world, they begin to demand things that appeal to a humanistic viewpoint. And understanding the church becomes identical to the world that it is supposed to reach.[7]

Raymond F. Collins describes men in the last days as "crass egocentrists."[8] Walter Lock adds, "The true centre of life is changed. Self has taken the place of God, so all sense of the duty to others, whether man or God, disappears."[9] This self-absorbed, power hungry, all about me attitude is the prerequisite for the one-world ruler who will eventually demand that everyone in the world worship and obey him, under penalty of death (Rev. 13:4, 7, 15). The

---

[7] Woods, The De-evolution of Man Part I.

[8] Raymond F. Collins, *1 & 2 Timothy and Titus: A Commentary*, ed. C. Clifton Black, M. Eugene Boring, and John T. Carroll, The New Testament Library (Louisville, KY: Westminster John Knox Press, 2012), 247.

[9] Walter Lock, *A Critical and Exegetical Commentary on the Pastoral Epistles (I & II Timothy and Titus)*, International Critical Commentary (Edinburgh: T&T Clark, 1924), 105.

Antichrist is the ultimate globalist with worldwide dictatorial power, and the means to hold the entire world accountable to his self-centered demands.

In contrast, the apostle Paul reminds Christians living in the current society to live a lifestyle that is antithetical to the self-centered narcissism permeating the contemporary anti-God culture.

> Therefore, if there is any consolation in Christ, if any comfort of love, if any fellowship of the Spirit, if any affection and mercy, fulfill my joy by being like-minded, having the same love, being of one accord, of one mind. Let nothing be done through selfish ambition or conceit, but in lowliness of mind let each esteem others better than himself. Let each of you look out not only for his own interests, but also for the interests of others. (Phil. 2:1–4)

Lovers of Money

"Lovers of money" (*philarguros*) describes those who are avaricious and greedy. Socialism's lure, before it gets a foothold in a country, appears to be the answer to those who struggle to make payments. Those who struggle to pay their bills find free medical care, free schooling, and massive government handouts very attractive. Embezzlement, tax evasion, stealing, robbery, burglary, and other such crimes stem from a love of money, which is a root of all kinds of evil (1 Tim. 6:10). Eugene Minor, in *An Exegetical Summary on 2 Timothy*, provides the following uses of the Greek word *philarguros*, as used in multiple Biblical translations including: 'money-lover,' 'lover of money,' 'money loving,' 'fond of money;' 'loving wealth,' 'lover of riches,' 'covetous,' 'avaricious,' 'greedy.' This word is also translated as a verb phrase: 'to love nothing but money,' 'to love only money,' and 'to set affections on money.'[10] In the last days of the Church Age, people shall be lovers of money, resulting in individual corrupt behavior, and a society that promotes cut-throat ambition that tramples over others in the acquisition of personal wealth.

Boasters

The Greek word *alazon,* has the meaning of boaster or-

---

[10] Eugene Minor, *An Exegetical Summary of 2 Timothy*, 2nd ed. (Dallas, TX: SIL International, 2008), 86.

braggart,[11] and describes one of the annoying human characteristics that makes the average person cringe. This characteristic, along with the others, describes the extreme self-centered, self-aggrandized, humanistic attitude of sinful humankind, which becomes exaggerated the closer this world comes to the removal of the Church Age saints, and the inauguration of the Antichrist's one-world satanically charged global system (1 Thess. 4:13-18; 1 Cor. 15:50-51; Rev. 13).

Robert W. Yarbrough provides an insightful examination of the characteristic of *boasting* in the latter days.

> The same word (*alazōn*) appears in Rom. 1:30 (and nowhere else in the New Testament). The word can also be rendered "arrogant, audacious." The verb for "boasting" (*kauchaomai*) is frequent in Paul;s writings and is usually negative, except when "boasting" or placing confidence in God (2 Cor. 10:17) or Christ (Gal. 6:14). Overall, the New Testament attitude toward haughty verbal self-promotion is summarized in Jas 4:16: "As it is, you boast in your arrogant schemes. All such boasting is evil." The sole Apostolic Fathers' occurrence of the word (1 Clement 7:2) discourages boastfulness of the tongue on this ground: "For it is better for you to be found small but included in the flock of Christ than to have a preeminent reputation and yet be excluded from his hope." For Clement as for Paul, there are not only temporal but eschatological implications for such behavior.[12]

Yarbrough's commentary rightly points out that extreme boasting will yet occur as the result of the prophetic mandate of the increase in boasting in the last days. When the Antichrist and the *false prophet* take their positions as the global leaders during the second half of the seven-year Tribulation, also called the Great Tribulation, they will not only boast about themselves, they will demand the worship of all people, with the failure to comply resulting in execution (Luke 24:21; Rev. 13; Rev. 16:13; 19:20; 20:10). The current times are perilous (2 Tim. 3:1), but the Great Tribulation, and the satanic control that will

---

[11] William Arndt et al., *A Greek-English Lexicon of the New Testament and Other Early Christian Literature* (Chicago: University of Chicago Press, 2000), 41.

[12] Robert W. Yarbrough, *The Letters to Timothy and Titus*, ed. D. A. Carson, Pillar New Testament Commentary (Grand Rapids, MI; London: William B. Eerdmans Publishing Company; Apollos, 2018), 405.

exist, constitute the most horrific, catastrophic, and terrifying events this current world will ever experience.[13]

Proud

The next Greek word *hyperēphanos,* has the meaning of being arrogant, haughty, or proud.[14] Pride characterizes many in the current society, which not only testifies to the fact of what Paul stated would occur in the last days of the Church Age, but it warns that this narcissistic behavior would increase the closer society comes to the rapture of the church, which will close out the Church Age. We turn again to Robert W. Yarbrough, who provides excellent insight into this cultural characteristic of the last days of the Church Age.

> Paul uses this word *hyperēphanos* in Rom 1:30. It occurs three other times in the NT (Luke 1:51; Jas. 4:6; 1 Pet. 5:5). James and Peter quote the word from the LXX *Septuagint*, where it occurs over three dozen times. Nearly a dozen denunciations of the arrogant in various Psalms employ this word. God's opposition to the proud is axiomatic in the Old and New Testament alike; it seems to be a human fault in all places and times. This does not mean that Timothy may simply sigh and resign himself to it, for God just as assiduously responds to it. The pastoral call is to shepherd people away from embrace of this vice.[15]

One has only to hear a political speech or listen to someone touting their personal accomplishments in a gathering of friends, a business meeting, or even a religious setting to see how a prideful attitude rears its sinful head. It has been said, *self-assessments are always flattering*. Now, that is a generalization, but unfortunately,

---

[13] The Scripture reveals that the world will literally be burned up with fire at the end of Christ's millennial kingdom (2 Peter 3:10-13) when God establishes the eternal New Heavens, New Earth, and New Jerusalem (Rev. 21:1-2). "But the day of the Lord will come as a thief in the night, in which the heavens will pass away with a great noise, and the elements will melt with fervent heat; both the earth and the works that are in it will be burned up. Therefore, since all these things will be dissolved, what manner of persons ought you to be in holy conduct and godliness, looking for and hastening the coming of the day of God, because of which the heavens will be dissolved, being on fire, and the elements will melt with fervent heat? Nevertheless we, according to His promise, look for new heavens and a new earth in which righteousness dwells" (2 Peter 3:10–13)

[14] Arndt et al., 1033.

[15] Yarbrough, *The Letters to Timothy and Titus*, 405.

the statement is altogether true way too many times, and no wonder, for the Scriptures clearly state that pride is a prominent characteristic of men in the last days of the Church Age.

Blasphemers

Blasphemer is a translation of the Greek word *blasphemos*, which describes one who defames, denigrates, demeans, or slanders another. It describes those who may believe that God exists, yet they disrespect and dishonor Him with their words. People may realize that God exists, yet their conduct rejects the giving of respect and honor to the very One who created them. However, this word actually incorporates a much broader concept than blasphemy against the Lord.

> The root word, *blasphēmos*, can be used for speech that maligns people, God, or both—Acts 6:11 uses it to describe "blasphemous words against Moses and against God." Paul describes himself with the same word in saying he "was once a blasphemer and a persecutor and a violent man" (1 Tim. 1:13). The Septuagint (the Greek translation of the Old Testament) uses tend to stress malignment of God rather than humans. This is also true of the noun form (*blasphēmia*) in its eighteen New Testament occurrences. Paul may be saying that these people are slanderous in their speech generally, whether about God or about other people.[16]

Eugene Minor found extra-biblical sources that translate the word *blasphamos* as blasphemer, reviler, and defamer. This word is also used as an adjective and translated as abusive, rude, insulting, and verbally abusive. It characterizes men who are slanderous; who rail against both God and men, using scornful language to insult them.[17] Based on the use of the word in the context of the last days, it is no mystery why defamation lawsuits regarding slander and libel are prevalent in civil and criminal litigation. The last days of the Church Age are overwhelmingly marked by selfish motives, where people in general, and especially powerful leaders take pleasure in bashing others, as the stage is being set for the horrific blasphemy that characterizes the future satanic leadership during the seven-year Tribulation (Rev. 13:5-6).

---

[16] Yarbrough, *The Letters to Timothy and Titus*, 405–406.
[17] Eugene Minor, *An Exegetical Summary of 2 Timothy*, 87.

Disobedient to Parents

The government and public schools increasingly restrict parental authority and aggressively promote children's alleged rights over those of the parents. Disobedience in children is outwardly expressed as defiance, noncompliance, rebellion, and insubordination. Children sue parents in the current society on an increasing basis. Elder abuse is a cultural disgrace where children not only ridicule and abuse parents verbally, but physically as well. The Scriptures clearly provide God's mandate regarding how parents must be treated. "Children, obey your parents in the Lord, for this is right. 'Honor your father and mother,' which is the first commandment with promise: 'that it may be well with you and you may live long on the earth'" (Eph. 6:1–3). The apostle Paul quotes Exodus 20:12 and Deuteronomy 5:16, which document God's perspective (the only one that truly matters) regarding how God commands children to treat their parents.

The Scriptures make it clear that the Christian is no longer under the law, nor justified by the law, but Christians are absolutely justified by the grace of God (Rom. 6:14-15; Gal. 2:21, 5:4). Yet the same Bible makes it clear that the moral law of God remains unchanged. Though there are 613 commandments in the Mosaic law, most of those commandments are not part of God's moral law. The Mosaic law includes commandments regarding keeping the sacrificial system, feasts, dietary requirements, purification and cleansing, Temple use requirements, and other topics that do not deal with God's moral commands. God's moral law stands on its own apart from the Mosaic law. In the Ten Commandments, God commanded the Jews to obey their parents. God has always expected children to obey their parents from the time of Adam and Eve to the present. Though the Mosaic law is no longer in effect during the Church Age (Rom. 6:14), the Biblical command to honor one's parents remains in place as reiterated by the apostle Paul. "Children, obey your parents in the Lord, for this is right. 'Honor your father and mother,' which is the first commandment with promise: 'that it may be well with you and you may live long on the earth'" (Eph. 6:1–3).

Disobedience to parents can be the result of the parents' failure to bring their children up in the nurture and admonition of the Lord (Eph. 6:4). God instituted a very specific methodology for Jewish parents to follow in rearing their children in the Mosaic law.

"Hear, O Israel: The LORD our God, the LORD is one! You shall love the LORD your God with all your heart, with all your soul, and with all your strength. "And these words which I command you today shall be in your heart. You shall teach them diligently to your children, and shall talk of them when you sit in your house, when you walk by the way, when you lie down, and when you rise up. You shall bind them as a sign on your hand, and they shall be as frontlets between your eyes. You shall write them on the doorposts of your house and on your gates. (Deut. 6:4–9)

Though Christians are not under the law, the practical application found in this profound instruction bears consideration for the Christian parent to implement. Teaching God's Word to one's children and providing them an example of a parent who loves the Lord and His Word, will reap real-time and eternal benefits for children. God's Word never returns void (Isa. 55:11; Rom. 10:17).

Subsequent chapters discuss in more detail the globalists' move to dismiss parental authority as the world moves toward a government-controlled system to rear children. The secular, anti-God, anti-Bible schools, in concert with the government's current hostility toward Christianity, even to the point of classifying Christians who believe in the sanctity of life and parental authority as domestic terrorists,[18] points to the extremely perilous times that the apostle Paul made very clear would be evident during the last days of the Church Age. Though God's people have no idea when Jesus Christ will come in the clouds to snatch up the one most fortunate generation of Christians (1 Thess. 4:13-18), they can certainly point to the current situation in America, and other places around the world, where parental authority is fading, and replaced with disregard, disrespect, and disobedience to parents. These are indeed perilous times.

---

[18] Lindsay Kornick, Fox News, AP's fact check falsely claims NSBA never requested protesting parents to be labeled as 'domestic terrorists'; Published October 6, 2021 8:49pm EDT; https://www.foxnews.com/media/ap-factcheck-claims-nsba-never-labeled-parents-domestic-terrorists; accessed September 6, 2022; 8:52PM.

Ryan Foley, Biden's education secretary urged NSBA to write letter labeling parents domestic terrorists: emails; The Christian Post; Wednesday, January 12, 2022; https://www.christianpost.com/news/biden-admin-miguel-cardona-urged-nsba-label-parents-domestic-terrorists-emails-show.html, accessed September 6, 2022, 8:56 PM CST.

Unthankful

"Unthankful" (*acharistos*) is a failure to give or verbalize thanks or appreciation. Eugene Minor discovered the Greek word translated in various writings and Bible translations as *ungrateful, devoid of gratitude,* and *with no sense of gratitude to any*. This same word can also be translated as a verb phrase: *to have no gratitude*. Unthankful carries the meaning of being ungrateful for the kindness and benefits that one receives.[19]

Robert W. Yarbrough once again provides an insightful analysis of the Biblical meaning of unthankful.

> The concept is not obscure: people who should be thankful, whether to God or to others, are neither. Fundamental to both OT and NT spirituality is the posture called for by Paul: "Give thanks [= be grateful] in all circumstances; for this is God's will for you in Christ Jesus" (1 Thess 5:18). In the OT this exhortation often takes the form of encouragement to praise (over a hundred times in the LXX *[Septuagint: Greek translation of the OT])*. The world stands under God's wrath, Paul writes, because "although they knew God, they neither glorified him as God nor gave thanks to him" (Rom 1:21). People are frequently ungrateful, despite all that God provides.[20]

Unthankful characterizes those in the current culture who have an entitled mindset. People who believe God, country, and parents owe them, do not see things with a thankful attitude, but with a selfish, you-better-provide-for-me attitude, which is the antithesis of a Biblical worldview. Unthankful, entitled people, personify the brashness that is prevalent in the current culture. Many who live in America believe the government owes them free medical care, free schooling, free food, rent assistance, energy assistance, and the list goes on. Able-bodied people who believe that government funds, which come from taxpayers who work hard, should be given to them for whatever their reasons, once again confirms that people in the last days are self-absorbed, prideful, entitled, and yes, unthankful.

There are individuals with serious physical and or mental health issues that need assistance with resources. Individuals that

---

[19] Eugene Minor, *An Exegetical Summary of 2 Timothy*, 87.
[20] Robert W. Yarbrough, *The Letters to Timothy and Titus*, 406.

comprise this category, and have no ability to go to work and earn compensation, are not the ones pointed out in this section. Those who do suffer from disabilities and special needs should find care from family, friends, and government assistance. Yet, the fact remains that all people should thank God for His provisions (Eph. 5:20; Col. 3:15; 1 Thess. 5:18).

Unholy

The Greek word *anosios*, means to be in opposition to God or what is sacred, and translators properly translate the word as *unholy*. Unholy carries the meaning that certain actions make beings or places off limits to their agents *and* invites the connotation of moral turpitude: *wicked,* i.e., revolting to God or to a well-minded person.[21] Profane, irreligious, irreverent, impious, devoid of piety, godless, wicked, and having no respect for divine things all define the term *unholy*.[22] Unholy "also carries the idea not so much of irreligion as of gross indecency. It was used of a person who refused to bury a dead body or who committed incest. The unholy person is driven by self-love to gratify his lusts and passions of whatever sort, as fully as possible with no thought to propriety, decency, or personal reputation."[23]

God's Word commands God's people to be holy, and to separate from unholy, sinful, secular cultural norms.

> As obedient children, not conforming yourselves to the former lusts, as in your ignorance; but as He who called you is holy, you also be holy in all your conduct, because it is written, "Be holy, for I am holy." 1 Pet. 1:14-16

The term *unholy* simply means lacking holiness, which translates in practical living to people following carnal behavior, without regard for the behavior God expects. Unholy living expands in many directions resulting in carnal, sinful, anti-God behavior, which certainly supports the statement of the apostle Paul that in the later days, perilous times will come (2 Tim. 3:1).

Unloving

"Unloving" is translated from the Greek word a*storgos*, meaning one who is lacking in good feelings for others, thereby

---

[21] Arndt et al., 86.
[22] Eugene Minor, *An Exegetical Summary of 2 Timothy*, 87.
[23] MacArthur Jr., *2 Timothy*, 114.

jeopardizing the maintenance of relationships (political and familial) that are essential to a well-ordered society; *hardhearted, unfeeling, without regard for others.*"[24]

Unloving translates *astorgos*, a negative adjective form of the verb *storgē*, which commonly was used of family, social, and patriotic love. The noted theologian Benjamin Warfield described it as "that quiet and abiding feeling within us, which, resting on an object as near to us, recognizes that we are closely bound up with it and takes satisfaction in its recognition." It is not natural for people to love God or the things and people of God, but it *is* natural for them to love their own families. To be *astorgos* is therefore to be "without natural affection" (KJV). Just as the self-loving person is without common decency, he also is without common affection. He cares nothing for the welfare of those who should be dearest to him. His only interest in them is for what he believes they can do for him. To be unloving is to be heartless.[25]

Paul uses the same word in Rom. 1:31. It points to abject godlessness, since love is at the core of God's identity and of what he calls for from people—in particular, from his people. A capacity for love is part of the image of God; when people suppress it and even replace it with the opposite, it is a sign of a hard and sinister turn away from their Creator.[26]

Once again, the apostle Paul points to the extremely selfish nature of humans in an anti-God society.

This lack of love in the last days of the Church Age eventually morphs into a lawless society that prevails during the seven-year Tribulation. The satanic globalist, the Antichrist, will run a chaotic, lawless society, where hatred, violence, and massive numbers of murders are the norm, not the exception. Jesus Himself, a few days before His crucifixion, spoke to His disciples prophetically regarding the horrific conditions that are yet to take place during the Tribulation.

"Then they will deliver you up to tribulation and kill you, and you will be hated by all nations for My name's sake. And then many will be offended, will betray one another, and will hate

---

[24] Arndt et al., 145–146.
[25] MacArthur Jr., *2 Timothy*, 114.
[26] Robert W. Yarbrough, *The Letters to Timothy and Titus*, 407.

one another. Then many false prophets will rise up and deceive many. And because lawlessness will abound, the love of many will grow cold. But he who endures to the end shall be saved. (Matt. 24:9–13)

Later in this book, we will cover in greater detail the rise of lawlessness in America. Globalism will eventually lead to anarchy, and the prerequisite is already in place in the unloving society of the later days of the Church Age, which appear to be upon us.

Unforgiving

The next Greek word *aspondos*, speaks of one who is unwilling to negotiate a solution to a problem involving a second party, *irreconcilable*.[27] One of the most disturbing things in the current Church Age is that many Christians refuse to forgive others. The lack of forgiveness is epidemic, resulting in resentments, family and church splits, and conflicts with neighbors, schoolmates, and work associates. The concept of humbling oneself, and forgiving the unruly person, is rare in both the secular and Christian realms. Why does this sad condition of the heart exist even among Christians? The answer is simple, yet disturbing. In the later days of the Church Age, people will refuse to forgive others, and will instead live in disobedience to God.

The apostle Paul exhorts the Christian to move beyond selfish behavior and forgive those who offend.

> Therefore, as the elect of God, holy and beloved, put on tender mercies, kindness, humility, meekness, longsuffering; bearing with one another, and forgiving one another, if anyone has a complaint against another; even as Christ forgave you, so you also must do. But above all these things put on love, which is the bond of perfection.
> (Col. 3:12–14)

May God convict those who choose to hold grudges and exercise an unforgiving spirit, resulting in one of the seven things God hates, disunity among the brethren (Prov. 6:19).

Slanderers

Diabolos, the Greek word translated in this passage as "slanderers," means *slanderous*, one who engages in slander, and is

---

[27] Arndt et al., 144.

also used for the title of the principal transcendent evil being *the adversary/devil.*[28]

Gossip is often thought of as being relatively harmless, but at best it is unkind, harmful, and ungodly. Malicious gossip is a sin of an even more evil and destructive sort. Whereas the irreconcilable person tends to disregard and neglect others, malicious gossips make a point of harming others. Whether to promote their own interests, to express jealousy or hatred, or simply to vent their anger, they take perverse pleasure in damaging reputations and destroying lives.

Malicious gossips translates *diabolos*, which, even to the person unacquainted with Greek, suggests the severity of this evil, with our English derivative "diabolical." *Diabolos* means "accuser" and is used thirty-four times in the New Testament as a title for Satan. Engulfed and blinded by self-love, malicious gossips do the very work of Satan.[29]

Slander is the oral presentation of something that is false, resulting in harm to the person slandered. Libel speaks to the offense of putting into writing a false accusation or statement regarding another person. This behavior results in many people, including Christians filing defamation suits. Some of this behavior is criminal, and some results in civil suits, which are defined as noncriminal litigation. This is another indicator of the selfish, mean-spirited, ungodly, prevalent behavior in the later days.

God's Word is very specific regarding what should come out of a Christian's mouth. In one very long sentence, the apostle Paul outlines what Christians should allow themselves to state, and the associated attitude.

And He Himself gave some to be apostles, some prophets, some evangelists, and some pastors and teachers, for the equipping of the saints for the work of ministry, for the edifying of the body of Christ, till we all come to the unity of the faith and of the knowledge of the Son of God, to a perfect man, to the measure of the stature of the fullness of Christ; that we should no longer be children, tossed to and fro and carried about with every wind of doctrine, by the trickery of men, in the cunning craftiness of deceitful plotting, *but,*

---

[28] Arndt et al., 226.
[29] MacArthur Jr., *2 Timothy*, 115.

> *speaking the truth in love*, may grow up in all things into Him who is the head—Christ—from whom the whole body, joined and knit together by what every joint supplies, according to the effective working by which every part does its share, causes growth of the body for the edifying of itself in love. (Eph. 4:11–16)

The essence of what one should speak is the *truth*, and the delivery of the *truth* must be with the attitude of *love*. This is a non-negotiable command. Failure to treat others with respect, and instead willfully speak falsely against someone with the intent to hurt their feelings and potentially cause them harm (on purpose or as an unintended consequence) is another unfortunate characteristic that the perilous times of the later days have come.

Without self-control

The Greek word *akratas*, means *without self-control, dissolute,*[30] lacking in self-control, uncontrolled, unrestrained, violent, licentious, profligate, dissolute, and with no control over their own passions. Though the word indicates lack of self-control in a broad sense, it especially refers to lacking control of bodily desires, one's own drives and impulses, one's passions; it means to be profligate, or dissolute. However, it has far more than just sensual implications and includes intemperateness, and lack of control of the tongue, the appetite, and all other aspects of our life.[31]

This one concept has very far-reaching implications: sexual promiscuity, violence, substance abuse, stealing, slander, libel, cursing, hatred, refusal to get along with others, and so on. The apostle Paul reminds Christians regarding behaviors they must remove, which requires walking with the Lord, and personal discipline.

> That you put off, concerning your former conduct, the old man which grows corrupt according to the deceitful lusts, and be renewed in the spirit of your mind, and that you put on the new man which was created according to God, in true righteousness and holiness. (Eph. 4:22–24)

> But now you yourselves are to put off all these: anger, wrath, malice, blasphemy, filthy language out of your mouth. Do not

---

[30] Arndt et al., 38.
[31] Eugene Minor, *An Exegetical Summary of 2 Timothy*, 88.

lie to one another, since you have put off the old man with his deeds, and have put on the new man who is renewed in knowledge according to the image of Him who created him. (Col. 3:8–10)

The apostle Paul provides the answer for those who believe self-discipline is an impossible task. Philippians 4:13 states, "I can do all things through Christ who strengthens me." He further states under the inspiration of the Holy Spirit, "No temptation has overtaken you except such as is common to man; but God is faithful, who will not allow you to be tempted beyond what you are able, but with the temptation will also make the way of escape, that you may be able to bear it" (1 Cor. 10:13).

Brutal

Anēmeros is the Greek word translated as fierce, brutal, and savage.[32] Brutal is "better translated 'without gentleness.' People would become like untamed beasts in the last days. Think of an animal that just devours its prey with no sense of sympathy, no sense of mercy, no sense of consciousness, no sense of anything other than that animal's appetite and that, in essence, is what people become like without God."[33] Once again, this characteristic speaks to the violent tendencies during the later days of the Church Age. Perilous, dangerous times are the norm in many urban environments; the violence finds its way into rural areas as well.

The horrific violent crimes that fill the headlines are too awful to describe. However, hiding from the truth, and attempting to persuade yourself that you or those you care about and love are not potential victims in this brutal society is to deny reality. Every day brutal criminals, whose hearts are calloused and insensitive, attack innocent people and commit horrific crimes including murder. This scary, yet all too frequent occurrence of violent, brutal crimes, validates what Paul stated would be evident in the later days.

Raymond Collins provides instructional thoughts on this characteristic of the later days.

> Classic authors used the adjective to describe those who could not contain their anger (Thucydides), their tongue

---

[32] Swanson, *Dictionary of Biblical Languages with Semantic Domains: Greek*.

[33] Woods, The De-evolution of Man, Part 2, 2-21-16 2 Timothy 2:2b-3 Lesson 22.

(Aeschylus), or their love for wine (Xenophon, Aristotle). "Uncivilized" (*anēmeroi*) is a term that is used of wild and savage animals or of uncultivated plants that grow wildly. Used derogatorily of humans, it describes people who lack common politeness and gentleness, people who act as if they are not civilized. Those who lack any love for the good would be those whom contemporary authors might describe as having no orientation whatsoever toward the moral good.[34]

What a sad state of affairs that in the midst of the age of grace the world is degenerating into a vile, brutal, uncaring culture where public safety is becoming more of an exception than the rule. We are indeed living in perilous, dangerous times.

Despisers of good

The Greek word *aphilayathos*, means *without interest in the public good;* a description of persons who are the opposite of public expectation.[35] The Bible uses the word *good* 796 times, in multiple contexts, in contrast to the word *bad*, which appears only 44 times. Paul states in Galatians 6:10, "Therefore, as we have opportunity, let us do good to all, especially to those who are of the household of faith." In Ephesians 2:10, Paul writes, "For we are His workmanship, created in Christ Jesus for good works, which God prepared beforehand that we should walk in them." In Ephesians 4:29–32, Paul exhorts believers in appropriate behavior by stating, "Let no corrupt word proceed out of your mouth, but what is good for necessary edification, that it may impart grace to the hearers. And do not grieve the Holy Spirit of God, by whom you were sealed for the day of redemption. Let all bitterness, wrath, anger, clamor, and evil speaking be put away from you, with all malice. And be kind to one another, tenderhearted, forgiving one another, even as God in Christ forgave you." Many such passages in the inspired Scriptures define the standard for godly living in the last days of the Church Age.

Those who despise what is good embrace that which is antithetical to godly, Biblical behavior. A summary study of Romans 1 reveals the three-step path towards despising all that is good. First, the apostle Paul refers to general revelation in nature that all people

---

[34] Raymond F. Collins, *1 & 2 Timothy and Titus: A Commentary*, ed. C. Clifton Black, M. Eugene Boring, and John T. Carroll, The New Testament Library (Louisville, KY: Westminster John Knox Press, 2012), 248.

[35] Arndt et al., 157.

observe, which reflects the existence of a Creator. The wonders and intricacies of the physical universe should lead a person to conclude that there must be a God (Rom. 1:20). The Bible says, however, that they "suppress the truth in unrighteousness". That is, they reject God's general revelation of Himself. They often, instead, embrace evolution and degenerate into idolatry, inventing their own gods (Rom. 1:23-25). The rejection of God leads to the second step of spiritual degeneration, which is obsession with vile passions. Paul reveals exactly why the current society is embracing what he calls *vile passions* (Rom. 1:26), which he pointedly stated was women having intimate relations with women, and men having intimate relations with men. That which God stated was good in Genesis 1-2, including the marriage of one man to one woman, is rejected in a society where vile passions replace intimacy in marriage. Paul concludes with a summary of the final rejection of all that is good, and the horrible third step of ungodly, degenerate behavior.

> And even as they did not like to retain God in their knowledge, God gave them over to a debased mind, to do those things which are not fitting; being filled with all unrighteousness, sexual immorality, wickedness, covetousness, maliciousness; full of envy, murder, strife, deceit, evil-mindedness; they are whisperers, backbiters, haters of God, violent, proud, boasters, inventors of evil things, disobedient to parents, undiscerning, untrustworthy, unloving, unforgiving, unmerciful; who, knowing the righteous judgment of God, that those who practice such things are deserving of death, not only do the same but also approve of those who practice them. (Rom. 1:28-32)

The prophet Isaiah summed up this issue by stating, "Woe to those who call evil good, and good evil; Who put darkness for light, and light for darkness; Who put bitter for sweet, and sweet for bitter!" (Isa. 5:20)

Traitors

Prodotas is the Greek word translated *traitor*, or *betrayer*,[36] which is one of the worst behaviors known to humankind, and will be the norm in the last days. Richard Yarbrough provides an instructive analysis of this last days characteristic.

---
[36] Arndt et al., 867.

"Treacherous." This translation of a form of *prodotēs* (traitor, betrayer) preserves symmetry with other words in the list, which are mostly adjectives. Yet, it is not an adjective but a noun: "[These people are] traitors, betrayers." "Treacherous" (NIV) certainly captures the thought, but the wording is perhaps even more denunciatory. The two other NT uses of the word describe Judas, "who became a *traitor*" (Luke 6:16), and those who were about to stone Stephen ("*betrayers* and murderers" of "the Righteous One"; Acts 7:52 NASB). Paul is not flagging insignificant foibles or describing abstract qualities.[37]

Betrayal is nothing new in society. However, in the last days, betrayal becomes commonplace. Honor, duty, family, country, freedom, and God are words that use to carry great meaning in America. Men and women have gone to war and given their lives to fight for those principles. The globalist mentality replaces those concepts with a centralized dictator who is the only one that all people must follow or suffer retribution. This is the exact scenario that will come to fulfillment during the seven-year Tribulation period (Rev. 13).

Jesus Himself described the out-of-control behavior that will take place during the Tribulation. "Then they will deliver you up to tribulation and kill you, and you will be hated by all nations for My name's sake. And then many will be offended, will betray one another, and will hate one another" (Matt. 24:9–10). The prerequisite behavior is in place during the perilous later days of the Church Age that will exponentially increase after the Church Age and during the satanically charged end times that will come to fulfillment during the catastrophic seven-year Tribulation.

Headstrong

"Headstrong" comes from the Greek word *propetas*, and literally means falling down or forward; pertaining to being impetuous, *rash, reckless, thoughtless.*[38] In addition, the word carries

---

[37] Robert W. Yarbrough, *The Letters to Timothy and Titus*, 409.
[38] Arndt et al., 873.

the meaning of reckless in speech and action,[39] foolhardy, and heady, an old English concept in the KJV.[40]

Dr. Woods provides an excellent visual of the concept of the root meaning of this word, which is actually to *lean forward*. "Paul says in the last days people would 'lean forward,' they are using 'lean forward' to describe so-called progress. But Paul says 'in the last days' people would not only 'lean forward,' they would fall forward, that basically means quick to run ahead rather than to think. It is talking about a population of people that are impulse driven; rash would be another translation of this."[41]

The current culture practices rash, impulsive behavior on a continual basis. One can hardly drive down any urban street or expressway without someone tailgating, speeding, or becoming enraged if another driver is going the speed limit or accidentally cuts them off. The enraged impulsive driver may shoot the other driver, cut them off, force them to stop, or violently assault them, even though they may have simply made an honest mistake.

Domestic violence is a scourge on society. Men, and yes women, become enraged with their spouse, significant other, children, parents, or guardians and impulsively lash out, not only with screaming and yelling, but with violent attacks that end in serious injury or death. This headstrong, impulsive, rash behavior ruins relationships, splits families, destroys friendships, and is another indicator of the last days of the Church Age. It also sets the tone for the chaos that becomes the norm during the seven-year Tribulation.

Thousands of people are murdered and violently assaulted every year simply because someone was offended. The offended person, instead of thinking through their actions and the repercussions of them, acts rashly, pulls out a weapon, and seriously harms or kills the person, or physically beats them. The horrific rise in crime and lawlessness is covered in a later chapter. Needless to

---

[39] Walter Lock, *A Critical and Exegetical Commentary on the Pastoral Epistles (I & II Timothy and Titus)*, International Critical Commentary (Edinburgh: T&T Clark, 1924), 106.

[40] Eugene Minor, *An Exegetical Summary of 2 Timothy*, 2nd ed. (Dallas, TX: SIL International, 2008), 89.

[41] Andy Woods, The Call to Persevere, February 28, 2016, 2 Timothy 3:4-9 Lesson 23 2-28-16, De-evolution of Man, Part 3, https://slbc.org/sermon/2-timothy-023-the-de-evolution-of-man-part-3/ , accessed September 7, 2022, 12:15PM.

say, people see in living color, virtually every day, headstrong, rash, impulsive behavior that results in horrific outcomes. The impulsive, all-about-me culture, is setting the stage for a massive increase in impulsive violence, where murder and assault will rise to an unprecedented level (Rev. 6:3-4).

Haughty
The next Greek word, *typhoomai*, carries the meaning of extremely proud, conceited, foolish, and stupid.[42] This characteristic of the last days accentuates the self-centered, prideful attitude that permeates the American culture. Certainly, there are many humble people, and many who suffer from depression that do not overtly personify a haughty, prideful attitude. However, sinful nature craves attention, validation, and the praise of others. The Scriptures remind believers in the Lord Jesus Christ to exercise humility in the same manner as Jesus.

> Let this mind be in you which was also in Christ Jesus, who, being in the form of God, did not consider it robbery to be equal with God, but made Himself of no reputation, taking the form of a bondservant, and coming in the likeness of men. And being found in appearance as a man, He humbled Himself and became obedient to the point of death, even the death of the cross. (Phil. 2:5–8)

Raymond Collins adds important thoughts regarding one who openly expresses a haughty attitude.

> The idea underlying the metaphor, if not the imagery, is similar to ideas expressed by Paul in 1 Corinthians. He used the verb *physioō*, "to puff up [with pride]," to describe those whose attitude was disruptive of good order in the community (1 Cor. 4:6, 18, 19; 5:2; 8:1; 13:4). The Pastor similarly uses the verb *typhoomai*, "to be surrounded by smoke," metaphorically to describe people whose ambition and vainglory leads them to be deluded (see 1 Tim. 3:6; 6:4). Philo also used the term with this metaphorical meaning, especially in describing an orator who is so caught up in the art of his rhetoric that he is unable to perceive the truth. For Philo, "pride" (*typhos*) is a source of many kinds of evil, even contempt for divine realities (see *Decalogue* 4–6).

---

[42] Swanson.

The name of the Egyptian god Typhon is derived from the verb *typhoomai*. Greek mythology speaks of Typhon, a many-headed (often a hundred snake heads) fiery monster who threatened the supremacy of Zeus. He was slain by a bolt of thunder and buried under Mount Etna. Typhon appears as a wicked god, the son of Gaia and Tartarus, in some Greek myths.[43]

The Scriptures warn those who choose to exhibit a prideful, haughty attitude. "Pride goes before destruction, and a haughty spirit before a fall" (Prov. 16:18). Though God warned about the outcome of the haughty person, Paul makes the case that prideful attitudes simply testify to the fact that the last days of the Church Age have come.

Lovers of pleasure rather than lovers of God

"Lovers of pleasure" comes from the Greek word *philadonos*, and carries the meaning of having a special interest in pleasure, *loving pleasure*,[44] pleasure-loving, preferring one's own pleasure, devoted to pleasure, and given over to pleasure.[45] The phrase stands on its own as it describes the spiritual conflict between doing what one desires instead of what God desires. Do I want to read the Bible or watch television, play video games, surf the internet, sleep, go to the bar, hang out, or whatever else brings pleasure? Do I choose to pray at least sometime during the day or night and seek God, or totally ignore the Lord and chat with someone else? Do I go to the local Bible-believing church on Sunday or do I sleep in, play sports, or engage in my favorite recreational activity? These are not only questions for non-Christians, but for Christians.

Those who have not received the free gift of eternal life by realizing that they are a sinner (Rom. 3:23), deserving of eternal separation from God in the lake of fire, also known as Hell (Rom.6:23; Rev. 21:8), and have not to this point embraced the fact that Jesus Christ, God's Son, came down from heaven's glory, took on the form of a human being, was subsequently crucified, buried, and rose from the dead three days later (1 Cor. 15:3-4) have no reason yet to engage in spiritual behavior. However, when people understand the concepts just stated, which are the elements of the gospel, and

---

[43] Raymond F. Collins, *1 & 2 Timothy and Titus: A Commentary*, 249.
[44] Arndt et al., 1057.
[45] Eugene Minor, *An Exegetical Summary of 2 Timothy*.

decide to embrace by faith what Jesus did for them, by accepting the free gift of eternal life, then there should be a change in their desire to become lovers of God rather than lovers of pleasure.

The apostle Paul provides the extremely important methodology for someone to change their desires from seeking pleasure to seeking a relationship with Jesus Christ. Carefully read the following two verses. "For by grace you have been saved through faith, and that not of yourselves; it is the gift of God, not of works, lest anyone should boast" (Eph. 2:8–9). Let us add a few helping phrases to the verses to define exactly what Paul is stating. For by grace,[*God's free unmerited gift*], you have been saved, [*saved from sin and the penalty of sin*], through faith, [*faith is believing something to be true that you cannot see*], and that not of yourselves, [*nothing you do can take you to heaven including going to church, baptism, the Lord's table, being good to others, etc.*]; it is the gift of God, [*a gift is something you reach out and take, nothing else is required*], not of works, [*Paul once again makes it clear nothing you do part from faith has any merit with God in securing heaven as your home*], lest anyone should boast, [*God wants us only to recognize what His Son Jesus Christ did for us, as Jesus' death, burial and resurrection paid the entire penalty for our sin*]. If you have never received the gift of eternal life by placing your faith in what Jesus did for you, would you consider doing so at this very moment?

I love the verse John 3:16, which helps one understand what Jesus did. "For God so loved the world, that He gave His only begotten Son, that whosoever believes in Him should not perish, but have everlasting life." Consider the following helps. For God so loved the world [*(Rich) put your name in the blank*], the world, that He, [*God the Father*], gave His only begotten Son, [*God sent His Son Jesus Christ to this earth for the sole purpose of paying the sin debt that every person has*], that whosoever [*(Rich) put your name in the blank*], believes in Him, [*believes in His death, burial and resurrection*], should not perish [*or spend eternity in the lake of fire/Hell*], but have everlasting life [*enjoying God's eternal presence*]. If you have never received the free gift of eternal life, how about doing it right now? Maybe you would like to let the Lord know what you are doing in your heart right now. I invite you to let the Lord know your heart's desire and am providing a simple prayer you may want to speak to the Lord. The prayer is not a special incantation, nor will simply reciting it get you to Heaven, but, if you truly by faith are ready to receive the gift of eternal life, you may want to thank the Lord with these thoughts.

> *Dear God, I understand that I am a sinner, and nothing good that I have done will pay for my sins. I also know that because I have sinned, that I not only do not deserve to go to Heaven, but there is nothing I can do to pay my sin debt. I fully realize I deserve eternal punishment and separation from you for eternity. However, I believe by faith that Jesus Christ is Your Son, and that He came down from Heaven, took on a human body, and was subsequently crucified, buried, and rose from the dead three days later to pay the entire penalty for my sin. I have by faith received your free gift of eternal life. Thank you for saving me from my sins, and the penalty of sin, and promising to take me to Heaven when I die.*

If you just placed your faith in Christ and received His free gift of eternal life, may I encourage you to contact me at Rich@ProphecyFocusMinistries.com, and I will send you free of charge some helpful resources to get you started in your walk with God.

Having a form of godliness but denying its power

The word *form* comes from the Greek word *morphosis*, which means being formally structured, *embodiment, formulation, form,* of teachers of error *who maintain a form of piety* (2 Tim. 3:5).[46] The simplistic way of defining this characteristic of the later days is someone seemingly associated with God, but not authentically knowing Him. Cultural Christianity might be one of the most diabolical tools of Satan in these last days of the Church Age. Children grow up going to church, they hear the right things, and they learn how to act like a Christian. They know the right lingo to use. They might even go to a so-called Christian school where the administrators and teachers tell them how they should act and what God requires of them. Many young people are indoctrinated with harsh do's and don'ts, and they know what is expected of them in a Christian culture, but their hearts are far removed from the religious lifestyle they are encouraged to live.

---

[46] Arndt et al., 132.

George Barna, in cooperation with Arizona Christian University regarding the worldview of alleged Bible-believing pastors, reports the following statistics.

But a new nationwide survey among a representative sample of America's Christian pastors shows that a large majority of those pastors do not possess a biblical worldview. In fact, just slightly more than a third (37%) have a biblical worldview and the majority—62%—possess a hybrid worldview known as Syncretism. The new findings come from the American Worldview Inventory 2022, conducted by the Cultural Research Center at Arizona Christian University, and administered to 1,000 Christian pastors to better understand the worldviews that drive their thinking and behavior.[47]

The result of cultural Christianity is that there are many "wolves in sheep's clothing"; that is, many shepherds (pastors) who are misleading their flocks (congregations), turning them away from authentic Biblical Christianity. This is the essence of globalism, and the one-world religion, which will become a reality during the Tribulation. The apostle John writes that the world, except for those who come to faith in the Lord Jesus, will worship Satan and the Antichrist, whom John calls *the beast*, during the Great Tribulation. (Matt. 21:24; Rev. 13:4, 8). The Antichrist will demand to be worshiped when he implements the one-world government, the one-world economy, and the one-world religion (Rev. 13:15).

The world, including America, is overrun with churches, religions, and people who base their personal beliefs on their own personal desires, not on Biblical truth. This is a form of godliness, but in essence, is a ruse. Many individuals have replaced Biblical Christianity, and the associated Biblical worldview, with a syncretistic pluralism that combines the Bible and secularism. This is the globalists' dream come true, as those who hold to socialism, Marxism, and a worldwide system, replace the rightful authority of the Bible with the demands of secular humanism. God does not comply with the cultural demands of contemporary society. The Scriptures clearly state that Jesus said, "I am the way, the truth, and the life. No one comes to the Father except through Me" (John 14:6).

---

[47] George Barna, Release #5: Shocking Results Concerning the Worldview of Christian Pastors, May 10, 2022, https://www.arizonachristian.edu/wp-content/uploads/2022/05/AWVI2022_Release05_Digital.pdf, accessed September 7, 2022, 7:26 PM CST.

Then Peter, filled with the Holy Spirit, said to them, "Rulers of the people and elders of Israel: If we this day are judged for a good deed done to a helpless man, by what means he has been made well, let it be known to you all, and to all the people of Israel, that by the name of Jesus Christ of Nazareth, whom you crucified, whom God raised from the dead, by Him this man stands here before you whole. This is the 'stone which was rejected by you builders, which has become the chief cornerstone.' Nor is there salvation in any other, for there is no other name under heaven given among men by which we must be saved." (Acts 4:8–12)

Secular society wants to go to heaven on their terms, including their religion, morality, ethics, and unbiblical beliefs. The God of the Bible has determined the path that leads to heaven; that is, by trusting in His Son, who left heaven, took on human form, was horribly treated, and ultimately gave His life for the remission of sins. This truth is politically incorrect but biblically spot on.

And from such people turn away!

"Turn Away" *(apotropo)* carries the definition of purposely avoiding or associating with someone, *turn away from, avoid*.[48] God makes this statement to warn the Christian community that the nineteen characteristics of the last days of the Church Age are enticing, and have the ability to corrupt God's people if embraced. As the Church Age comes to a close, God's people must stand firm on Biblical principles, and not fall prey to the globalists who are working day and night to establish a one-world government, one-world economy, and one-world religion. These things will unequivocally come to fulfillment when Satan, Antichrist, and the false prophet dominate the world scene during the great Tribulation (Revelation 13).

---

[48] Arndt et al., 124.

PREREQUISITES FOR THE ONE-WORLD SATANIC SYSTEM

CHAPTER TWO
DECEITFUL DOCTRINE

I charge you therefore before God and the Lord Jesus Christ, who will judge the living and the dead at His appearing and His kingdom: Preach the word! Be ready in season and out of season. Convince, rebuke, exhort, with all longsuffering and teaching. For the time will come when they will not endure sound doctrine, but according to their own desires, because they have itching ears, they will heap up for themselves teachers; and they will turn their ears away from the truth, and be turned aside to fables. But you be watchful in all things, endure afflictions, do the work of an evangelist, fulfill your ministry. (2 Tim. 4:1–5)

The apostle Paul was approaching the final days of his life when he delivered this very solemn message to Timothy, his son in the faith (1 Tim. 1:2). Paul understood the conditions that would exist in the later days of the Church Age, as he wrote this letter under the inspiration of the Holy Spirit (2 Tim. 3:16) nearly two millennia ago. Paul impresses on Timothy the necessity to equip the final generations of Christians, who will live through the perilous last days of the Church Age. He provides a set of nine commands, which, if God's servants will obey them, will help them to be effective for the cause of Christ while facing extreme opposition from those who reject a biblical worldview.

In the previous chapter, we looked at the horrific conditions that will exist on this earth during the later days of the Church Age, and now it is incumbent upon us to get the biblical counsel on how those of us in the midst of these perilous, dangerous times must choose to live our lives. Despite the fact of persecution and suffering projected upon believers in the Lord Jesus Christ in the last days, Paul makes the plea for Timothy to follow nine imperatives amid an increasing marginalizing of the gospel of the Lord Jesus Christ. Why? Despite the extremely difficult environment in this post-Christian era, God's people must still stand strong in the faith. Christians must encourage one another to do everything possible to fulfill the Lord's mission, which is to reach out to those, who at this point in their lives, have either rejected the gospel, or literally have not heard the gospel (Luke 19:10; 1 Tim. 1:15). God's people must encourage those who have yet to receive the free gift of eternal life to place their faith in the death, burial, and resurrection of Jesus Christ, providing the exclusive way to heaven (Eph. 2:8-9; Titus 3:5-6). No one knows when they will breathe their last breath. Therefore, every person who has yet to place their faith in Jesus Christ should do so quickly.

The implementation of socialism, Marxism, and finally the one-world system, when Satan will absolutely inaugurate his ultimate globalist, anti-God agenda, the closer the world, and yes, America, comes to the final days of the Church Age. Based on the degradation of society, which is setting the prophetic stage for the biblical end times scenario, the more important it is for God's people to put on the full armor of God. Christians must prepare themselves to get in the spiritual battle (Eph. 6:10-18), and proclaim the only hope for one's eternal destiny, which is the gospel of the Lord Jesus Christ (Rom. 3:20; 1 Cor. 15:1-4; Eph. 2:8-9; Titus 3:5-6).

The apostle Paul presents a very pointed list of commands he expects Timothy to follow, without exception. Second Timothy 4 begins with three powerful words, *I charge you*. The Greek word for *charge* means "to exhort with authority in matters of extraordinary importance, frequently with reference(s) to higher powers and/or suggestion of peril, *solemnly.*"[49] Dr. Andy Woods provides instructional insight on the use of the word.

> This word "charge" is very interesting in the Greek, it's *marturomai*, where we get the word martyr incidentally, and it speaks of a charge or of a command at the highest level of intensity. In fact, that's why the New American Standard Bible translates this as "I solemnly charge," charge in and of itself wouldn't be strong enough a word so the English translation adds the word "solemnly", but these are both English words derived from the single word *marturomai*.[50]

Paul continues the instruction by stating, "therefore before God and the Lord Jesus Christ." The Scripture leaves no doubt regarding the authority behind Paul's exhortation, as he pointedly names two members of the Trinity, God the Father and Jesus Christ.

---

[49] William Arndt et al., *A Greek-English Lexicon of the New Testament and Other Early Christian Literature*, 233.

[50] Andy Woods, 2 Timothy 030 – Why Preach The Bible? – Part 5, 2 Timothy - The Call To Persevere, May 8, 2016, Sermon, Sugarland Bible Church, Sugarland Texas, https://slbc.org/sermon/2-timothy-030-why-preach-the-bible-part-5/, accessed September 14, 2022, 9:00 am CST.

Timothy knew immediately that Paul was not simply providing good counsel or his opinion. Paul put Timothy on notice that he must fulfill the approaching list of commands, as they carry the weight of Divine inspiration. Paul, when he wrote to the Romans, stressed the fact that following the Lord Jesus is a personal sacrifice, but a reasonable one (Rom. 12:1).

Second Timothy 4:1 continues with, "who will judge the living and the dead at His appearing and His kingdom." The final phrase in verse one provides a challenge to determine the exact timing when Jesus will judge the living and the dead. The Scriptures reveal that there are two more times in the future when Jesus will come towards the earth. The next time Jesus comes towards the earth is what dispensational theologians refer to as the Rapture, which is the removal or snatching away of one generation of Christians, dead and alive to provide them with an eternal glorified body (1 Thess. 4:13-18; 1 Cor. 15:50-58). Jesus does not literally touch down on the earth as Paul explains. "For the Lord Himself will descend from heaven with a shout, with the voice of an archangel, and with the trumpet of God. And the dead in Christ will rise first. Then we who are alive and remain shall be caught up *(raptured)* together with them in the clouds to meet the Lord in the air. And thus we shall always be with the Lord" (1 Thess. 4:16-17). At the Rapture, one generation of Church Age believers will be taken to heaven without dying. They will meet the Lord Jesus in the clouds, not on the earth.

Paul reveals in 2 Corinthians 5:9–10 "Therefore we make it our aim, whether present or absent, to be well pleasing to Him. For we must all appear before the judgment seat of Christ, that each one may receive the things done in the body, according to what he has done, whether good or bad." Fortunately, the Lord provides a clarification of this passage in 1 Corinthians 3:9-15, which reveals that God will judge all believers after the Rapture and reward them for the positive things they accomplished for the Lord.

> For we are God's fellow workers; you are God's field, you are God's building. According to the grace of God which was given to me, as a wise master builder I have laid the foundation, and another builds on it. But let each one take heed how he builds on it. For no other foundation can anyone lay than that which is laid, which is Jesus Christ. Now if anyone builds on this foundation with gold, silver, precious stones, wood, hay, straw, one's work will become clear; for the Day will declare

it, because it will be revealed by fire; and the fire will test each one's work, of what sort it is. If anyone's work which he has built on it endures, he will receive a reward. If anyone's work is burned, he will suffer loss; but he himself will be saved, yet so as through fire. (1 Cor. 3:9–15)

Paul clearly states that God will hold Christians accountable for the works they performed. Yet God's mercy and grace will be displayed as He disposes of the poor decisions believers made on earth and rewards them for the positive things accomplished for the sake of the gospel. However, is this what Paul is referring to in 2 Timothy 4:1?

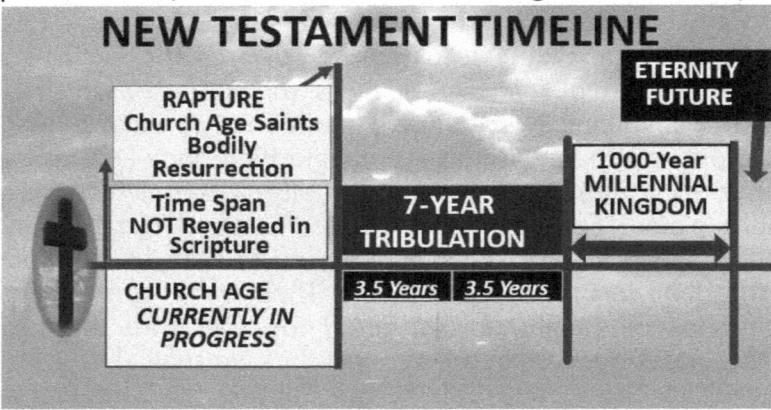

NEW TESTAMENT TIMELINE

RAPTURE Church Age Saints Bodily Resurrection		ETERNITY FUTURE
Time Span NOT Revealed in Scripture	7-YEAR TRIBULATION	1000-Year MILLENNIAL KINGDOM
CHURCH AGE CURRENTLY IN PROGRESS	3.5 Years | 3.5 Years	

Figure 2.1

Once again, we turn to the scholarly analysis of Andy Woods, who provides instructional commentary on when the judgment of 2 Timothy 4:1 takes place.

> Now when will this judgment take place? He tells us here as we move into the end of verse 1, He is, "to judge the living and the dead," well, when is this going to happen, "by His appearing and His kingdom." You will notice that Paul says the judgment is yet future. It is connected with Christ's appearing. The Greek word translated "appearing" is where we get the English word "epiphany," the revelation of the appearance of God. So this is a reference to the Second Advent of Christ. It is not speaking of the rapture here, but the return of Jesus Christ at the end of the seven-year

Tribulation period, to establish his long-awaited kingdom on planet earth.[51]

Five Biblical Commands for the Later Days

Paul emphatically gave the opening words of his charge to Timothy by accentuating that his authority is from God. Paul further states that Timothy's obedience to these imperatives would have eternal consequences on those who hear him (2 Tim. 4:1). The practical application is for all believers to take heed and obey the charge, with even more urgency, as we draw near to the final days of the Church Age (Dan. 9:27; Matt. 24:4-26; Rev. 13).

> **Charge for God's Servants**
> **Considering the Rejection of Sound Doctrine**
> **In the Later Days of the Church Age**
> 1. Preach the word
> 2. Be ready in season and out of season
> 3. Convince
> 4. Rebuke
> 5. Exhort
> 6. Be watchful in all things
> 7. Endure afflictions
> 8. Do the work of an evangelist
> 9. Fulfill your ministry

Figure 2.2
Preach the Word!

Paul commands Timothy to *preach the word*. Preach (*karusso*) means "to make an official announcement, *announce, make known* by an official herald or one who functions as such, to make public declarations, *proclaim aloud.*"[52] However, the importance lies in what Timothy is to herald, which is *the word*. The word, (*logos*) is defined as a communication whereby the mind finds expression, *word*.[53] *Logos* is also used to refer to a statement, that which is said (John 4:41); speech, the act of speaking (Acts 14:12); gospel, the content of what is preached about Christ (Acts 19:20; Col. 3:16; Mark 16:20); treatise, systematic treatment of a subject (Acts

---

[51] Andy Woods, 2 Timothy 030 – Why Preach The Bible? – Part 5, 2 Timothy - The Call To Persevere.
[52] William Arndt et al., 543.
[53] William Arndt et al., 599.

1:1); Word, Message, a title for Christ (John 1:1, 14; 2 Tim. 4:2; 1 John 1:1; Rev. 19:13), account, a record of assets and liabilities (Phil. 4:17); reason, a cause for something (Matt. 5:32; Acts 10:29; 1 Peter 3:15); event, matter, thing (Acts 8:21); appearance, to seem to be (Col. 2:23); accusation, and legal charge of wrongdoing (Acts 19:38).[54] Spiros Zodhiates adds important information to the study of *the word*.

> Of the divine declarations, precepts, oracles, relating to the instructions of men in religion, the Word of God, i.e., the divine doctrines and precepts of the gospel, the gospel itself (Luke 5:1; John 17:6; Acts 4:29, 31; 8:14; 1 Cor. 14:36; 2 Cor. 4:2; Col. 1:25; 1 Thess. 2:13; Titus 1:3; Heb. 13:7). With "of God" implied (Mark 16:20; Luke 1:2; Acts 10:44; Phil. 1:14; **2 Tim. 4:2**; James 1:21; 1 Pet. 2:8; Rev. 12:11); the word of truth (2 Cor. 6:7; Eph. 1:13; 2 Tim. 2:15; James 1:18); the word of life (Phil. 2:16); the word of salvation (Acts 13:26); the word of the kingdom (Matt. 13:19); with the kingdom implied (Matt. 13:20; Mark 4:14); the word of the gospel (Acts 15:7); the word of the cross (1 Cor. 1:18); the word of His grace (Acts 14:3; 20:32). In the same sense of Christ, the word of Christ (John 5:24; 14:23, 24; Col. 3:16); the word of the Lord (Acts 8:25).[55]

The apostle John helps to define *the word*. "In the beginning was the Word (*logos*) and the Word (*logos*), was with God, and the Word (*logos*) was God. He was in the beginning with God. All things were made through Him, and without Him nothing was made that was made. In Him was life, and the life was the light of men" (John 1:1–4). The Scriptures identify the Word (*logos*) as Jesus Christ and expand on that truth to define the entire canon of Scripture (the 66 books of the Bible) as the very words of God. "All Scripture is given by inspiration of God, and is profitable for doctrine, for reproof, for correction, for instruction in righteousness, that the man of God may be complete, thoroughly equipped for every good work" (2 Tim. 3:16–17).

---

[54] James Swanson, *Dictionary of Biblical Languages with Semantic Domains: Greek (New Testament)* (Oak Harbor: Logos Research Systems, Inc., 1997).

[55] Spiros Zodhiates, *The Complete Word Study Dictionary: New Testament* (Chattanooga, TN: AMG Publishers, 2000).

Luke records Paul's statement regarding preaching the whole counsel of God, referring to the Scriptures.

> Therefore I testify to you this day that I am innocent of the blood of all men. For I have not shunned to declare to you the whole counsel of God. Therefore, take heed to yourselves and to all the flock, among which the Holy Spirit has made you overseers, to shepherd the church of God which He purchased with His own blood. For I know this, that after my departure savage wolves will come in among you, not sparing the flock. Also from among yourselves men will rise up, speaking perverse things, to draw away the disciples after themselves. Therefore watch, and remember that for three years I did not cease to warn everyone night and day with tears. (Acts 20:26–31)

The Word, the Bible, the Scriptures, the whole counsel of God, synonymously define what the apostle Paul mandated that Timothy, and every other teacher and preacher of Jesus Christ, proclaim. With the rapid approach of the globalists' agenda, including their anti-God, anti-Bible, and anti-Christian schema, it is imperative in these last days of the Church Age that Christians embrace every opportunity to proclaim God's Word to whoever will listen. This is nothing less than an imperative from God Himself (2 Tim. 4:1-2).

Paul develops the command to preach the Word with additional commands. The writers of *The New American Commentary* provide insight on this issue.

> Five aorist imperatives in this verse set forth commands with the crisp forcefulness of a military order. The first command, "Preach the Word," is the basis for all others. The command urged Timothy to declare the gospel. That was the word on which he had to focus. Every command that follows in this verse told Timothy how he should proceed about the task of preaching the word. To "preach" does not imply that an ordained minister is to stand behind a stately pulpit and expound Scripture. It called Timothy to a public heralding of the gospel message, whether done in a mass meeting or person-to-person.[56]

---

[56] Thomas D. Lea and Hayne P. Griffin, *1, 2 Timothy, Titus*, vol. 34, The New American Commentary (Nashville: Broadman & Holman Publishers, 1992), 242–243.

Therefore, Paul develops the command to preach the word with the following imperatives.

Be Ready in Season and of Season

The first imperative commands Timothy to be prepared to preach "the word of God" at all times. *In season* comes from the Greek word *eukaíroēs*, which is an adverb meaning opportune, convenient, opportunely, conveniently, in season (Mark 14:11; 2 Tim. 4:2). *Out of season* comes from the root word *akaírōs*, meaning inopportunely, impracticably, with difficulty.[57] Paul exhorted Timothy to always be on duty and ready to speak, whether or not the opportunity seemed right. Paul may have looked back on his life realizing how quickly the time had passed, and therefore, he states, "See then that you walk circumspectly, not as fools but as wise, redeeming the time, because the days are evil" (Eph. 5:15–16).[58]

When is the preaching of God's word *in season?* In a Christian society, where people embrace a biblical worldview, one could conclude that they are always *in season* for preaching the Scriptures. However, when the culture turns away from Christianity and the Bible and becomes secular, then the concept of *out of season* carries more meaning.

This brings us to the very purpose of this book. Christians (those who still embrace the Lord Jesus Christ) are a numerical minority in America and around the world. God calls the remnant of Christians to not only recognize the rapid deterioration of the contemporary culture leading to socialism, but to embrace every opportunity to spread the gospel of Jesus Christ. Christians must be on guard not to fall prey to secularizing biblical truth by embracing syncretistic and pluralist secular norms, which distort and corrupt their biblical worldview. God's people are facing a crisis in the current degenerating society, which embraces a narcissistic, all-about-me worldview. God's people must challenge the self-destructive thinking most of the populace embraces and proclaim that the Word of God is indeed truth. That every individual obtain a personal relationship with Jesus Christ is imperative to them having the assurance of

---

[57] Spiros Zodhiates, *The Complete Word Study Dictionary*.
[58] Bruce B. Barton, David Veerman, and Neil S. Wilson, *1 Timothy, 2 Timothy, Titus*, Life Application Bible Commentary (Wheaton, IL: Tyndale House Publishers, 1993), 220.

eternal life in heaven (John 3:16-17; Eph. 2:8-9). The devastating scriptural reality is that anyone who refuses to accept by faith the gift of salvation will experience the alternative destination, which is the eternal lake of fire (Rev. 21:8). Christians must ask themselves if they are ready to proclaim the truth of the gospel in the current out of season society, where the populace marginalizes the gospel, and persecution of Christians is on the rise. Every believer in Jesus Christ must challenge themselves to boldly proclaim the gospel, which is *out of season* in the current society.

Convince

Convince (*elégchō*) in the New Testament means to convict, to prove one in the wrong, and thus to shame him.[59]

John MacArthur provides insightful commentary regarding the word *convince*, which could also be translated as *reprove*. MacArthur synchronizes the command to reprove with Paul's subsequent command to *rebuke*.

> The preacher's continuing responsibility is to expose, reprove, and rebuke sin. Sin is that which totally separates unbelievers from God and which temporarily separates believers from close fellowship with their Lord. Paul therefore counseled believers in Ephesus, "Do not participate in the unfruitful deeds of darkness, but instead even expose them" (Eph. 5:11).
>
> He warned Titus about those sinners who infiltrate the church: "There are many rebellious men, empty talkers and deceivers, especially those of the circumcision, who must be silenced because they are upsetting whole families, teaching things they should not teach, for the sake of sordid gain.... For this cause reprove them severely that they may be sound in the faith" (Titus 1:10–11, 13).
>
> Sin must be addressed among believers as well. In his first letter to Timothy, Paul commanded, "Those who continue in sin, rebuke in the presence of all, so that the rest also may be fearful of sinning" (1 Tim. 5:20).[60]

---

[59] Spiros Zodhiates, *The Complete Word Study Dictionary: New Testament* (Chattanooga, TN: AMG Publishers, 2000).

[60] John F. MacArthur Jr., *2 Timothy*, MacArthur New Testament Commentary (Chicago: Moody Press, 1995), 178.

Paul's commands certainly are not politically correct, but they are biblically spot on. Watered-down preaching characterizes many alleged Bible-believing churches around the country, where entertainment, emotionally driven music, and story-driven messages, temporarily move people to a supposed spiritual experience. However, after leaving the service, the people return to their same old secular lifestyle. It is this type of preaching that Paul was charging Timothy to expose and attack.

The Scriptures indicate that during the last days of the Church Age apostasy creeps into local churches, resulting in leaders (pastors, elders, deacons, and ministry heads) who embrace worldly standards, such as wealth, popularity, lust, entertainment, self-centeredness, and emotionalism. As a result, this sinful behavior becomes evident in those who attend their churches. Paul stated, "imitate me, just as I also imitate Christ" (1 Cor. 11:1). Those words should challenge every person in leadership to continually strive to determine what Jesus would do in any given situation, and then determine to live out that example.

Paul, under the inspiration of the Holy Spirit, strongly enforces the command of God to convince and reprove God's people to embrace the Word of God. Paul's exhortation is directly applicable in today's contemporary culture, which is currently on a collision course with the anti-God globalist agenda that is infiltrating the country, including local churches, and the individuals who attend them. Anyone currently attending a church that does not preach from the scriptures every service, should consider that church suspect. If one does not hear biblical truths, provided in context from an appropriate biblical text, including convicting scriptural encouragement to live for the Lord seven days a week, by displaying a godly lifestyle and a biblical worldview, they should strongly consider leaving, never to return. There are many excellent Bible-centered churches, but there are unfortunately exponentially more churches that either do not use the Bible at all, or use it out of context. Remember Paul's proclamation that in the last days of the Church Age, perilous, dangerous times will come (2 Tim. 3:1), and it is incumbent upon believers in the Lord Jesus Christ to make the most out of every breathing moment of their life, to serve the Lord, and to embrace a church that preaches the full counsel of God, even if the messages sting on occasion, and are not politically correct.

Rebuke

"Rebuke" (*epitimao*) means to express strong disapproval of someone, reprove, censure, speak seriously, and to *warn* in order to prevent an action or bring one to an end.[61] Jesus provides several key examples of rebuke.

> And He [Jesus] began to teach them that the Son of Man must suffer many things, and be rejected by the elders and chief priests and scribes, and be killed, and after three days rise again. He spoke this word openly. Then Peter took Him aside and began to rebuke Him. But when He had turned around and looked at His disciples, He rebuked Peter, saying, "Get behind Me, Satan! For you are not mindful of the things of God, but the things of men." (Mark 8:31–33)

Peter, attempting to protect the Lord Jesus, makes a significant error, as he did not understand the sovereign plan of God regarding the necessity of the death, burial, and resurrection of Jesus to accomplish the plan of redemption. Peter strongly attacks the Lord verbally and rebukes Him for uttering the prophetic words that must be fulfilled. The scenario quickly turns, as Jesus, knowing exactly what had to take place, realizes that Satan himself was behind Peter's rebuke. Therefore, Jesus rebukes Peter and goes to the root of the problem, He commands Satan to get behind Him. This is a sharp, pointed rebuke, and provides an example of what the Lord expects of the servants of God, who at times must address an issue with a rebuke.

The scenario provides an important lesson: if you choose to rebuke someone, make sure your facts are correct. Peter's failure to comprehend what Jesus stated regarding His death, burial, and resurrection resulted in his blurting out an uncalled-for rebuke against the Lord Jesus. Certainly, Jesus was able to quickly correct Peter, but if we rebuke someone based on a false assumption, the person is likely to be offended. The Bible says, "A brother offended is harder to win than a strong city, and contentions are like the bars of a castle" (Prov. 18:19).

Multiple times in the gospel narratives Jesus rebuked demons, which makes sense, as the mission of Satan and the demonic world is to oppose the Lord Jesus and all that He represents. (Matt. 17:18; Mark 1:25; 9:25; Luke 4:35; 4:41; 9:42). Jesus also

---

[61] William Arndt et al., 384.

rebuked His disciples for their failure to believe the reports of those who saw Him after He had risen (Mark 16:14). In addition, Jesus described how a believer in the Lord Jesus should respond when offended by another person. "Take heed to yourselves. If your brother sins against you, rebuke him; and if he repents, forgive him. And if he sins against you seven times in a day, and seven times in a day returns to you, saying, 'I repent,' you shall forgive him" (Luke 17:3–4). Therefore, the Scriptures endorse rebuking someone for wrongdoing, even at the risk of offending the person. Caution should be taken to ensure the facts are correct and to weigh the consequences of being wrong about the matter. The Lord expects teachers and preachers of the Word of God to rebuke an erring Christian. However, this is not a license for a pastor to lord over God's people (1 Peter 5:3) as a dictator. The servant leader must be willing to speak the truth, but with the express attitude of love (Eph. 4:15).

The preacher of the Scriptures must find the biblical balance between loving those who are willing to listen, and rebuking those who are following a path to potential disaster through ungodly living. Timothy, and subsequently every servant of God who speaks to individuals or the masses, has the God-given responsibility to hold accountable those engaging in sinful behavior. The one performing the rebuke should strive to help those in error make a conscious decision to turn from their sin, and follow the Lord. This is vitally important in the last days of the Church Age, as in these perilous, dangerous times, God's people are tempted to embrace the secular norms of society. This is the globalist's agenda, to minimize the Christian message, and to pull people into the anti-God, anti-Bible, satanic system, which is headed straight to the one-world government, religion, and economy.

Exhort

"Exhort" (*parakaleō*) means to ask for earnestly, beg, plead (Ac 28:20), invite (Lk 8:41); call together (Ac 28:20), encourage, console, urge (Eph 6:22).[62] In addition, the word carries the meaning to ask to come and be present where the speaker is, call to one's side,

---

[62] James Swanson, *Dictionary of Biblical Languages with Semantic Domains: Greek (New Testament)* (Oak Harbor: Logos Research Systems, Inc., 1997).

of need, to urge strongly, appeal to, urge, and exhort, which is the meaning incorporated in 2 Timothy 4:2. [63]

Donald Guthrie brings out an expanded use of the word *exhort*. "The last word *encourage* is a translation of *parakaleō*, which can also mean 'exhort.' Both these meanings are applicable to the preacher's work, but if this duty is taken with the preceding two charges, the former meaning (encourage) would be more applicable."[64] Guthrie concludes that when one must deliver a strong charge and rebuke, the next step is to encourage the recipient. There certainly is a place for supporting and encouraging the person who endured a rebuke. However, is this the appropriate use of the word in the context of 2 Timothy 4:2?

Jay Adams provides a very pointed analysis of Paul's charge to Timothy to exhort when preaching the word.

> Timothy is to urge people to believe and follow the teachings of God's Word. Like it or not, that means putting pressure on them. Paul was not loathe to do that very thing. In this letter in which he is counseling Timothy, he puts extraordinary pressure on him. At every turn he is urging him to accept and carry on the ministry he is leaving behind. Take a look at Philemon sometime and notice the unusual amount of pressure (urging) of various sorts that Paul exerts on the recipient of that letter! A minister of the Word has authority, and there are times to exert it. Authority and pressure can be improperly brought to bear on others, that is true, but follow Paul in doing so and you will not go wrong. It would be to your benefit, and the benefit of your counselees, to make a study of the ways and means that the apostles legitimately urged others to do God's will. Counseling involves much urging. Certainly, the apostles did not simply explain matters and leave it to the counselee to take it from there. The word translated urge can mean persuade; but, basically, it means to use all legitimate means available to assist another in fulfilling a biblical command.[65]

---

[63] William Arndt et al., 764–765.

[64] Donald Guthrie, *Pastoral Epistles: An Introduction and Commentary*, vol. 14, Tyndale New Testament Commentaries (Downers Grove, IL: InterVarsity Press, 1990), 185.

[65] Jay E. Adams, *I Timothy, II Timothy, and Titus*, The Christian Counselor's Commentary (Cordova, TN: Institute for Nouthetic Studies, 2020), 80–81.

Adams suggests a balanced approach that includes exhorting the person to do the right biblical thing and then encouraging the person in their walk with the Lord. Pointing out inappropriate, unbiblical behavior in the current anti-God culture is a mandate of Scripture. Once the erring person understands the issue and determines to make a change, the godly servant leader should positively reinforce the proper behavior with encouragement, and so much more as society pushes against all that is good and godly.

Paul completes this powerful section of commands with two specific qualifiers, "with all longsuffering and teaching" (2 Tim. 4:2). "Longsuffering" (*makrothymia*) carries the meaning of remaining tranquil while awaiting an outcome; *patience, steadfastness, endurance*, the state of being able to bear up.[66] The work of a dedicated servant of God is very taxing from a spiritual warfare perspective. Ephesians 6 provides the perfect analogy of putting on spiritual armor every day to endure the harsh conditions of spiritual battle. The secular culture constantly attacks the biblical worldview. Therefore, God's people must daily put on the spiritual armor for the ongoing battle of fighting evil, sharing the gospel, and discipling believers in the Lord Jesus. The Christian life is not a sprint, but a grueling marathon that will not let up until death or the Rapture occurs. This immutable truth requires that those who *preach the Word,* do so with longsuffering.

Not only must God's people exercise longsuffering, but they must do so while *teaching* God's Word. "Teaching" (*didachē*) simply means providing instruction. The Scriptures also use the word to convey the presentation of doctrine, specifically the principles that the Bible literally reveals (Mt 16:12; Ac 5:28; 17:19).[67] The writer of Hebrews states, "For the word of God is living and powerful, and sharper than any two-edged sword, piercing even to the division of soul and spirit, and of joints and marrow, and is a discerner of the thoughts and intents of the heart" (Heb. 4:12). God's Word, the Bible, is the most powerful tool for changing a person's mindset. Preaching (exegeting) the Word (after careful study per 2 Tim. 2:15) and subsequent longsuffering while teaching the Word, are God's means for confronting those walking in spiritual error. God's Word, properly

---

[66] William Arndt et al., 612.
[67] James Swanson, *Dictionary of Biblical Languages with Semantic Domains: Greek (New Testament)* (Oak Harbor: Logos Research Systems, Inc., 1997).

taught, will bring conviction and potential change in the erring person, as God's Word never returns void (Isa. 55:10-11).

The unfortunate truth regarding Bible-believing Christians is that they are constantly under the influence and outright attack of secular society. This often results in God's people succumbing to false doctrines and secular deviations from God's truth. Syncretism is the fusion of secular ideas with biblical truth. When weak Christians embrace doctrinal error that appeals to their carnal sin nature, they often look for a church or pastor who also embraces that error. The new environment enforces what the erring person wants to hear and believe, and leads them further from the truth. The corruption of sound biblical doctrine is a tragedy in the contemporary church in the last days of the Church Age (2 Tim. 3:1).

Andy Woods once again provides an excellent analysis of why the current conditions require the church leadership to stay focused on biblical truth.

> What Paul is saying is this will become normal in the church. You see, in the realm of spirituality, this is normal. You gravitate towards places that tell you or reaffirm your pre-existing ideas. What you discover, particularly when you pastor a local church is a lot of people want their ideas reinforced. And if you are committed to the Scripture what you discover is that the Word of God does not reinforce any human viewpoint, it tears it down. The Bible is a wrecking ball that is going after, not the building itself but the foundation. It is called renewing your mind. And yet if you're married to a false idea, you simply say well, that spiritual leader is not telling me what I want to hear, I'm going to go down the street and I'm going to find my own ministerial calf maker and they are in surplus and abundance.[68]

The apostle Paul summarizes the spiritual conditions that exist in the last days of the Church Age.

> For the time will come when they will not endure sound doctrine, but according to their own desires, because they have itching ears, they will heap up for themselves teachers; and they will turn their ears away from the truth, and be turned aside to fables. (2 Tim. 4:3-4)

---

[68] Andy Woods, 2 Timothy - The Call To Persevere, May 22, 2016, Sermon, Sugarland Bible Church, Sugarland Texas, https://slbc.org/sermon/2-timothy-031-itching-ears-of-the-last-days/accessed September 14, 2022, 9:52 am CST.

How tragic it is that during the later days of the Church Age there will be a dearth of solid biblical teaching in the churches. The god of this world, Satan (2 Cor. 4:4), is working frantically in this post-Christian era, to replace the truth of God's Word with corrupt, anti-God philosophies that are setting the stage for the globalist one-world religion, government, and economy.

Four Additional Biblical Commands for the Later Days

Be Watchful in all things – Sober

"Be watchful" (*nēphō*) means to be sober-minded, clear-headed, not drunk (1Th 5:6, 8; 2Ti 4:5; 1Pe 1:13; 4:7; 5:8; Mt 6:28), restrained, and self-controlled.[69]

To be sober-minded, to take things seriously, and to realize that life is not a game but has serious consequences, are concepts embraced by some segments of society. However, these ideals are becoming less common in a culture where many more people pursue entertainment, sports, recreation, vacations, and playtime. The consequences of this cultural shift are addressed in subsequent chapters of this book. This culture not only embraces a carefree lifestyle, but its all-about-me attitude often leads to violence when narcissistic, entitled people believe the world owes them whatever they desire. Andy Woods provides intriguing commentary on this very issue.

> It's amazing some of the things that are being triggered today in our society related to mob violence and people just willing to riot so fast over disagreements about this, that or the other. That's the characteristic of the last days. We, as God's people, are not rioters, we are people that function under sobriety, functioning under self-control. It's interesting here, he says, be sober in some things.... Oh, I'm sorry, it doesn't say that. It says "be sober in all things." Think of all of the things that challenge us and get us away from a clear God-filled mind: materialism, where we spend our lives pursuing things, thinking that that is somehow going to make us happy. Out of control emotions, allowing our emotional moods to dictate to us rather than reigning and governing our

---

[69] James Swanson, *Dictionary of Biblical Languages with Semantic Domains: Greek (New Testament)*.

emotions under God. Sexual impulses, wanting to cast aside God's standard for sexuality and instead gratify ourselves in any number of ways.[70]

The ramifications of a self-centered, undisciplined society are chaos, and a lack of productivity. This has significant spiritual application, as the less focused the Christian community is on Jesus Christ and living out a biblical lifestyle, the less effective it will be in reaching others with the gospel and discipling believers. Satan and his demonic army applaud the lack of commitment of the complacent Christian culture. Paul encourages Timothy to think with purpose. Two thousand years after Paul's exhortation, society continues to move away from biblical lifestyles and turns to a pleasure-loving, narcissistic lifestyle. Therefore, it is incumbent on God's people to realize that time on this earth is very short, and then determine to be sober-minded and vigilant in serving the Lord, as the globalist influence becomes stronger in these last days.

Endure afflictions

"Endure afflictions" (*kakopathéō*) has the meaning of suffering ill, to suffer evil or afflictions, to be afflicted (2 Tim. 2:9; James 5:13), to endure or sustain afflictions (2 Tim. 2:3; 4:5), endure hardships.[71]

Many Christians, since the first century, have suffered persecution to the point of physical assaults, imprisonment, and martyrdom. Americans have enjoyed, at least to this point, a society that is generally accepting of Christians. There are isolated incidents of churches that have come under governmental scrutiny or the disdain of their community, but imprisonment, physical violence, and martyrdom have been the exception rather than the rule. However, Paul made it clear that in the last days, perilous, dangerous times will come (2 Tim. 3:1). Will America change into a completely anti-God, anti-Christian country? Will socialism, Marxism, and eventually a one-world order change not only America but the entire globe? The apostle John affirms that globalism and the one-world government will indeed become the future of the entire world (Rev. 13). Does that

---

[70]Andy Woods, 2 Timothy 032 – No Regrets, 2 Timothy 4:5-7, Lesson 33, June 5, 2016, Sermon, Sugarland Bible Church, Sugarland Texas, https://slbc.org/sermon/2-timothy-032-no-regrets/, accessed September 14, 2022, 10:45 am CST.

[71]Spiros Zodhiates, *The Complete Word Study Dictionary: New Testament*.

mean that American Christians will experience increased persecution, and be forced to endure increasing afflictions before the Rapture of the Church Age saints? The unfortunate answer, yet the one that corresponds with Paul's letter to Timothy, is an emphatic yes.

Bruce Barton provides the following commentary.

The same Greek verb is used in 2 Timothy 2:3, where Paul wrote, "Share in suffering like a good soldier of Christ Jesus." The suffering, hardship, persecution, and struggles would only intensify in the days and months ahead. Many in Timothy's ministry would look to Timothy as their example. Timothy would have to endure. In fact, like his mentor Paul, Timothy did experience imprisonment."[72]

Robert W. Yarbrough adds the following thoughts.

"Endure hardship" commands what Paul has described as his own experience in jail—but God's Word continues its free course of movement. He has already called Timothy to join him in "suffering for the gospel" (1:8), to be strong in grace (2:1), and to be prepared for persecution (3:12). The call to hardship repeats an established theme of this epistle."[73]

Paul stresses that afflictions for Christians will not decrease, but actually increase. "Yes, and all who desire to live godly in Christ Jesus will suffer persecution. But evil men and impostors will grow worse and worse, deceiving and being deceived" (2 Tim. 3:12–13). Christians should not be surprised at the increasing trend to marginalize them and their biblical worldview. The globalists must continue their destructive practices to destroy the Christian influence and set the stage for the corrupt one-world satanic system. The Bible foretells the deteriorating safety of God's people as the world moves toward the establishment of a one-world leader, the Antichrist (1 John 2:18; Rev. 13:1-9). The positive message for God's people is that increased afflictions signal the imminent return of the Lord Jesus Christ, and in that
Christians should rejoice.

---

[72] Bruce B. Barton, David Veerman, and Neil S. Wilson, 222.
[73] Robert W. Yarbrough, 441.

Do the work of an evangelist

An "evangelist" (*euangeliostas*) may be defined as *one who preaches the good news*,[74] one who declares the good news (Rom. 10:15). An evangelist, a preacher of the gospel, was often not limited to any particular place, but traveled as a missionary to preach the gospel and establish churches (Acts 21:8; Eph. 4:11; 2 Tim. 4:5).[75] Across the country, Bible-believing churches tend to stress either strong verse-by-verse Bible teaching, practical contemporary topical studies, or evangelism. Rarely does a church have a balanced approach where excellent Bible teaching and evangelism take place. Many pastors embrace strong reformed views and so-called Calvinism, where evangelism seldom occurs, based on the theological belief that God will sovereignly force *the elect* to accept the gift of eternal life. Other pastors are focused completely on evangelism, and virtually every service is focused on leading people to faith in Jesus Christ, leaving most attendees with very little understanding of the sixty-six books of the Bible, and the twelve major doctrines in Scripture.

The conundrum is that evangelism is very difficult for many pastors and church attendees to execute. Attempting to start a conversation with a person with the intent of sharing the gospel is very intimidating to many Christians, including pastors. Therefore, Paul exhorts Timothy to do the work of an evangelist, regardless of how easy or formidable the challenge may be. In 2 Corinthians, Paul provides a very convicting and motivational message regarding the necessity of evangelism.

> Therefore, if anyone is in Christ, he is a new creation; old things have passed away; behold, all things have become new. Now all things are of God, who has reconciled us to Himself through Jesus Christ, and has given us the ministry of reconciliation, that is, that God was in Christ reconciling the world to Himself, not imputing their trespasses to them, and has committed to us the word of reconciliation. Now then, we are ambassadors for Christ, as though God were pleading through us: we implore you on Christ's behalf, be reconciled to God. For He made Him who knew no sin to be sin for us,

---

[74] Barclay M. Newman Jr., *A Concise Greek-English Dictionary of the New Testament.* (Stuttgart, Germany: Deutsche Bibelgesellschaft; United Bible Societies, 1993), 75.

[75] Spiros Zodhiates, *The Complete Word Study Dictionary: New Testament.*

that we might become the righteousness of God in Him. (2 Cor. 5:17–21)

The Lord stresses the fact, that not only did He command the apostle Paul and Timothy to take part in evangelism, but every person who subsequently received the gift of eternal life. Each person who places their faith in Jesus Christ for eternal life is now a called-out *ambassador*, commissioned to spread the good news of what Jesus accomplished through His death, burial, and resurrection. Christians who refuse to tell others the gospel message are outright refusing to accomplish the mission of Jesus Christ and are contributing to the marginalization of Christianity, which is exactly what the globalists desire as an outcome.

What is the mission of Jesus Christ? "For the Son of Man has come to seek and to save that which was lost" (Luke 19:10). "This is a faithful saying and worthy of all acceptance, that Christ Jesus came into the world to save sinners" (1 Tim. 1:15).

What is the gospel? "Moreover, brethren, I declare to you the gospel which I preached to you, which also you received and in which you stand, by which also you are saved, if you hold fast that word which I preached to you—unless you believed in vain. For I delivered to you first of all that which I also received: that Christ died for our sins according to the Scriptures, and that He was buried, and that He rose again the third day according to the Scriptures" (1 Cor. 15:1–4).

Why is the gospel needed? "For all have sinned and fall short of the glory of God" (Rom. 3:23). If every person received the just penalty for their sin, they would spend eternity in the place of eternal torment. "But the cowardly, unbelieving, abominable, murderers, sexually immoral, sorcerers, idolaters, and all liars shall have their part in the lake which burns with fire and brimstone, which is the second death" (Rev. 21:8). "For the wages of sin is death, but the gift of God is eternal life in Christ Jesus our Lord" (Rom. 6:23).

Exactly how does one gain the absolute assurance of going to heaven when they breathe their last breath?

Please allow me for the moment to address you personally. If you were to die in the next moment, where would you go? Are you 100% sure that when you take your last breath God will immediately take you to heaven? In the preceding paragraphs, the gospel was explained, which is God's plan of how one can, without a shadow of a doubt, go directly to heaven at their death.

Let us look one more time at God's specific plan for how to go to heaven. We will examine four elements of the gospel. First, every person is a sinner (Rom. 3:23). Every person inherited the sin nature from their father based on Adam's sin, the first man God created. "Therefore, just as through one man *[Adam]* sin entered the world, and death through sin, and thus death spread to all men, because all sinned" (Rom. 5:12). Second, every person deserves eternal separation from God and eternal punishment in the lake of fire or hell because of their sin (Rom. 6:23; Rev. 21:8). However, God does not desire that anyone spend eternity in hell. Third, God provided the only way for one to get to heaven when Jesus Christ, God's Son, left heaven's glory, came down to this earth, took on the body of a human being, and subsequently, willing went to the cross where He was crucified to pay for your sins. "God demonstrates His own love toward us, in that while we were still sinners, Christ died for us" (Rom. 5:8). Jesus died because He loves YOU and wants to take YOU to heaven when you die. Not only did Jesus give His life for YOU, but He was buried, and three days after His crucifixion, Jesus was resurrected victorious over death (1 Cor. 15:3-4). Jesus paid the entire penalty for your sin, which is why the fourth and final point of the gospel is very specific on what YOU must do. "For by grace *[God's free unmerited gift]* you have been saved *[saved from your sin and the penalty of sin]* through faith *[faith is believing without anything else being done]* and that not of yourselves; it is the gift of God, not of works *[nothing besides faith]* lest anyone should boast" (Eph. 2:8–9). There is literally nothing anyone can do to earn heaven! Eternal life in heaven is a *free gift*, available to anyone who believes and accepts by faith what Jesus did for them. Have you ever placed your faith in Jesus Christ and received the gift of eternal life? May I encourage you to stop for a moment, ponder this eternal truth, and receive by faith the gift of eternal life. Are you ready to accept Jesus Christ as your personal Savior? Then right where you are, by faith, believe in what Jesus did for you through His death, burial, and resurrection.

Fulfill your ministry

"Fulfill" (*plērophoreomai*) means to be completely certain, fully assured, convinced, or persuaded (Rom. 4:21; 14:5; Col. 4:12; Eph. 3:19), to make happen, fulfill (Luke 1:1), proclaim fully, (2 Tim.

4:17), accomplish, fulfill completely (2 Tim. 4:5).[76] In addition, *fulfill* in the Scriptures also means to complete a period of time, to bring to completion that which was already begun, to bring to a designed end, such as to *fulfill* a prophecy, an obligation, a promise, a law, a request, a purpose, a desire, a hope, a duty, a fate, a destiny, etc.; it means to bring to completion an activity that one has been involved in from its beginning, and to have the number made complete.[77] This lengthy description of the word *fulfill* accentuates the necessity of not quitting or turning back from what God has called you to do, which is your ministry.

Your "ministry" (*diakonia*) refers to service rendered in an intermediary capacity, *mediation, assignment,* performance of a service, functioning in the interest of a larger public *service, office* such as the prophets and apostles; the rendering of specific assistance.[78] Richard Yarbrough provides helpful commentary on this command.

> As for "discharge all the duties of your ministry," these seven words could be expressed in just three: "fulfill your ministry." "Fulfill" (from *plērophoreō*) is a word used only once in the [New Testament] outside of Paul's writings. Here it means to carry out completely; to leave nothing undone; to execute tasks with the high standards and fidelity to Christ that Paul has called for throughout the epistle. In v. 17 Paul will use the same word to describe how he "fully proclaimed" the gospel message with God's help and was thus spared from the lions. Timothy should be faithful unto death in every aspect of his *diakonia* (service, pastoral labors, ministry), the same word Paul uses to describe his work for the Lord (1 Tim. 1:12; 2 Tim. 4:11).[79]

It is imperative, in these last days of the Church Age, that God's people use their spiritual gifts, talents, and resources to serve the Lord. Christian complacency provides an easy path for the globalists to advance their anti-God, anti-Bible agenda. Every pastor, elder, deacon, church ministry leader, and Christian that fails to fulfill their ministry, adds one more win to the deterioration of society. The

---

[76] James Swanson, *Dictionary of Biblical Languages with Semantic Domains: Greek (New Testament)*.

[77] William Arndt et al., 827–829.

[78] William Arndt et al., 230.

[79] Robert W. Yarbrough, 442.

philosophy that God only calls pastors and missionaries to the ministry is completely false. The apostle Paul emphatically states that those called to specific positions within the church are for the express purpose of helping all Christians take part in the ministry.

> And He Himself gave some to be apostles, some prophets, some evangelists, and some pastors and teachers, *for the equipping of the saints for the work of ministry, for the edifying of the body of Christ*, till we all come to the unity of the faith and of the knowledge of the Son of God, to a perfect man, to the measure of the stature of the fullness of Christ; that we should no longer be children, tossed to and fro and carried about with every wind of doctrine, by the trickery of men, in the cunning craftiness of deceitful plotting, but, speaking the truth in love, may grow up in all things into Him who is the head—Christ—from whom the whole body, joined and knit together by what every joint supplies, according to the effective working by which every part does its share, causes growth of the body for the edifying of itself in love. (Eph. 4:11–16)

Andy Woods provides a chilling analysis of what can occur when God's people fail to fulfill their ministry.

> Judges 2:10 says, "All that generation also were gathered to their fathers; and there arose another generation after them who did not know the LORD, nor yet the work which He had done for Israel." If you want a real world example of it take a trip to Europe. Europe, the cradle of the Protestant Reformation, Europe, the home of beautiful Christian architecture, beautiful Christian art, massive cathedrals that once were the worship home of thousands of worshippers, and today 1% or less of Europe is Christian. In fact, the fastest growing religion in Europe today, as we all know, is not Christianity which is on the way out, it is Islam. And if you were alive during the days of Luther and Calvin and all of the things God did you would never suspect that the day would come when Europe would become a post-Christian society. And I just say that with heaviness in my heart and warning, I don't really care what the secularists are teaching you at the public schools.
>
> There has never been a country in the history of mankind, other than the nation of Israel itself, that has started on such

a firm biblical base as the United States of America. That's just a fact. A perfect country—no, but a biblically based country. And you look at today, you look at the youth and how little they know or understand and sometimes even care about the things of God. It's shocking. It's frightening the things that are happening. And yet we, here at this church have the ability in some minor way to possibly be used in the providence of God to reverse an unsettling trend. You do not think your life matters, you do not think you're significant? The fact of the matter, beloved, is God wants to use us more than most of us want to be used. God wants to bless us more than most of us even want to be blessed. And let's fulfill our purpose as we press into our design and complete our assignment in God.[80]

It has been said, all that it takes for evil to succeed is for good men and women to do nothing. The first two chapters in this book set forth the biblical commands that Christians in these last remaining days of the Church Age must embrace and execute, lest the churches around the world, and yes, in America, continue their downward spiral, allowing the hyper-aggressive globalists to move ahead unobstructed toward a one-world satanic system.

The next chapter provides a detailed biblical prophetic chronology of God's established, unchangeable, frightening plan, stating exactly what will take place on this earth to establish the one-world government, religion, and economy, according to Revelation 13. The subsequent chapters will move into the plethora of current events that are setting the stage for Bible prophecy to be fulfilled. The prophetic Word of God is not speculation or meant for entertainment. God's prophetic Word is absolute truth. Dr. John Walvoord wrote a book entitled *Every Prophecy of the Bible*, where he details 1,000 prophecies from Genesis to Revelation. God fulfilled 500 of those prophecies exactly as written, leaving 500 end times prophecies remaining, which God will bring to fulfillment exactly as written.[81] There is no other book in the history of humanity that can claim inerrancy. The time is now for God's people to not only realize "that in the last days perilous times will come" (2 Tim. 3:1), but to embrace and follow the nine commands listed in 2 Timothy 4:1-5.

---

[80] Andy Woods, 2 Timothy 032 – No Regrets, 2 Timothy 4:5-7.
[81] John F. Walvoord, *Every Prophecy of the Bible* (Colorado Springs, CO; Chariot Victor Publishing, 1999), 7.

SECTION TWO:
THE PROPHETIC MANDATE FOR THE SATANIC ONE-WORLD SYSTEM

CHAPTER THREE
GOD'S PROPHETIC TIMELINE

The apostle Paul, in 2 Timothy 2:15, states, "Be diligent to present yourself approved to God, a worker who does not need to be ashamed, rightly dividing the word of truth." The King James Version uses the word "study" in place of "be diligent," stressing the necessity of the diligent study of God's Word. Many pastors and Bible teachers do not teach the prophetic Word in their church because, they say, it is too hard to understand and causes confusion among their people. The book of Revelation makes the following rebuttal to those who refuse to study it and digest its deep prophetic truths. "Blessed is he who reads and those who hear the words of this prophecy, and keep those things which are written in it; for the time is near" (Rev. 1:3). Therefore, it is imperative in these last perilous days of the Church Age, which are leading up to the one-world government, economy, and religion, that God's people understand the detailed chronological end times calendar. The fact is, God's prophetic Word requires diligent study. However, when a reader interprets the Scripture based on its historical, contextual, grammatical, and literal meaning, its truth and accuracy become apparent. The greatest mistake the student of the Bible can make is to allegorize or spiritualize prophecy, instead of determining the literal meaning of each passage.

The title of the book of Revelation comes from the Greek word *apokalypsis,* which means to make fully known, *revelation, disclosure*, of revelations of a particular kind, through visions, the disclosure of secrets belonging to the last days (1 Pet. 4:13).[82] Apocalyptic style writing uses symbolism that has a prophetic nexus, but the Scriptures will at some point define the literal meaning. For example, what comes to mind when you read about a dragon in Revelation? Revelation 12 uses the word "dragon" multiple times before defining the being to whom it refers.

---

[82] William Arndt et al., *A Greek-English Lexicon of the New Testament and Other Early Christian Literature* (Chicago: University of Chicago Press, 2000), 112.

And war broke out in heaven: Michael and his angels fought with the dragon; and the dragon and his angels fought, but they did not prevail, nor was a place found for them in heaven any longer. So the great dragon was cast out, that serpent of old, called the Devil and Satan, who deceives the whole world; he was cast to the earth, and his angels were cast out with him. (Rev. 12:7–9)

Understanding that the "dragon" is a metaphor for Satan is important for interpreting Revelation 12, and understanding what God prophesied will take place in the future seven-year Tribulation.

Readers of the Bible must study it carefully to gain a thorough understanding of how God dealt with different people groups in different ways at different times throughout history. This simple concept is the basis for the more impressive word, *hermeneutics*, which is the study of how to properly interpret the Scriptures. Failure to follow a specific set of guidelines when interpreting the Bible will likely result in erroneous conclusions.

Before we discuss the intriguing topics of current events and Bible prophecy in the next sections of this book, it is necessary to have a basic understanding of God's chronological timeline. This book is not designed to be an exhaustive theological study of the prophesied end times events. However, understanding the prophetic timeline will greatly enhance the meaning of the events taking place on a global basis, which are setting the stage for the fulfillment of Bible prophecy.

SUMMARY OF GOD'S PROPHETIC CALENDAR

The importance of understanding God's prophetic calendar as detailed in Scripture cannot be overstated. Despite significant theological differences among Bible expositors, biblical prophecy reveals a very precise timeline when one interprets the Bible from the dispensational model. The dispensational model declares that the Bible should be interpreted literally, as well as historically, contextually, and grammatically. This model stands in sharp contrast to those who interpret the Bible as allegory or attempt to spiritualize the text.[83]

God provides the timeline for the creation of the universe in Genesis 1-2. There is much debate among theologians and Bible scholars regarding the exact amount of time God took to create the entire universe. The periods of time that various scholars suggest are based on whether one believes that God created everything in a literal six-day period, or that creation took place over a much longer period of time, as held by those embracing the big bang theory, evolution, or theistic evolution. The following passage from Exodus supports the literal six-day timeline described in Genesis.

> "Remember the Sabbath day, to keep it holy. Six days you shall labor and do all your work, but the seventh day is the Sabbath of the LORD your God. In it you shall do no work: you, nor your son, nor your daughter, nor your male servant, nor your female servant, nor your cattle, nor your stranger who is within your gates. For in six days the LORD made the heavens and the earth, the sea, and all that is in them, and rested the seventh day. Therefore, the LORD blessed the Sabbath day and hallowed it. (Ex. 20:8–11)

Exodus 20 clearly states that God created the universe in six literal days. The next issue is determining the actual age of the earth, based on the secular world attempting to establish a timeline of the history of the world that is inconsistent with God's Word. God revealed the age of creation in Genesis 5 and 11 (see Appendix 1) through two detailed genealogies from Adam to Noah in Genesis 5, and from Noah's son Shem to Abraham, in Genesis 11. The two genealogies provide, in chronological order, the age at which each man fathered a particular son, then the age at which those sons fathered a particular son, and so on. Based on this information, we can determine the approximate year in which God created Adam.

---

[83] This author wrote a detailed book on the prophetic timeline, *Daniel's Gap Paul's Mystery, What Paused the Prophetic Calendar* (Franklin, WI.; Prophecy Focus Ministries, 2016). The book covers the various interpretive models of Scripture and compares the various views on eschatology including positions on the Rapture, Tribulation, and the Millennium. There is also a detailed section comparing the dispensational interpretive model and covenant theology. It is strongly suggested that failure to understand these issues results in the student, teacher, and preacher of the Scriptures falling short of God's imperative to *study the Scriptures*, and to *rightly divide* or *rightly handle the Word of truth* (2 Tim. 2:15).

The genealogies do not provide the month and the day on which the sons were born; therefore, the dating has a plus or minus variable to account for that. The reasonable conclusion is that, based on the genealogical records in Genesis 5 and 11, God created the earth in approximately 4,004 B.C. (see Figure 3.1). The first 2,000 years of history take place between Genesis 1 and 11.[84] The next 2,000 years of history take place from Genesis 12 through Malachi, the last book of the Old Testament (see Figure 3.2).[85] One of the major events in the Old Testament is the giving of the Mosaic Law, which took place at Mount Sinai in 1445 B.C.[86] Following the completion of Malachi in 430 B.C.,[87] God was silent for 400 years. God restored communication with humanity at the time of the incarnation of the Lord Jesus Christ, and subsequently provided further revelation to the New Testament authors.[88]

| ADAM 4004 BC
NOAH 2885 BC
SHEM 2384 BC

GENTILES
2,000 YEARS | ABRAHAM 1995 BC
DAVID 1034 BC
JESUS 4 BC

GENTILES & JEWS
2,000 YEARS | CHURCH AGE
AD 30/33

1 Cor. 10:32

GENTILES JEWS & CHRISTIAN
2,000 YEARS |

CHRONOLOGY

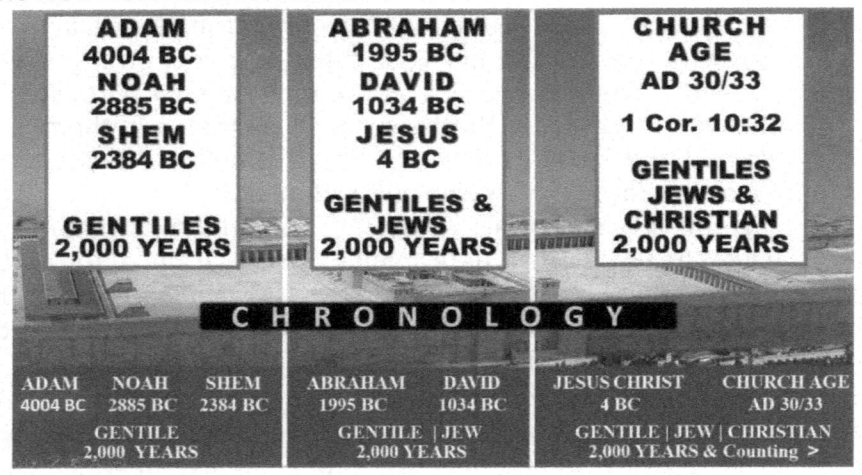

ADAM 4004 BC	NOAH 2885 BC	SHEM 2384 BC	ABRAHAM 1995 BC	DAVID 1034 BC	JESUS CHRIST 4 BC	CHURCH AGE AD 30/33
GENTILE 2,000 YEARS			GENTILE | JEW 2,000 YEARS		GENTILE | JEW | CHRISTIAN 2,000 YEARS & Counting >	

Figure 3.1

The next major events on God's chronological timeline were the death, burial, and resurrection of Jesus Christ, followed by the start of the Church Age, also known as the age of grace. The Church

---

[84] Ed Hindson and Thomas Ice, *Charting the Bible Chronologically* (Eugene, OR.: Harvest House Publishing, 2016), opening chart, no page number noted.

[85] Ibid.

[86] Ibid.

[87] Craig A. Blaising, "Malachi," in *The Bible Knowledge Commentary: An Exposition of the Scriptures*, ed. J. F. Walvoord and R. B. Zuck, vol. 1 (Wheaton, IL: Victor Books, 1985), 1573.

[88] Ed Hindson and Thomas Ice, *Charting the Bible Chronologically*, 12.

Age, which began nearly 2,000 years ago, will come to an end when God removes all Christians, both dead and alive, from the earth at the Rapture (that is, the catching up of the body of Christ) (1 Thess. 4:13-18; 1 Cor. 15:51-54).[89]

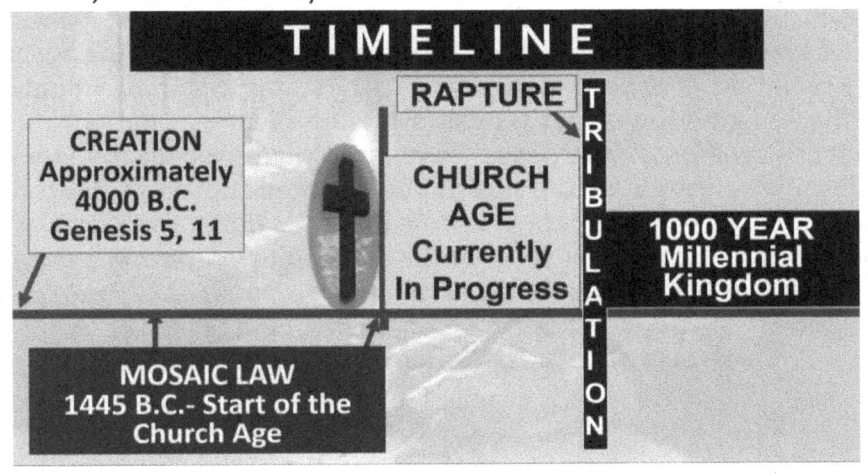

```
                          TIMELINE
                          ┌──────────┐
                          │ RAPTURE  │  T
┌──────────────┐          └──────────┘  R
│   CREATION   │          ┌──────────┐  I
│ Approximately│          │  CHURCH  │  B
│   4000 B.C.  │     +    │   AGE    │  U   ┌──────────────┐
│ Genesis 5, 11│          │ Currently│  L   │  1000 YEAR   │
└──────────────┘          │ In Progress│ A   │  Millennial  │
                          └──────────┘  T   │   Kingdom    │
                                        I   └──────────────┘
        ┌──────────────────────┐        O
        │     MOSAIC LAW       │        N
        │ 1445 B.C.- Start of the│
        │      Church Age      │
        └──────────────────────┘
```

Figure 3.2

Shortly after the Rapture, God reinstates the Old Testament, Jewish prophetic timeline. That timeline starts when the Antichrist confirms a covenant (peace treaty) with the Jewish people (Dan. 9:27). The Tribulation period, also called the seventieth week of Daniel's prophecy, contains a series of judgments God will pour out on the earth for seven literal years (Rev. 4:2-19:21). We refer to these as the seal, trumpet, thunder, and bowl judgments (Rev. 6-16). The seven-year Tribulation period is when the globalist agenda becomes reality. This is precisely why the events taking place worldwide that have a globalist agenda are extremely important for Christians to understand. Never in the history of the world has there been such a proliferation of events that so closely align with the scenarios outlined in biblical prophecy. Understanding current events and

---

[89] The detailed argument for the pretribulation rapture of the Church Age saints, also known as the body of Christ, is in *Daniel's Gap Paul's Mystery, What Paused the Prophetic Calendar* (Franklin, WI.; Prophecy Focus Ministries, 2016). This book contains Scriptures' most compelling argument for the pretribulation, which is understanding how the Church Age fits literally between Daniel 9:26-27, and synchronizes perfectly with the mystery church, detailed in Col. 1:24-29 and Eph. 3:1-7. The reason for the many different theological positions on the end times is the failure of many to understand Daniel's 70-week prophecy and the Church Age gap that exists between Daniel 9:26-27.

analyzing them from a biblical perspective, should excite every Christian with the reality that Jesus Christ's coming in the clouds to gather His saints to heaven cannot be far off.

God's chronological prophetic timeline has one major point at which the world will dramatically change. When the Antichrist arrives on the world scene, one of the things he will do is bring peace to Israel (Dan. 9:27). However, Daniel 9:27 states that in the middle of the seventieth-week of Daniel (a literal seven-year period), the Antichrist will break the peace treaty, and then execute the worst holocaust in history on the Jewish people. The Scriptures state that two-thirds of all Jewish people will die (Zech. 13:8-9), . The Bible calls the final three and a half years of that seven-year period, the Great Tribulation (Matt. 24:21) (see Figure 3.3).

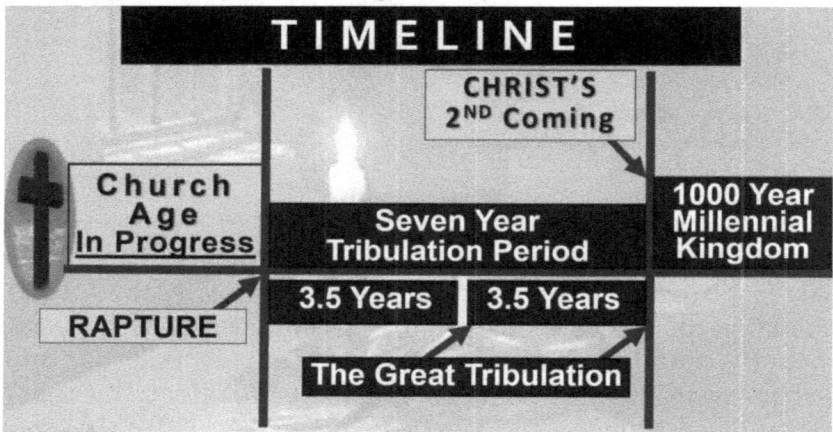

Figure 3.3

SATAN'S SPIRITUAL FALL

How art thou fallen from heaven, O Lucifer, son of the morning! *how* art thou cut down to the ground, which didst weaken the nations! For thou hast said in thine heart, I will ascend into heaven, I will exalt my throne above the stars of God: I will sit also upon the mount of the congregation, in the sides of the north: I will ascend above the heights of the clouds; I will be like the most High. (Isaiah 14:12-14)

Everything God created was perfect. Lucifer is no exception to that fact. God created Lucifer as a perfect angel, a masterpiece. The Lord, in His infinite wisdom, determined the angels would have a free will to decide if they would remain faithful to their Creator, or make the foolish decision to rebel against the One who gave them their very existence. Isaiah graphically describes Lucifer's rebellion against God. The adage, pride comes before a fall, is vividly illustrated in Lucifer's prideful, narcissistic diatribe. Lucifer, also named the Serpent, the dragon, and yes, Satan (Rev. 12:9; 20:2), is the ultimate promoter of himself. Satan engages in war against all that oppose his evil anti-God agenda (2 Cor. 4:4).

Isaiah reveals that Lucifer gave five prideful statements that each began with the words, "I will."
- I will ascend into heaven
- I will exalt my throne above the stars of God
- I will sit on the mount of the congregation on the farthest sides of the north
- I will ascend above the heights of the clouds
- I will be like the Most High

The statements clearly set the context for Satan's war in heaven. The accuser of God's people will have access to God in heaven during the first half of the Tribulation, and his mission will be to discredit those who claim the Lord Jesus as their Savior. The apostle John prophesied the exact time when God will end Satan's access to the heavens, which is at the midpoint of the Tribulation.[90]

THE GREAT TRIBULATION [91]

Satan's War in Heaven

The Great Tribulation, defined as the last 3.5 years of the seven-year Tribulation period, the most devastating time period since the catastrophic worldwide flood in Genesis 6, takes place after an event which occurs in heaven between Satan, his demonic army, the elect angel Michael and the elect angels. When the student of Bible prophecy understands the devastating turn of events for Israel, the Jewish people, and all inhabitants of the earth at this pivotal time, many of the current events will come into focus as God is setting the stage for Bible prophecy to be fulfilled. God is currently putting the biblical scenario in place that leads to the absolute guarantee of the Satanic one-world government, economy, and religion of Revelation 13.

---

[90] David M. Levy, *Revelation, Hearing the Last Word* (Bellmawr, NJ.: The Friends of Israel Gospel Ministry, 1999), 137.

[91] Chapter three is taken in part from: Richard R. Schmidt, *Tribulation to Triumph,* Hales Corners, WI: Prophecy Focus Ministries, 2019

The event that brings great clarity to what the Antichrist executes at the midpoint of the Tribulation is found in Revelation 12. The question Revelation 12 answers is, "Why does the Antichrist, after three and a half years of support for the Jewish people, suddenly take a negative, hateful, violent turn towards the Jewish people?" This chapter uncovers the Antichrist's abominable acts against the Jewish people, and why he will violently turn against them. Jesus prophesied this catastrophic event in the Olivet Discourse (Matt. 24:15).

To fully understand the Antichrist's actions as described in Matthew 24:15, the Abomination of Desolation against the Jewish people and God's temple, it is imperative to set the context by first turning to the apostle John in Revelation 12-13. We will examine Satan's war in heaven, his defeat, and the catastrophic outcome on earth. Satan's prophesied loss of access to heaven is the impetus for Satan's and the Antichrist's subsequent apocalyptic abominable acts from the mid-Tribulation until Satan's final demise in the lake of fire (Rev. 19:20).

| Matthew 24:1-13 | Matthew 24:14-25:46 |
| Mark 13:1-13 | Mark 13:14-23 |

Revelation 12:7–13:18
Satan's War in Heaven

Figure 3.4

> And war broke out in heaven: Michael and his angels fought with the dragon; and the dragon and his angels fought, but they did not prevail, nor was a place found for them in heaven any longer. So the great dragon was cast out, that serpent of old, called the Devil and Satan, who deceives the whole world; he was cast to the earth, and his angels were cast out with him.
>
> Then I heard a loud voice saying in heaven, "Now salvation, and strength, and the kingdom of our God, and the power of His Christ have come, for the accuser of our brethren, who accused them before our God day and night, has been cast down. And they overcame him by the blood of the Lamb and by the word of their testimony, and they did not love their lives to the death. Therefore rejoice, O heavens, and you who dwell in them! Woe to the inhabitants of the earth and the

sea! For the devil has come down to you, having great wrath, because he knows that he has a short time. (Rev. 12:7-12)

Revelation 12 describes a battle that takes place at the midpoint of the Tribulation. Michael and the elect angels will battle Satan and the demonic angels, and expel them from heaven.

God reveals in the writings of Isaiah the prophet, the corrupt character of Lucifer, whose name was subsequently changed to Satan. Isaiah points out five rebellious, anti-God, narcissistic statements made by Lucifer that are instructional in understanding why God orders the war in heaven against Satan and the demonic, fallen angels.

Satan's Access to God Ends

And war broke out in heaven: Michael and his angels fought with the dragon; and the dragon and his angels fought, but they did not prevail, nor was a place found for them in heaven any longer. So the great dragon was cast out, that serpent of old, called the Devil and Satan, who deceives the whole world; he was cast to the earth, and his angels were cast out with him. ¹⁰Then I heard a loud voice saying in heaven, "Now salvation, and strength, and the kingdom of our God, and the power of His Christ have come, for the accuser of our brethren, who accused them before our God day and night, has been cast down. And they overcame him by the blood of the Lamb and by the word of their testimony, and they did not love their lives to the death. (Rev. 12:7-11)

Satan and the demons will face off with Michael and the elect angels. A war in heaven will take place, which, to the human mind, seems an unlikely event. Christians tend to view heaven as a place of peace in the presence of God, but the apostle John paints a much different picture. John does not describe the weapons that the angelic, spirit beings use to fight each other. However, the war in heaven is an apocalyptic certainty.

The apostle Paul provides insight into how Christians must war against spiritual adversaries. "For though we walk in the flesh, we do not war according to the flesh. For the weapons of our warfare are not carnal but mighty in God for pulling down strongholds" (2 Cor. 10:3-4). The most powerful weapon in the Christian's spiritual arsenal is the Word of God (Heb. 4:12). However, Scripture strongly intimates that a literal physical battle will ensue between the elect and evil angels.

Our minds can only imagine how invisible spirit beings will war against each other. Artists for centuries have painted pictures that depict armor-clad angels slashing at each other with swords. The fact remains, spirit beings cannot be injured or killed, making human weapons ineffective in an angelic war. Despite the limitations of the human mind to comprehend the battle, the outcome is certain. The elect of heaven permanently evict Satan and the demonic army. Heaven receives a great cleansing, as Satan, the false, malicious, accuser of God's people, will once and for all be cast out. Satan's constant day and night ranting in heaven against God's children as "the accuser of the brethren" will meet a sudden and glorious end in the heavenlies (vs. 10).

Satan's War on Earth

Therefore rejoice, O heavens, and you who dwell in them! Woe to the inhabitants of the earth and the sea! For the devil has come down to you, having great wrath, because he knows that he has a short time. (Rev. 12:12)

Heaven's victory will result in a catastrophic attack on the inhabitants of earth. God uses a very strong word in pronouncing a "woe" upon the earth and the sea, which involves the entire world. The word "woe" is an interjection of grief or indignation, and the word's meaning in the grammatical structure of Revelation 12:12 pronounces misery, and pities those who will experience the actions associated with the woe (Matt. 11:21; 23:13; Mark 13:17; Luke 6:24; Jude 1:11).[92] David Levy rightly states, "The world, already under the wrath of God, must now face the uncontrollable anger of Satan as he pours out the most irrational hatred possible against humanity."[93]

Satan knows, "that he has but a short time." This issue comprises the most important fact regarding why Satan's hatred for God and the Jewish people reaches epic proportions during the last half of the Tribulation. He knows that he only has three and a half years to thwart God's prophetic plan to inaugurate His kingdom on earth. Satan knows he must make every effort to annihilate the

---

[92] Joseph H. Thayer, *Thayer's Greek-English Lexicon of the New Testament* (Peabody, MA.: Hendrickson Publishers, 1896-2002), 461.
[93] Levy, 141.

Jewish people and prevent God's covenant promises to the Jewish people from being fulfilled.

God's unconditional eternal covenants, including the Abrahamic, Land, Davidic, and New Covenants, cannot be fulfilled if the Jewish people cease to exist. Therefore, Satan will attack the Jewish people, and God's program, with a fierce intensity, with his ultimate goal of protecting himself from eternal punishment (Rev. 20:10). Satan knows the content of the Scriptures, as proven by his twisted use of them when tempting Eve in the Garden of Eden and Jesus in the wilderness (Gen 3:1-5; Matt. 4:6). Satan knows that despite God's prophetic Word having always been fulfilled exactly as written, he must try to put an end to God's perfect record.

> Now when the dragon saw that he had been cast to the earth, he persecuted the woman who gave birth to the male Child. But the woman was given two wings of a great eagle, that she might fly into the wilderness to her place, where she is nourished for a time and times and half a time, from the presence of the serpent. So the serpent spewed water out of his mouth like a flood after the woman, that he might cause her to be carried away by the flood. But the earth helped the woman, and the earth opened its mouth and swallowed up the flood which the dragon had spewed out of his mouth. And the dragon was enraged with the woman, and he went to make war with the rest of her offspring, who keep the commandments of God and have the testimony of Jesus Christ. (Rev. 12:13–17)

The Satanic Trinity

Revelation 13 summarizes Satan's plan during the last three and a half years of the Tribulation to completely disrupt the earth and all its inhabitants. The three main figures in Revelation 13 are Satan, called the "dragon" (Rev. 13:2,4,11), the Antichrist, called the first "beast" (13:1-4, 12, 14, 15, 18), and the false prophet (Rev. 13:3; 19:20; 20:10), called "another beast" (13:11). These three individuals could properly be called the satanic trinity.

This apocalyptic passage reveals that Satan is the powerful, leader within the satanic trinity. The Antichrist is the satanically empowered, anti-God, anti-Israel, anti-Jewish, anti-believers in the Lord Jesus Christ enemy of all that is good and godly. The false prophet (second beast) (Rev. 16:13; 19:20; 20:19) is the evil one tasked to promote the worship of the Antichrist.

The satanic trinity will literally take over the world, and form a one-world government, economy, and religion (Rev. 13). Globalism will become a reality. The satanically run global system will culminate in a barbaric, violent dictatorship, resulting in the worst cultural conditions ever experienced on earth. This period will truly be the "Great Tribulation" (Matt. 24:21).

The student of the Olivet Discourse (Matt. 24-25; Mark 13; Luke 21) will gain a great deal of background information for the text when carefully studying Revelation 13. Everything that occurs in the Olivet Discourse is directly linked to the work of the satanic trinity. The student must keep in mind that God uses evil leaders, and Satan himself, to accomplish His sovereign will. God will sovereignly allow Satan, the Antichrist, and the false prophet to disrupt the entire world (Prov. 16:4; Pa. 115:3; Isa. 14:24; 45:7; Jer. 10:23; Lam. 3:37; Amos 3:6; Eph. 1:11).

We will examine Revelation 13 to learn what the satanic trinity will accomplish, specifically during the last half of the Tribulation. The key point to remember in the study of Revelation 13 and the Olivet Discourse, is that both passages are describing eschatological events exclusively. The satanic trinity does not exist until after the Rapture of the Church Age saints (1 Thess. 4:13-18; 1 Cor 15:50-54), and the Tribulation begins (Dan. 9:27).

Satan and the Antichrist

> Then I stood on the sand of the sea. And I saw a beast rising up out of the sea, having seven heads and ten horns, and on his horns ten crowns, and on his heads a blasphemous name. Now the beast which I saw was like a leopard, his feet were like the feet of a bear, and his mouth like the mouth of a lion. The dragon gave him his power, his throne, and great authority. And I saw one of his heads as if it had been mortally wounded, and his deadly wound was healed. And all the world marveled and followed the beast. So they worshiped the dragon who gave authority to the beast; and they worshiped the beast, saying, "Who is like the beast? Who is able to make war with him?"
> And he was given a mouth speaking great things and blasphemies, and he was given authority to continue for

forty-two months. Then he opened his mouth in blasphemy against God, to blaspheme His name, His tabernacle, and those who dwell in heaven. It was granted to him to make war with the saints and to overcome them. And authority was given him over every tribe, tongue, and nation. All who dwell on the earth will worship him, whose names have not been written in the Book of Life of the Lamb slain from the foundation of the world. If anyone has an ear, let him hear. He who leads into captivity shall go into captivity; he who kills with the sword must be killed with the sword. Here is the patience and the faith of the saints. (Rev. 13:1-10)

Revelation 13:1-10 describes the first two members of the satanic trinity, Satan and the Antichrist. The verses are written in an apocalyptic style, which uses symbolism to portray literal people, places, and things. William Varner provides insight into biblical apocalyptic literature.

> Apocalypse, from the Greek *apokalupsis,* is literally an "unveiling." As a literary term, it describes a genre that flourished in intertestamental Jewish writings from the third century BC through the first century AD. The main characteristics of apocalyptic literature mark most of these writings. A disclosure of heavenly secrets is made to a biblical character through an angelic mediator by means of highly symbolic language. These visions usually describe a direct divine intervention in wicked human affairs whereby sinners are judged and the righteous are rewarded. [94]

Therefore, the text uses the symbolism of "the sand of the sea," a "beast," "seven heads," "ten horns," "ten crowns," and a "dragon" (Rev. 13:1-2). In addition, similes (comparisons using the words "like" and "as") are used to describe the beast, including he was "like unto a leopard, and his feet were as *the feet* of a bear, and his mouth as the mouth of a lion" (13:2).

The first two verses in Revelation 13 could be explained as follows.

And I *[the apostle John]* stood upon the sand of the [Mediterranean] sea, and saw a beast *[the Antichrist]* rise up out of

---

[94] William Varner, "Apocalyptic Literature," in Dictionary of Premillennial Theology A Practical Guide to the People, Viewpoints, and History of the Prophetic Studies, ed. Mal Couch (Grand Rapids: Kregel Publications, 1996), 53-54.

the sea *[mass of humanity]*, having seven heads *[possibly referring to the seven major empires cited in Scripture: Egypt, Assyria, Babylon, Medo-Persia, Greece, Rome, Revived Rome; or to the rulers of the future seven nations that will survive out of the ten original confederate nations, which give their authority to the Antichrist]* and ten horns *[future Tribulation period ten-nation confederacy]*, and upon his horns ten crowns *[governmental authority]*, and upon his heads the name of blasphemy *[signifying anti-God rulers]*. ²And the beast *[Antichrist])* which I *[the apostle John])* saw was like unto a leopard *[representing the attributes of the Grecian Empire (Daniel 7:6)]*, and his feet were as *the feet* of a bear *[representing the attributes of the Medo-Persian Empire (Daniel 7:5)]*, and his mouth as the mouth of a lion *[representing the attributes of the Babylonian Empire (Daniel 7:5)]*: and the dragon *[Satan]* gave him *[Antichrist]* his power, and his seat, and great authority.[95]

Revelation 13:1-2, refers to three of the four beasts discussed in Daniel 7, which are the lion, the bear, and the leopard. Daniel 7:7 describes the fourth beast: "After this I saw in the night visions, and behold, a fourth beast, dreadful and terrible, exceedingly strong. It had huge iron teeth; it was devouring, breaking in pieces, and trampling the residue with its feet. It was different from all the beasts that were before it, and it had ten horns.". The fourth beast represents the Roman Empire, which morphs into the yet future Revived Roman Empire.

At this point, the careful reader may start to question whether something is missing in the chronology of Daniel 7 and Revelation 13. I agree that something is missing, and it constitutes the most important issue for the proper interpretation of God's prophetic calendar.

History bears record to the chronology of Daniel 7 as follows. The Babylonian Empire lasted from 605 BC to 538 BC. The Medo-Persian Empire, represented by the bear, lasted from 538 BC to 331 BC. The empire of Greece, represented by the leopard, was in place from 331 BC to 168 BC. Rome conquered Greece in 146 BC and remained in power until AD 476. Now the interpretive challenge comes to light. Why is there a massive gap of time between the end of the Roman Empire and the start of the prophesied Revived Roman Empire? The answer is that God interrupted His Old Testament

---

[95] Walvoord, Every Prophecy in the Bible, 562-563.

Jewish prophetic calendar and inserted the mystery Church Age, which was never prophesied in the Old Testament (Eph. 3:1-7; Col. 1:24-29; Rom. 16:25-26). I discuss this issue in detail in my book, *Daniel's Gap Paul's Mystery, What Paused the Prophetic Calendar*.[96]

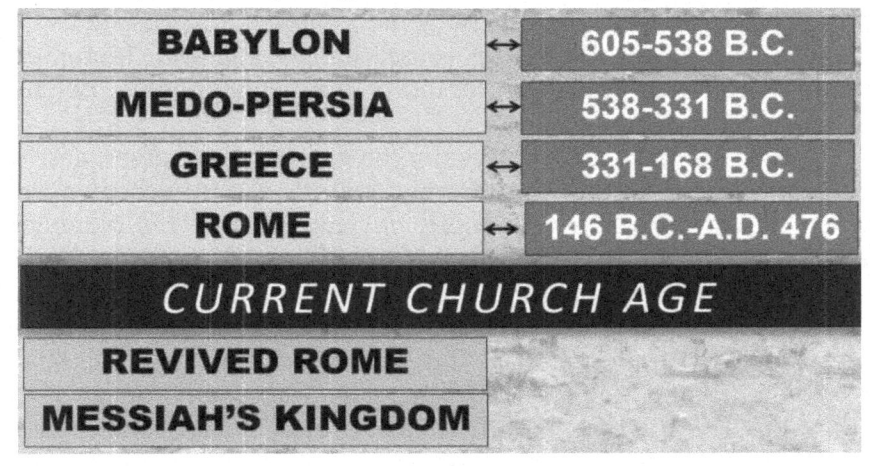

BABYLON	↔	605-538 B.C.
MEDO-PERSIA	↔	538-331 B.C.
GREECE	↔	331-168 B.C.
ROME	↔	146 B.C.-A.D. 476
CURRENT CHURCH AGE		
REVIVED ROME		
MESSIAH'S KINGDOM		

Figure 3.5

When studying Daniel 7 and Revelation 13 it becomes evident that a large gap of time exists in God's Old Testament prophetic calendar, specifically between the Roman Empire and the Revived Roman Empire. When we understand that God inserted the current Church Age into the midst of the Old Testament prophetic timeline, the gap makes sense. God's placement of the mystery Church Age into the timeline explains exactly why there has been a nearly two-thousand-year gap in God's prophetic calendar. In addition, this theological conclusion explains why God paused the pattern of prophecy in predicting the empires from Babylon through Rome. God did not reveal which dominant world powers would arise after Rome lost its dominant position. The Church Age political powers fall outside of the Old Testament prophetic calendar. This truth vividly

---

[96] God's Old Testament Jewish prophetic timeline in Daniel 9:24-27 comprises the most important text for determining exactly how the prophetic calendar unfolds. The book *Daniel's Gap Paul's Mystery, What Paused the Prophetic Calendar,* by Richard R. Schmidt, Hales Corners, WI, Prophecy Focus Ministries, 2016, is the only known volume that specifically addresses Daniel 9:24-27 and how the mystery Church Age (Eph. 3:1-7; Col. 1:24-29; Rom. 16:25-26) fits in the gap between Daniel 9:26-27.

explains why a time gap exists between Daniel 2:40 and 41, and Daniel 7:7a and 7b.

The existence and timing of the Church Age explain exactly why the Olivet Discourse was not written to the Church Age saints, as the church did not exist at that time, nor was it discussed in the Gospels. The Olivet Discourse is specific to the Old Testament prophetic calendar and is addressed to the Jewish people, not the church.

Revelation 13:2 says, "the dragon gave him his power, and his seat, and great authority." Simply stated, Satan provides the Antichrist with his throne, where he will practice his diabolical dictatorship. David Aune adds an important insight.

> The reference to the throne of the dragon calls to mind the throne of Satan mentioned in Rev. 2:13, metaphorically located in Pergamon. The throne of the beast is again mentioned in Rev. 16:10, where the fifth angel pours out his bowl on the throne of the beast, causing its kingdom to be in darkness.[97]

A key concept to grasp when delving into the mind of Satan is to understand that his motivation during the Tribulation is to gain dominion over God and all that He has created. Satan's original rebellion against God was based on the Devil's loss of dominion over the earth to Adam and Eve (Gen. 1:26-28). Satan's career for the past six thousand years is to not only regain his place as the anointed, powerful cherub, but to ascend to the next level and take over as God Himself. Based on the infallible Scriptures, Satan will never achieve his goal, but he will cause catastrophic grief on the earth until the day when God once and for all sends him to his eternal torment in the lake of fire (Rev. 20:10).

The Worship of Antichrist and Satan
The Wound

> And I saw one of his heads as if it had been mortally wounded, and his deadly wound was healed. And all the world marveled and followed the beast. So they worshiped the dragon who gave authority to the beast; and they worshiped the beast,

---

[97] David E. Aune, "Revelation 6-16" in Word Biblical Commentary, general ed. Bruce M. Metzger, OT ed. John D. W. Watts, James W/ Watts, (Nashville, TN.: Thomas Nelson Publishers, 1998), 736.

saying, "Who is like the beast? Who is able to make war with him?" (Rev. 13:3–4)

A logical question to ask when studying prophecy is, "Why will all the people of the earth who reject Jesus Christ accept a one-world religion during the Great Tribulation?" The current world has a plethora of religions, and in the case of Christianity, there are dozens of denominations and theological nuances. Revelation 13:3-4 gives an important insight into how the one-world satanic religion forms.

Expositors of Revelation 13:3 have differing opinions on the section of the verse, "And I saw one of his heads as it were wounded to death; and his deadly wound was healed." John Walvoord provides a summary of the exegetical conundrum.

> Through the history of the church this description has suggested to various expositors the revival from the dead of some great personage of the past to assume this role, including such people as Judas Iscariot, Nero, and in more modern times, Mussolini, Hitler, and Stalin. The fact that there are so many possible candidates seems to militate against this explanation. It also has the problem that if Satan cannot rise one from the dead, it would require God to raise this person from the dead to fulfill his role.[98]

There are those who argue that the wound did not result in physical death, but was an apparent legitimate catastrophic injury. Satan does have miraculous, but limited abilities. Therefore, Satan certainly could cause the appearance of the alleged fatal wound to be immediately healed, causing a frenzied, worldwide belief in his power, and the power of the Antichrist. The text is clear that the people will not only worship the Antichrist because of this apparent miracle, but they will also worship Satan (the dragon), based onthepower he gives to the Antichrist.

Mark Hitchcock argues that the wound will indeed be a fatal one, and the Antichrist will literally be raised from the dead. Hitchcock provides three main arguments to support this conclusion. First, the restraining work of the Holy Spirit on earth will be lifted, allowing Satan to perform things that currently he cannot (2 Thess. 2:6-7). Second, Jesus and the apostles Paul and John use the same language describing the future miracles of Satan that they used to describe the miracles Jesus performed (Matt. 24:24; Mark 13:22; 2

---

[98] Walvoord, Every Prophecy of the Bible, 564.

Thess. 2:9; Rev. 13:13-15; 16:13-14; 19:20). Third, in texts referring to the resurrection of Christ and the Antichrist, similarities in language are used (Rev. 2:8; 5:6; 13:3; 17:8).[99]

The Antichrist, the powerful political leader who brokers a pseudo peace for Israel (Dan. 9:26), will develop into a powerful spiritual leader as he takes control of the one-world satanically empowered religion.

The Period of Worship

> And he was given a mouth speaking great things and blasphemies, and he was given authority to continue for forty-two months (Rev. 13:5).

The timing in apocalyptic passages has led to many allegorical interpretations. The apostle John unequivocally states that the Antichrist's blasphemous one-world religion will last "forty-two months." Since there are 12 months in a year, 42 months equates to three and a half years. Scripture provides two other ways for determining that the last half of the Tribulation is a literal three-and-a-half year period.

First, Scripture refers to the last half of the Tribulation as "time, times and half a time" (Dan. 7:25; 12:7; Rev. 12:14). This interesting formula in biblical times refers to one year "time," plus two years "times," plus six months or half of one year "half a time." Adding the three parts of the equation together provides the answer of three and a half years.

Second, the Bible refers to a three-and-a-half-year period as "one thousand two hundred and sixty days" (Rev. 11:3; 12:6). Sir Robert Anderson points out the Jewish year followed the lunisolar period of 360 days, unlike the 365 days in our current calendar.[100] Floyd Nolan Jones adds, "the data in Genesis does indicate that the original creation years were 360 days long (Gen. 7:11, 24; 8:3-4). Furthermore, the Book of Revelation indicates that the 360-day year will be restored during Christ Jesus' 1,000-year millennial reign on the earth (Rev. 12:6, 13-14; 13:4-7)."[101] Therefore, the hermeneutical principle stands that the Scripture must be interpreted literally unless there is an obvious contextual reason to

---

[99] Hitchcock, 324-328.
[100] Anderson, 99-100.
[101] Floyd Nolan Jones, *The Chronology of the Old Testament* (Green Forest, AR.: Master Books, 2004), 225.

conclude that God is using symbolism in a text. The Bible incorporates three different mathematical statements to consistently verify that the Tribulation consists of two equal parts of three and a half years. Therefore, the Great Tribulation, when the satanic trinity is operating, will last for a literal three-and-a-half-year period.

Antichrist's Hatred for God

> Then he opened his mouth in blasphemy against God, to blaspheme His name, His tabernacle, and those who dwell in heaven (Rev. 13:6)

Antichrist's motivation for his horrific acts of violence against humanity stem from Satan's hatred of God's positional authority. During the last half of the Tribulation, when Satan controls the Antichrist and raises him up to be the fierce dictator of the world, the Antichrist will impose a *monotheistic* theology and demand that all people worship him. The Antichrist will vehemently fight against the true and only God. The apostle John looks to the eschatological future and reveals that the Antichrist "opened his mouth in blasphemy against God, to blaspheme his name."

The apostle John uses forms of the word blasphemy four times in the first six verses of Revelation 13, which refers to the anti-God speech and acts of the Antichrist. Thayer points out that blasphemy consists of "impious and reproachful speech injurious to the divine majesty."[102] Blasphemy is the ultimate disrespectful hate speech against God.

Antichrist's Hatred for God's Dwelling

The satanically empowered Antichrist hates everything that bears the name of God, including His dwelling place in heaven. The word "tabernacle" as used in the King James Version and the New King James Version carries the meaning in modern English of the place where God resides. The English Standard Version more rightly translates the word "dwelling place," which expresses the root meaning of the word in the current twenty-first-century vernacular. God's dwelling place with the Hebrew children during their journey

---

[102] Thayer, 102-103

from Egypt to the promised land was in the tabernacle, or dwelling place of God (Ex. 29:43).[103]

The Antichrist further expresses His hatred of God by verbally lashing out at the inhabitants of heaven. This comes as no surprise, for Satan and his demons were cast out of heaven a short time earlier at the mid-Tribulation, when they lost their heavenly battle against the archangel Michael and the elect angels (Rev. 12:7-9). The satanically empowered Antichrist will hate what Satan hates, and that includes God, His dwelling place, and all angels and people who love the Lord.

Antichrist's Hatred for the Saints

"It was granted to him to make war with the saints and to overcome them. And authority was given him over every tribe, tongue, and nation" (Rev. 13:7).

Persecution against God's people has been a constant throughout history. However, during the Great Tribulation, God makes it clear that an all-out war will take place between the Antichrist and the saints of God on earth. John's use of the word "war" bears the exact meaning of what will take place when the full fury of the satanically charged Antichrist is unleased. All who place their faith in the Lord Jesus and refuse to follow and worship the Antichrist during the Great Tribulation will be martyred for their faith, unless they can go underground and avoid Antichrist's one-world governmental system (Rev. 13:15-18).

Some years ago, I attended a Bible prophecy conference in Illinois. A well-known prophecy speaker stated that in all likelihood, more than ninety percent of earth's population will die during the Tribulation. He reminded us that Jesus spoke about the massive number of people who will die during the Tribulation. Jesus stated, "And except those days should be shortened, there should no flesh be saved: but for the elect's sake those days shall be shortened" (Matt. 24:22). Scholars conclude that the comment Jesus made was specific to the seven-year period of the Tribulation. There is nothing in Scripture that indicates that the number of hours in the days will be shortened.[104]

---

[103] Thayer, 577-578.
[104] Walvoord, "Christ's Olivet Discourse on the End of the Age, Part III, Signs of the End of the Age," 322.

The book of Revelation records four major sets of judgments that will take place during the Tribulation. The seven seal judgments (Rev. 6:1-17), the seven trumpet judgments (Rev. 8:1-9:21; 11:13-19), the seven thunder judgments (which God instructed the apostle John not to write about) (Rev. 10), and the seven vial or bowl judgments (Rev. 16:1-21), which will result in a catastrophic number of deaths. Two judgments alone result in the death of one-half of the earth's population: the fourth seal judgment will result in one-fourth of the earth's population dying as a result of violence, famine, plagues, and wild beasts (Rev. 6:7-8), and the sixth trumpet results in one-third of the earth's population dying as a result of fire, smoke, and sulfur being spewed from the mouths of a 200 million-member demonic army (Rev. 9:13-21). Therefore, between these two judgments alone, half of the world's population will die.

Revelation 12-13 brings great clarity to verses such as Matthew 24:9-12 in the Olivet Discourse.

> "Then they will deliver you up to tribulation and kill you, and you will be hated by all nations for My name's sake. And then many will be offended, will betray one another, and will hate one another. Then many false prophets will rise up and deceive many. And because lawlessness will abound, the love of many will grow cold.

The student of prophecy should carefully consider the gravity of the devastating judgments and events that will occur in the eschatological future. God did not provide the prophetic Word, and explanation of future events, simply to inform. The Lord anticipates His saints, present and future, to vigorously act as His ambassadors, contending for the faith, and sharing the greatest news ever given to humanity, that Christ Jesus came into the world to save sinners (2 Cor. 5:20; 1 Tim. 1:15). God's people who understand great prophetic truths, and yet forsake the mission of sharing the gospel, make their dedication suspect.

> Therefore we make it our aim, whether present or absent, to be well pleasing to Him. For we must all appear before the judgment seat of Christ, that each one may receive the things done in the body, according to what he has done, whether good or bad. Knowing, therefore, the terror of the Lord, we persuade men; but we are well known to God, and I also trust are well known in your consciences. (2 Cor. 5:9-11)

Antichrist's Scope of Followers

> It was granted to him to make war with the saints and to overcome them. And authority was given him over every tribe, tongue, and nation. All who dwell on the earth will worship him, whose names have not been written in the Book of Life of the Lamb slain from the foundation of the world. (Rev. 13:7-8)

The Antichrist's global influence, which he will gain during the Tribulation, is one of the most astounding facts in Bible prophecy. Many a powerful leader has arisen that gained the great support of a multitude of people. However, no single person has ever had the entire world submit to their leadership. The Antichrist's power will extend "every tribe, tongue, and nation" (vs. 7). Simply stated, everyone whose name is absent from the "book of life" (vs. 8), will submit to the Antichrist.

"Globalism," a concept that has gained contemporary political and economic leverage, will become an absolute apocalyptic reality during the Tribulation. The impact of globalism will enter the religious sphere, as the satanically charged Antichrist deceives the entire world, and forms his one-world political, economic, and religious system.

John Walvoord provides valuable insight into interpreting the challenging text of Revelation 13:10 "He who leads into captivity shall go into captivity; he who kills with the sword must be killed with the sword. Here is the patience and the faith of the saints."

> The invitation here is not addressed to the churches as in Revelation 2-3, since the church has already been raptured, but to individuals. The saints can rest in the fact that God honors sincere faith in coming to Him. Though this may not prevent them from being martyred, it assures them, nevertheless, eternal blessing in the presence of God. On the other hand, those who are wicked and who deserve punishment will receive it in time or in eternity. The saints, recognizing that God is not settling all accounts in this world, should have patience and endurance, trusting God who is handling their personal lives.[105]

---

[105] Walvoord, Every Prophecy of the Bible, 566-567.

Satan, Antichrist, and the False Prophet

Then I saw another beast coming up out of the earth, and he had two horns like a lamb and spoke like a dragon. And he exercises all the authority of the first beast in his presence, and causes the earth and those who dwell in it to worship the first beast, whose deadly wound was healed. He performs great signs, so that he even makes fire come down from heaven on the earth in the sight of men. And he deceives those who dwell on the earth—by those signs which he was granted to do in the sight of the beast, telling those who dwell on the earth to make an image to the beast who was wounded by the sword and lived. He was granted power to give breath to the image of the beast, that the image of the beast should both speak and cause as many as would not worship the image of the beast to be killed. He causes all, both small and great, rich and poor, free and slave, to receive a mark on their right hand or on their foreheads, and that no one may buy or sell except one who has the mark or the name of the beast, or the number of his name. Here is wisdom. Let him who has understanding calculate the number of the beast, for it is the number of a man: His number is 666. (Rev. 13:11-18)

The False Prophet's Description

Then I saw another beast coming up out of the earth, and he had two horns like a lamb and spoke like a dragon. (Revelation 13:11)

The beast, referred to in other passages as the "false prophet" (Rev. 16:13; 19:20; 20:10), is the third member of the satanic trinity. Together, Satan, the Antichrist, and the false prophet will produce the most terrifying one-world religious, economic, and political system that has ever existed.

This apocalyptic text uses symbolic language to describe the second beast, "he had two horns like a lamb, and he spoke like a dragon" (Rev. 13:11). The "lamb" suggests a sweet, calm, cuddly, endearing persona. However, the two horns on its head speak to its authority and power.This apparently sedate lamb has more of a personality than one might suspect.

```
              ┌─────────┐
             /    ≠     \
            /  ─────────  \
           /               \
          /  THE SATANIC    \
         /      FALSE        \
        /      TRINITY        \
       /                       \
      /     REVELATION 13       \
     /_____\
```

SATANIC TRINITY   **MIMICS**

Satan ⟷ DRAGON: Rev. 13:2 4, 11 ⟷ *God the Father*

Antichrist ⟷ FIRST BEAST: Rev. 13:1-4, 12, 14,15,18 ⟷ *God the Son-Jesus Christ*

False Prophet ⟷ SECOND BEAST: Rev. 13:11 ⟷ *God the Holy Spirit*

Figure 3.6

Surprisingly, this lamb speaks with the voice of a dragon. The charismatic personality of the false prophet has a fierce, powerful, dictatorial side that is not to be trifled with. Jesus warned of false prophets when He stated, "Beware of false prophets, who come to you in sheep's clothing, but inwardly they are ravenous wolves" (Matt. 7:15). The Lord's use of "ravenous" wolves perfectly describes the false prophet, who will cause the deaths of an untold number of people who refuse to worship the Antichrist (Rev. 13:15).

Grant Osborne provides an excellent summary of the work of the second beast.

> Like the Antichrist, the false prophet is the agent of the dragon and speaks with his voice. This is another parody of Christ, who speaks with the voice of the Father (John 5:25-30; 7:16-18). The "voice like a dragon" probably also refers to the same deceptive, lying words that the "ancient serpent" uses to lead the world astray (12:9). The Antichrist was given "a mouth to speak blasphemies, and ... opened his mouth in order to blaspheme God and to slander His name (13:5-6). The second beast will speak with the same voice.[106]

---

[106] Grant R. Osborne, *Revelation* in *Baker Exegetical Commentary on the New Testament* (Grand Rapids, Ml.: Baker Academic, 2006), 512.

The False Prophet's Mission
> And he exercises all the authority of the first beast in his presence, and causes the earth and those who dwell in it to worship the first beast, whose deadly wound was healed. (Rev. 13:12)

The false prophet will possess the same supernatural satanic power as the Antichrist. The importance of this passage should never be underestimated, as it provides one of the most powerful texts on the horrific environment that will exist during the Great Tribulation. The student of prophecy should be awestruck by the reality of this critical prophecy. The world controlled by Satan, and his two possessed workers, having global power and authority is an absolutely distressing thought. Those who come to faith in Jesus Christ during the Tribulation will face violent persecution and a probable martyr's death. The Scriptures reveal that a group of Jewish and Gentile believers in Jesus Christ that will survive the Tribulation. Zechariah specifically states that one-third of the Jewish people will survive (Zech. 13:8-9). Matthew reveals that an unknown number of Gentile believers will also survive the Tribulation judgments and enter into the millennial kingdom in human bodies (Matt. 25:31-46).

There are very few people on earth who embrace the thought of death, much less a violent death. I have spoken with many an aged Christian who longs for the Rapture, and even death. Their bodies are suffering from the effects of age, and death offers the wonderful hope of being absent from the old sin-sick, deteriorating body, and being present with the Lord (2 Cor. 5:8). However, most people, including Christians, are not looking forward to the experience of death. Humans have a desire to live and survive. What happens to a person who is forced to live in a dictatorial environment with the constant threat of punishment or death? Think about that question and allow the gravity of it to sink deep into your mind.

Life under the rule of the satanic triniity will be characterized by fear, desperation, and a constant state of panic . Revelation 13 accentuates the need for God's people today to actively tell others the greatest news ever given, that Christ Jesus came into this world to save sinners (1 Tim. 1:15). The apostle Paul speaks to the important position that every Christian has in Christ. "Now then, we are ambassadors for Christ, as though God were pleading through us: we implore *you* on Christ's behalf, be reconciled to God. For He made

Him who knew no sin *to be* sin for us, that we might become the righteousness of God in Him" (2 Cor. 5:20-21).

The Rapture of the Church Age saints could happen at any moment (1 Thess. 4:13-18; 1Cor. 15:50-54). Those left behind will face the atrocities and horrors of a world in utter chaos for the seven-year Tribulation. Those who ultimately trust Jesus Christ as their personal Savior will suffer persecution and probable martyrdom, but the good news is they will immediately go into the presence of the Lord at death. Those who refuse to place their faith in the Lord Jesus will live in a world of hunger, violence, and chaos, and face the strong probability of a terrifying death (Rev. 4-18).

The False Prophet's Methodology
Wonders & Miracles

> He performs great signs, so that he even makes fire come down from heaven on the earth in the sight of men. And he deceives those who dwell on the earth—by those signs which he was granted to do in the sight of the beast, telling those who dwell on the earth to make an image to the beast who was wounded by the sword and lived. He was granted power to give breath to the image of the beast, that the image of the beast should both speak and cause as many as would not worship the image of the beast to be killed. (Rev. 13:13–15)

The Old and New Testaments both record periods of signs, wonders, and miracles. The purpose of supernatural events was to authenticate those God chose to speak on His behalf. God will allow the satanic trinity to perform miraculous, supernatural signs to gain the attention of all people and nations. God will accomplish His sovereign will in allowing satanic deception to occur, resulting in judgment upon those who refuse to trust in Him and His Son.

Jesus addressed the issue of deception in the Olivet Discourse (Matt. 24:5, 11, 24; Mark 13:6, 22). The supernatural signs of the Antichrist and the false prophet will be so convincing that even the believers in Jesus Christ, referred to as the elect (Matt. 24:24), will be nearly deceived into believing in the satanic duo.

The apostle John provides insight into the marvelously deceptive signs that the satanic trinity will perform. First, the false prophet will bring "fire down from heaven" (Rev. 13:13). Grant Osborne provides an excellent summary of the false prophet's miraculous signs.

Deuteronomy 13:1-4 and 2 Thess. 2:9 speak to the counterfeit miracles, signs and wonders that typify false teachers and prophets throughout history but especially the work of this paragon of evil at the end of history... In particular, the false prophet parodies Elijah, who called down fire from heaven both at Mount Carmel (1 Kings 18:36-39) and with the soldiers sent to arrest him (2 Kings 1:10-14). In Revelation this miracle is performed both by the two witnesses (11:5) and by God himself at the destruction of Satan's army (20:9). However, the false prophet calls down fire from heaven (...in front of the people), which the NIV rightly translates "in full view of men." It is not a religious act but a public-relations performance intended to enhance the worship of the false trinity.[107]

Second, the false prophet will perform other unnamed spectacular miracles, which will gain the approval of the world's populace. Satan can empower his prophets with the ability to perform miracles. Though the scope of the miracles is not specified in this passage, Scripture is replete with the deceptive wonders and miracles that Satan has empowered others to perform (Rev. 16:14; 19:20; Deut. 13:1-5; Matt. 7:22; 24:24; Mark 13:22; 2 Thess. 2:9).[108]

Third, the false prophet's opening miracles, which deceive the entire world, will be followed by his building an image of the Antichrist that will have supernatural abilities. David Levy provides an instructional summary regarding the image of the beast.

> The image erected by the people will seem to take on life: "And he [the false prophet] hath power [lit., was given power] to give life unto the image" (v. 15). Commentators are divided on whether this image actually will have life or only the appearance of life. Some believe that God will allow the false prophet to give life to the image because of its ability to speak and cause the death of those not worshipping it. Others believe that the word *life* (lit., *breath* or *spirit*) refers only to an appearance of life, similar to a computerized figure, and not to life itself. It has been documented that trickery, magic, and ventriloquism were used in the first century to gain a

---

[107] Osborne, 513-514.
[108] Alan F. Johnson, *Revelation*, in vol. 12. of *The Expositors Bible Commentary*, ed. Frank E. Gaebelein (Grand Rapids: Zondervan, 1981), 530.

following and worship by pseudo-religionists (Acts13:6-12; 16:16; 19:13-20).[109]

Mandatory Worship

He was granted power to give breath to the image of the beast, that the image of the beast should both speak and cause as many as would not worship the image of the beast to be killed. (Rev. 13:15)

This text is one of the most sobering and outright horrifying statements in the prophetic Scriptures. The false prophet's mission is to do whatever it takes to get all of humanity to worship the Antichrist. The false prophet has an image of the beast made, and through supernatural power or potentially through technological means, gives the image the ability to speak.

The text is implicitly clear and emphatic, that all people must worship the image of the beast. The punishment for those who refuse to worship the image of the beast is death (Rev. 7:9, 14;13:15; 20:4). There will be a great number of people who will refuse to worship the false satanic trinity and the image of the beast. Those who place their faith in the Lord Jesus Christ during the Great Tribulation will choose a martyr's death over denying their faith and potentially saving their life (Rev. 20:4).

The gravity of the situation at the midpoint of the Tribulation should not be underestimated. The satanic trinity will do everything possible to stop God's sovereign plan of preserving a Jewish remnant. However, the Lord will not allow Satan to annihilate His chosen people, and certainly not through the false prophet's scheme to force all people to worship the image of the beast. The apostle John reveals that God will miraculously take a Jewish remnant to the wilderness, where God will feed the people for "a thousand two hundred and sixty days" (Rev. 12:6, 14). The prophet Zechariah specifically states that God will protect and provide for one-third of the Jewish people during the Great Tribulation. "And it shall come to pass in all the land," Says the LORD, "That two-thirds in it shall be cut off and die, But one-third shall be left in it: I will bring the one-third through the fire, Will refine them as silver is refined, And test them as gold is tested. They will call on My name, And I will answer them.

---

[109] Levy, 157.

I will say, 'This is My people'; And each one will say, 'The LORD is my God.'" (Zech. 13:8-9).

Mandatory Mark

He causes all, both small and great, rich and poor, free and slave, to receive a mark on their right hand or on their foreheads, and that no one may buy or sell except one who has the mark or the name of the beast, or the number of his name. (Rev. 13:16–17)

Prophecy reveals that a one-world economic system is on the horizon. Those paying attention to the current economic situation from a global and local perspective are acutely aware of the serious issues. People pay attention to their money, and when they lack the funds to enjoy a pleasant lifestyle, they become disgruntled. When the populace faces severe economic depression, the propensity for outrage against the government and violence in the streets, dramatically increases. One has only to watch the contemporary crime trends to conclude that the highest rates of crime have a direct correlation to poverty. The most basic instinct in every person is survival.

The apostle John provides details regarding the future need for a worldwide ruler to come on the scene to bring order to a world that is in economic chaos. The Scriptures reveal that during the first half of the Tribulation, Jesus Christ will unleash on the world six seal judgments(Rev. 6), which leads to severely depressed global economic conditions. The seal judgments include, first, the coming of the Antichrist, who brings a strong political presence to a world already inundated with wars and violence, and economic woes (Rev. 6:1-2). The second seal discloses that violence will greatly increase resulting in people killing each other (Rev. 6:3-4). The third seal is extremely important in understanding the tremendous negativity in the world that will occur during the first part of the Tribulation. There will be a severe global famine (Rev. 6:5-6). People must eat, and when they are deprived of food, they will turn to violence to survive, guaranteed. The fourth seal is one of the most devastating judgments in Scripture, only paling to the worldwide Flood in Genesis 6-8. The apostle John states that one-fourth of the world's population will die from violence, famine, plagues, and wild beasts. There are currently 7.3 billion people on the earth. If the world's population is similar at the beginning of the Tribulation, 1.8 billion people will die during the first three and one-half years of the Tribulation. The impact of such devastation is incomprehensible. The fifth seal reveals that persecution will be severe against those who put their faith in the Lord Jesus Christ during the Tribulation (Rev. 6:9-11). The Antichrist will demand compliance with the one-world religion (Rev. 17). The sixth seal unleashes catastrophic events in nature. There will be massive earthquakes, the sun will be darkened, the moon will turn red, and stars will fall to the earth (Rev. 6:12-19). Great fear, violence, and death will prevail during the entire Tribulation period.

When the student of prophecy understands the horrific conditions on earth, commencing with the start of the Tribulation, it makes perfect sense that the Antichrist will have the perfect opportunity, as a powerful and apparently accepted political leader, to force a global economic system. People will beg for help to survive, and that is exactly what the Antichrist will provide.

The satanic trinity will have the infrastructure in place at the midpoint of the Tribulation to control virtually everyone on earth, except those who somehow manage to hide in an "underground" dwelling and avoid detection by the one-world government. The satanic trinity will force the masses, including the "small and great, rich and poor, free and bond," to receive an identifying mark on their right hand or forehead (Rev. 13:16). The purpose of the mark is to control the individual's ability to buy or sell anything (Rev. 13:17).

The exact technology used to place a mark on an individual's forehead or right hand is not specifically stated in Scripture. However, there is current technology that certainly fits the scenario described in Revelation 13:16-17. In March 2018, *Business Insider* reported that over 3,000 people in Sweden had small microchips, the size of a grain of rice, implanted in their body for the purpose of identification. The chips give users access locked machines and office and gym doors. The SJ rail line in Sweden started using microchip technology for riders several years ago. *Business Insider* states that there is no reason why the microchip technology could not be used just like a credit card. A Wisconsin vending machine company, Three Square Market, offered their employees the opportunity to have microchips implanted in their hands for the purpose of giving them access to vending machines, their work computers, and photocopiers. Fifty employees volunteered for the implants.[110]

Microchip technology raises serious concerns for the Christian community. Some question whether the Tribulation period has started. Others question if those who already have the microchips embedded in their body have received the "mark of the beast," and are forever doomed. The apostle John gave a strict warning regarding those who receive the mark of the beast.

> Then a third angel followed them, saying with a loud voice, "If anyone worships the beast and his image, and receives his mark on his forehead or on his hand, he himself shall also drink of the wine of the wrath of God, which is poured out full strength into the cup of His indignation. He shall be tormented with fire and brimstone in the presence of the holy angels and in the presence of the Lamb. And the smoke of their torment ascends forever and ever; and they have no rest day or night, who worship the beast and his image, and whoever receives the mark of his name" (Rev. 14:9-11).

The Revelation 13-14 scenario does not apply to people who currently have the microchip technology embedded in their bodies. God's prophetic timeline is key to understanding this issue. The current age, rightly called the Church Age, is distinct from the yet future Tribulation period when the satanic trinity will exercise their reign on earth. The Church Age is not a part of the Old Testament prophetic calendar (Dan. 9:24-27), but it is a mystery period inserted by God (Rom. 16:25-26; Eph. 3:1-7; Col. 1:24-29) causing a pause in the Jewish prophetic calendar between Daniel 9:26 and Daniel 9:27. The next event on God's calendar is the removal of the Church Age saints (1 Thess. 4:13-18; 1 Cor. 15:51-53). Shortly after the Rapture of the saints, the Antichrist will become known, as he will confirm a covenant with Israel, which starts the clock on the seven-year Tribulation. The mark of the beast will not occur until the midpoint of the Tribulation. Therefore, anyone embedding a microchip in his or her body during the current Church Age is not part of the Revelation 13-14 scenario.

---

[110] Business Insider, "Thousands of People in Sweden are Embedding Microchips Under Their Skin to Replace ID Cards," Alexandra MA, May 14, 2018, 8:09 AM ET, https://amp.businessinsider.com/swedish-people-embed-microchips-under-skin-to-replace-id-cards-2018-5, accessed January 16, 2019.

The current microchip technology provides a valid possibility i, however, as to how the future one-world government could apply a "mark" to each individual. While the technology may change before the Tribulation begins, the fact remains that people will be forced to receive the mark of the beast, or they will not be able to buy or sell (Rev. 13:15-18).

SECTION TWO: ONE-WORLD GOVERNMENT
CHAPTER FOUR
COVID-19 / CORONAVIRUS PANDEMIC

Many people, Christians included, are in a state of panic and fear, based on the repercussions, real or perceived, of the COVID-19 pandemic. The pandemic has existed for several years, and yet many questions and debates still exist regarding the virus. Where did the virus come from? How did and should the medical community treat the virus? What restrictions should remain in place locally and internationally? How will governments respond to the next global pandemic? Dr. Mark Hitchcock, a noted biblical scholar, provides insight into the start of the COVID-19 pandemic.

> On New Year's Eve 2019, health officials from China alerted the World Health Organization of a new form of pneumonia in the city of Wuhan, a megacity in the Central China region. A few days later, health officials announced they had identified a new strain of virus from the coronavirus family. It was labelled "2019-nCoV," more commonly known as COVID-19, or the coronavirus. The number of cases exploded in China, and then Italy and Spain were hit hard. The first COVID-19 death in the United States was on February 29, 2020. The US eventually surpassed China as the country with the most confirmed cases. New York City became the global epicenter.[111]

Dr. Hitchcock's brief statement starts the discussion on what is one of the most influential issues of the current generation. Dr. Hitchcock also provides his impression of America's initial reaction to COVID-19.

> Cable news shows in the US had coronavirus coverage 24/7. Store shelves were ransacked. Bottled water was scarce. Toilet paper was nowhere to be found. Quarantines were mandated. Cruise ships were stranded. Events of all kinds were cancelled. The NBA, NHL, and MLB all suspended their seasons. High school and college sports seasons were ended. The NCAA's March Madness was scratched. Schools closed. Restaurants suspended dine-in service. Bars shut down.

---

[111] Mark Hitchcock, *Corona Crisis*, (Nashville, TN.: W Publishing Group, 2020), 4.

> Pastors preached to empty pews and chairs as church services were broadcast via livestream. Streets emptied. Gatherings of more than ten people were forbidden. Global stock markets collapsed.[112]

Virtually every person reading Dr. Hitchcock's opening analysis can relate to it in multiple ways based on their experience of the early days of the pandemic.

Jeff Kinley, a noted prophecy author and scholar adds the following insights about the initial response to COVID-19.

> New phrases and concepts were injected into our vocabulary as *social distancing* and *sheltering in place* became the vernacular. Breathing masks became as common as cell phones, though the demand for them made them scarce early on. Signs with the number 6 lined the streets, reminding people to keep a distance of six feet from others to help prevent the spread of the disease. But there were also serious concerns about the *mental* health of citizens worldwide as billions were virtually banned from outside contact for weeks on end.[113]

What is the real impact locally and globally of the COVID-19 pandemic? Steve Miller provides a thought-provoking answer to this question.

> The longer that COVID-19 and its variant strains have persisted, the more normal it has become for governments to extend their emergency powers. At the same time, globalists have stepped up their calls for a great reset and reinventing the way government is done. The outcome of all this? People everywhere are becoming conditioned to the idea that increased government authority, coupled with a globalized approach to governance, are the answers to resolving the world's problems. Given the trajectory we are on, we can expect that every global crisis our world faces will become one more stepping-stone that draws us closer to the one-world order that will arise during the end-times.[114]

---

[112] Mark Hitchcock, *Corona Crisis,* XI-XII.

[113] Jeff Kinley, *After Shocks* (Eugene, OR.: Harvest House Publishers, 2021), 14.

[114] Steve Miller, *Foreshadows* (Eugene, OR.: Harvest House Publishing, 2022), 60.

The challenge is to examine the COVID-19 pandemic within the scope of Bible prophecy and determine how COVID-19 has and will impact the globalists' move towards a one-world government, economy, and religion. The strong suggestion, based on the facts presented in this chapter, is that the pandemic set the tone for future events as prophesied in the Scriptures, specifically the world's reaction regarding plagues, pestilences, and pandemics.

Unfortunately, there are those in secular and Christian circles who sensationalized the facts, and touted self-serving and erroneous statements that padded their egos and potentially their pocketbooks, while performing a disservice to the people who encountered their fallacious materials. Robert F. Kennedy, Jr. wrote the following in the foreword to *The Truth About COVID*-19.

> Government technocrats, billionaire oligarchs, Big Pharma, Big Data, Big Media, the high-finance robber barons, and the military industrial intelligence apparatus love pandemics for the same reason they love wars and terrorist attacks. Catastrophic crises create opportunities of convenience to increase both power and wealth.[115]

Mr. Kennedy, also made the following penetrating statement.

> As soon as they get hold of the levers of authority, tyrants impose Orwellian censorship and begin gaslighting disasters. But ultimately, they seek to abolish all forms of creative thinking and self-expression. They burn books, destroy art, kill writers, poets and intellectuals, outlaw gatherings, and at their worst, force oppressed minorities to wear masks that atomize any sense of community or solidarity.[116]

Many biblical and secular scholars have written on this highly charged emotional issue. However, conspiracy theories, heated emotions, and politics cannot deny the massive number of deaths from the coronavirus, the repercussions of which millions of people are living with, as they adjust to the loss of friends and family members.

I personally lost two of my close Christian mentors to severe cases of COVID-19. The deaths of these two men, whom I worked with closely, and loved as dear Christian brothers, was not only

---

[115] Joseph Mercola and Ronnie Cummins, *The Truth About COVID-19* (White River Junction, VT.: Chelsea Green Publishing, 2021), IX.
[116] Joseph Mercola and Ronnie Cummins, *The Truth About COVID-19,* IX, X.

shocking, but heartbreaking. Though I rejoice they are "absent from the body and present with the Lord" (2 Cor. 5:8), my heart still deeply misses them. Many others are enduring the same pain associated with the loss of their loved ones.

One of the serious issues associated with the response to the COVID-19 pandemic was the decision by the majority of hospitals, treatment centers, retirement homes, assisted living facilities, and other healthcare centers, to forbid visitors from seeing those under their care. As a pastor, forbidding family members, friends, and even clergy from visiting the sick and dying is cruel to all concerned. Surprisingly, on one occasion, hospital staff allowed me to enter the hospital room of a dear person who attended the church I pastor. The staff had me don the COVID-19 protective gear. I then entered the room with the spouse of the critically ill person. We silently cried together, and watched the labored breathing of our friend and loved one, which was heartbreaking. This dear person, a few days earlier, was vibrant, and in good physical condition. The couple had just retired and were preparing to travel the country and enjoy their lovely grandchildren. However, within 24 hours, this special person was dead.

I conducted several funerals of people who died of COVID-19 complications. Some people died while on ventilators, others refused ventilators and also succumbed to the disease process. The deaths were very real, and the devastated families and friends do not want to hear from the politicians, pharmaceutical companies, or the media, regarding their position on the reality, or lack thereof, of the COVID-19 pandemic.

There is a plethora of material documenting the politicization and false information surrounding COVID-19. Writing an accurate, truthful account regarding the origin, transmission, and confirmed cases of COVID-19 is virtually impossible based on the significant speculation intertwined with alleged factual information. Robert F. Kennedy, Jr. provides insight into what many people are feeling. "Instead of citing scientific studies to justify mandates for masks, lockdowns and vaccines, our medical rulers cite WHO, CDC, FDA and NIH-captive agencies that are groveling sock puppets to the industries they regulate. Multiple federal and international investigations have documented the financial entanglements with pharmaceutical companies that have made these regulators cesspools of corruption."[117] The greatest question asked during this confusing time is, *what is truth?*

This conundrum leads to the purpose of this chapter, which is to detail how governments around the globe used truth, lies, conspiracy theories, and speculation to change how the world functions. COVID-19 radically changed the world, and paved the way for how governments will respond to the next major event that impacts the world. Dr. Hitchcock rightly speaks to this issue. "COVID-19 is also speeding the rise of globalism. The pandemic intersects with the drive toward a one-world economy and government that will fall under the rule of a global strongman, the final Antichrist (Revelation 13:1-18). The global framework that must be in place for the Antichrist to rise to power is gaining momentum in the face of the pandemic."[118]

The world's reaction to COVID-19 is one of the most important scenarios in the history of the world with regard to setting the stage for globalism, the one-world government, economy, and religion described in Revelation 13. Dr. Hitchcock adds, "everywhere you look, more and more people are wondering if, in addition to all the other impact, coronavirus signals the beginning of the end. With the sudden surge of COVID-19, it is not uncommon to hear the words *apocalyptic, doomsday* or *last days* used to describe what's happening.[119]

There are numerous questions that remain unanswered after several years of dealing with the COVID-19 pandemic, even though some outlets have declared the pandemic no longer exists.
- Will you contract the coronavirus?
- If you contract the coronavirus, will you die?
- Will your employer dismiss you for refusing to receive the COVID-19, flu, or other vaccinations?
- Will you suffer catastrophic financial loss if laid off, or if your employer is forced to shut down based on actual sickness or government mandates?
- Is God judging the world?
- Are we living in the biblical Tribulation period?
- How are you supposed to live with the unbearable loss of a friend or relative who died of COVID-19?

---

[117] Joseph Mercola and Ronnie Cummins, *The Truth About COVID-19,* XI.
[118] Mark Hitchcock, *Corona Crisis*, 30-31.
[119] Mark Hitchcock, *Corona Crisis*, 7.

- Is God trying to teach us something through this pandemic?
- What can we do to prevent the loss of our freedoms with the onset of new government restrictions and mandates when future pandemics occur?
- Does the new normal mean the end of religious freedom?

Several of the questions may remain unanswered for those trying to learn the truth. However, historical documentation, current information, and Bible prophecy provide an excellent path to understanding what is taking place in the world today, and how it will impact each person. The operative issue is not where COVID-19 came from, or the actual outcomes surrounding the pandemic. The issue is understanding how governments around the world responded to the pandemic, and how that response is setting the stage for the implementation of a globalist one-world government, economy, and religion, which Scripture mandates as an outcome of God's wrath and judgment as prophesied in Revelation 13.

ECONOMIC IMPACT OF COVID-19

America made extensive progress in reducing the unemployment rate before COVID-19. President Trump unequivocally stated that the unemployment rate for the African American and Hispanic communities reached significantly lower rates than existed in the past. The conservative community applauded this news, as prosperity for many Americans, specifically those in minority communities, was happening for the first time in their lives. Many who wanted the opportunity to work but were denied in the past for a plethora of reasons, now had the opportunity to join the workforce and feel a sense of accomplishment.

The Trump White House released the following information that outlines what was the reality of a very positive unemployment rate until the COVID-19 sanctions impacted the economy.

Since the President's election, the economy has added over 6.4 million jobs—more than the population of Maryland. Steady job growth in combination with sustained year-over-year wage increases are not only positive signs for the economy: They also improve workers' quality of life and incentivize previously left-behind Americans to join the labor force.

The household survey finds that the unemployment rate fell to 3.5 percent in September, marking the 19th consecutive month at or below 4 percent unemployment. The unemployment rate is the lowest it has been since May 1969—over 50 years ago. All Americans are benefiting from the labor market's continued improvement. The lowest unemployment rates on record were matched or set in September 2019 for African Americans, Hispanics, and people with disabilities.[120]

The pandemic took the booming economy, and the wonderful opportunities it presented to millions of Americans, and destroyed many of the positive gains made in unemployment around the country. This heartbreaking reality left millions of Americans out of work. Many of the newly unemployed had just started working for the first time. In addition, many long-term employees permanently lost their jobs or experienced a temporary layoff.

Millions of Americans remain scared and frustrated with the current economic downturn. In addition to the financial impact of COVID-19, the Federal government under President Biden has radically increased spending, further exasperating the economic downturn and spiking the rate of inflation. Many Americans face losing what they have worked for their entire life. Investments are failing, bank accounts are dwindling, lifestyles are changing, and interest rates are rising, resulting in the stress that accompanies such dramatic changes.

Various reports document the rise in domestic violence that occurred both locally and internationally during the COVID-19 pandemic.

Violence against women increased to record levels around the world following lockdowns to control the spread of the COVID-19 virus. The United Nations called the situation a "shadow pandemic" in a 2021 report about domestic violence in 13 nations in Africa, Asia, South America, Eastern

---

[120] Council of Economic Advisors, U.S. Unemployment Rates Falls to 50-Year Low, October 4, 2019, https://www.whitehouse.gov/articles/u-s-unemployment-rate-falls-50-year-low/, accessed April 29, 2020.

Europe, and the Balkans.[121] In the United States, the American Journal of Emergency Medicine reported alarming trends in U.S. domestic violence,[122] and the National Domestic Violence Hotline (The Hotline) received more than 74,000 calls, chats, and texts in February, the highest monthly contact volume of its 25-year history.[123]

Many people lashed out at loved ones when their anxiety and fears became overwhelming. The unprecedented worldwide response to COVID-19 is a foreshadowing of what will exponentially take place when famine, violence, sickness, pestilence, plagues, and other repercussions of the satanic system come to fulfillment during the seven-year Tribulation.

COVID-19 is not the end of civilization. However, based on the unprecedented governmental response to COVID-19, the way society reacts to a large-scale crisis on a global scale, and most definitely America, has come to an abrupt end. Never in modern history has any generation experienced a worldwide lockdown as took place in reaction to COVID-19. Americans protested the sanctions imposed at the local, state, and federal levels of the government. Millions of people were laid off by their employers. An untold number of businesses shut down, and many either filed for bankruptcy or are facing that probability. Suicides skyrocketed as the economy faltered, and the hope of recovery and returning to normalcy is still suspect. Investors lost a staggering amount of money, and those living paycheck to paycheck are all but financially destroyed. The United States poured trillions of dollars into the bank accounts of millions of Americans, but the question remains, can America, and the world, recover from the unprecedented measures

---

[121] Measuring Shadow Pandemic, Violence Against Women During COVID-19, https://data.unwomen.org/sites/default/files/documents/Publications/Measuring-shadow-pandemic.pdf, accessed October 29, 2022, 3:10 pm, CST.

[122] Brad Boserup, MarkMcKenney, AdelElkbuli, Alarming Trends in US Domestic Violence During The COVID-19 Pandemic, The American Journal of Emergency Medicine, Volume 38, Issue 12, December 2020, Pages 2753-2755, https://www.sciencedirect.com/science/article/pii/S0735675720303077, accessed October 31, 2022, 9:20 am, CST.

[123] Liz Mineo, The Harvard Gazette, Shadow Pandemic of Domestic Violence, June 29, 2022, https://news.harvard.edu/gazette/story/2022/06/shadow-pandemic-of-domestic-violence/, accessed October 2, 2022, 7:50 PM, CST.

taken during the COVID-19 pandemic? Though world health leaders state that the worst of the pandemic is over, the financial repercussions are still devastating the world, based on the unprecedented measures multiple governments employed.

Robert F. Kennedy, Jr. provides an excellent summary of the impact of the coronavirus on multiple levels from a worldwide perspective.

> The suspension of due process, due notice, and comment rulemaking meant that none of the government prelates who ordained the quarantine had to first publicly calculate whether destroying the global economy, disrupting food and medical supplies, and throwing a billion humans into dire poverty and food insecurity will kill more people than it would save.
>
> For example, this cabal used the lockdown to accelerate construction of their 5G network of satellites, antennae, biometric facial recognition and "track and trace" infrastructure that they, and their government and intelligence agency partners, will use to mine and monetize our data for free, compel obedience to arbitrary dictates, and to suppress dissent. Their government/industry collaboration will use this system to manage the rage when Americans finally wake up to the fact that this outlaw gang has stolen our democracy, our civil rights, our country, and our way of life- while we huddled in orchestrated fear from a flu-like illness. Putting opiates-which kill 50,000 Americans annually- aside, pharmaceuticals are now the third biggest killer of Americans after heart attacks and cancer.[124]

HISTORICAL EXAMINATION OF DISEASE AND PLAGUES

History reveals a myriad of horrific plagues and pandemics that resulted in the deaths of multitudes of people. The outbreak of COVID-19, from a logical analysis, should not be viewed as an unusual, unprecedented event. The government's response to COVID-19 is what is unprecedented, but the actual number of people infected and who died from the disease is not an anomaly as historical records document.

---

[124] Joseph Mercola and Ronnie Cummins, *The Truth About COVID-19,* XIII.

When an unusual event occurs, such as a pandemic, the natural tendency of those going through the challenge is to view it as the worst possible scenario in history. To many people, the COVID-19 pandemic may in fact be the worst event they have faced in their lifetime. Combine the terrifying current situation with the massive amount of media and government attention given to COVID-19, and the natural response is all too often fear and panic. Therefore, examining the history of pandemics, plagues, and other events that have occurred, and the documented tragic results, provides a balanced approach to the current pandemic issue.

Many sources are available that provide information on past catastrophic events, which resulted in a massive loss of life. Our examination begins in the current era and centers only on the events that resulted in a large number of fatalities. The material will progress up to the current pandemic and give the most recent statistics available (see appendix 2).

The first major plague on record is the Antonine Plague, which occurred in the years between 165 and 180. Scholars speculate that the plague was an outbreak of either smallpox or malaria, and resulted in the deaths of 5 million people. The opinion of many of those living at the time may have been that they were in the biblical Tribulation period. Imagine living almost two thousand years ago and watching millions of people die. Doctors, nurses, and other medical professionals did not have a fraction of the knowledge possessed by our contemporary medical professionals. Medications were either non-existent or poor in quality. Fear and panic would have consumed many a person living under those conditions.[125]

Moving forward in history to the year 541, the Plague of Justinian occurred. The plague is also known as "Yersinia pestis bacteria," a plague resulting from bacteria transmitted by rats and fleas. The estimated number of deaths caused by the detestable plague was 30-50 million people. The estimated world population in

---

[125] Nicholas LePan, "Visualizing the History of Pandemics," Visual Capitalist, March 14, 2020, https://www.visualcapitalist.com/history-of-pandemics-deadliest/, accessed April 29, 2020.

the year 500 was 300 million people,[126] which equates to at least 10% of the world's population dying during this one plague.[127]

The next major loss of life took place between 735 and 737 due to the Japanese smallpox epidemic. The death toll from this disease was 1 million people. There is a stretch of 610 years before the next major plague hit in 1347, known as the Black Plague. The Black Plague lasted from 1347 to 1351, and was likened to the Plague of Justinian because both plagues were the result of bacteria transmitted to the populace by rats and fleas. The death toll from the Black Plague is estimated at a staggering 50 million people, estimated to be 60% of Europe's population at the time.[128] The world population in 1350 is estimated at 450 million people, meaning that nearly 11% of the world's population died during the Black Plague.[129]

> There were recurrences of the plague in 1361–63, 1369–71, 1374–75, 1390, and 1400. Modern research has suggested that, over that period of time, the plague was introduced into Europe multiple times, coming along trade routes in waves from Central Asia as a result of climate fluctuations that affected populations of rodents infested with plague-carrying fleas.[130]

The next major plague was the New World smallpox epidemic, which began in 1520. The plague was responsible for a massive 56 million deaths. In 1665, the Great Plague of London, which was also believed to be transmitted by vermin, resulted in the deaths of 100 thousand people. Likewise, the Italian plague from 1629 to 1631, which some in the medical community believed was transmitted by vermin, resulted in the deaths of 1 million people.[131]

From 1817 to 1923, there were six Cholera pandemics, which resulted in the deaths of over 1 million people. Cholera was a severe and fatal bacterial disease that infected the small intestine. The

---

[126] Vaughn Aubuchon, World Population Growth History (Vaughn's Summaries, History Summaries Human Population) https://www.vaughns-1-pagers.com/history/world-population-growth.htm, accessed April 17, 2020.

[127] LePan.

[128] LePan.

[129] Editors of Encyclopedia Britannica, Black Death Pandemic, Medieval Europe (Encyclopedia Britannica, Updated April 15, 2020) https://www.britannica.com/event/Black-Death/Cause-and-outbreak, accessed April 17, 2020.

[130] Ibid.

[131] LePan.

source of the bacteria was contaminated water supplies. Cholera was a very unpleasant way to die, as its victims suffered horrific vomiting and diarrhea.

The next major pandemics are categorized as influenza. The Russian flu, from 1889 to 1890, was believed to be of Avian origin. This strain of flu resulted in 1 million deaths. The Spanish flu, 1918-1919, was an H1N1 virus that pigs transmitted. This strain resulted in a catastrophic loss of life, estimated at 40-50 million causalities. The Asian flu, 1957-1958, known as the H2N2 virus, resulted in the deaths of 1.1 million people. The Hong Kong flu, 1968-1970, named the H3N2 virus, resulted in the deaths of 1 million people.[132]

The AIDS/HIV disease, which began in 1981 and still is infecting people at the present time, has resulted in the deaths of an estimated 25-35 million people. The disease originated in chimpanzees and then spread to people. This virus, according to the medical community, was mainly transmitted through sexual contact.[133]

The SARS outbreak, 2002-2003, caused by SARS coronavirus (SARS-CoV), was transmitted through bats. The death toll was 770. The Swine flu, 2009-2010, was, as the name implies, transmitted through pigs or swine. It was classified as the H1N1 virus and resulted in the deaths of 200,000 people. The Ebola virus outbreak occurred between 2014 and 2016, and was contracted from wild animals. The death toll reached an estimated 11,000 people. The MERS outbreak, 2015 through the present, was transmitted through bats and camels. MERS, which is caused by MERS coronavirus (MERS-CoV), has resulted in the deaths of 850 people.[134]

As of September 30, 2022, there have been just over 614 million confirmed cases of COVID-19 worldwide, including over 6 million deaths reported to the World Health Organization (WHO). A total of 12.6 billion vaccine doses were administered worldwide. In the United States of America, from January 3, 2020 to September 3, 2020, there have been nearly 95 million confirmed cases of COVID-19 with over 1 million deaths reported to the WHO. As of September

---

[132] Ibid.
[133] Ibid.
[134] LePan.

16, 2022, a total of over 604 million vaccine doses, including booster shots were administered.[135]

Statistics can be hard to digest, but understanding the history of pandemics reveals that COVID-19 is not unique historically, when it comes to great loss of life. COVID-19 is one of the current major focuses of the medical community, government agencies, and the media. The significant issue regarding COVID-19 is not that it is unique in history, but how the world responded to this pandemic.

PROPHETIC GUARANTEE OF DISEASE AND PLAGUES
One-Fourth of the World's Population Dies
When He opened the fourth seal, I heard the voice of the fourth living creature saying, "Come and see." So I looked, and behold, a pale horse. And the name of him who sat on it was Death, and Hades followed with him. And power was given to them over a fourth of the earth, to kill with sword, with hunger, with death, and by the beasts of the earth. (Revelation 6:7–8)

The book of Revelation 4:2-19:21 describes the devastating judgments God will impose on the world during the future catastrophic seven-year Tribulation period. God's opening set of seven judgments is called the seal judgments. The Scriptures reveal the first four seal judgments using metaphorical terms. Each judgment begins by naming the color of a symbolic horse, and the associated judgment.

The Bible describes the first seal judgment as a white horse with a rider who has a bow and no arrows. Dispensational scholars are near unanimous on interpreting seal one as the arrival of the Antichrist. Daniel 9:27 reveals that the specific event that starts Daniel's seventieth prophetic week, which is literally the seven-year Tribulation period, is when the Antichrist confirms a covenant (peace treaty) with the Jewish people (Rev. 6:1-2).

God reveals the second seal judgment as follows. "Another horse, fiery red, went out. And it was granted to the one who sat on it to take peace from the earth, and that people should kill one another; and there was given to him a great sword (Rev. 6:4). Therefore, the second horse represents a massive increase in

---

[135] WHO Coronavirus (COVID-19) Dashboard, World Health Organization, https://covid19.who.int/, accessed October 1, 2022, 7:19 PM, CST.

violence across the globe, resulting in an undisclosed number of deaths.

The Bible reveals the third seal judgment in Revelation 6:5–6. "When He opened the third seal, I heard the third living creature say, 'Come and see.' So I looked, and behold, a black horse, and he who sat on it had a pair of scales in his hand. And I heard a voice in the midst of the four living creatures saying, 'A quart of wheat for a denarius, and three quarts of barley for a denarius; and do not harm the oil and the wine.'" The symbolic rider on the black horse represents the devastating famine that God will impose upon the earth. Many people around the world have experienced empty shelves in grocery stores and empty stomachs. COVID-19 introduced all classes of people in America to grocery stores that were missing many products and food staples due to some people hoarding supplies, and suppliers not being able to produce the normal quantities due to sick people not coming to work.

The first three seal judgments describe events that lead to the fourth seal judgment, which is the focus of this section. The fourth seal judgment is literally of biblical proportion, and is the worst event that the Scriptures prophecy will occur since the worldwide Flood described in Genesis 6. The worldwide Flood resulted in God taking the lives of all but eight people in the world, due to the people's refusal to love the one true God, the God of the Bible. Carefully read the words of the fourth seal judgment, and allow the guaranteed, devastating results to penetrate your mind.

> When He opened the fourth seal, I heard the voice of the fourth living creature saying, "Come and see." So I looked, and behold, a pale horse. And the name of him who sat on it was Death, and Hades followed with him. And power was given to them over a fourth of the earth, to kill with sword, with hunger, with death, and by the beasts of the earth. (Rev. 6:7–8)

Dr. Mark Hitchcock provides an important analysis regarding the metaphorical pale horse the apostle John uses to describe the devastating fourth seal judgment. "The horse's color is ashen or pale. The Greek word is *chloros*, from which we get the English words *chlorine* or *chlorophyll*. Chloros usually denotes a pale green color and is used twice in Revelation to describe the color of grass and vegetation (8:7; 9:4). In Revelation 6:8, however, it pictures the color of a decomposing corpse."[136] God is making a point that is very difficult for most people, especially in America, to comprehend. The world's population is currently at 8 billion people.[137] When dividing 8 billion by four, the result is 2 billion people. Statistics reveal that on average, 60 million people die around the world each year.[138] Sixty million is 3% of 2 billion. When God brings the fourth seal judgment to fulfillment, if the population numbers are relatively the same as now, the increase in deaths will be over 90% of what currently takes place annually.

The statistics point to the undeniable fact that the worldwide reaction to COVID-19 is unprecedented in history, and set a new bar for how the world will react in the future to a real or perceived threat. Globalism, resulting in a one-world government, economy, and religion, is no longer difficult to comprehend. When governments shut down workplaces, schools, churches, and travel, and then mandated the wearing of masks, social distancing, and limits on congregating, the world's population became keenly aware that they were being controlled in ways they never would have thought possible. COVID-19 set the stage for what will one day morph into the actual globalist goal of a one-world government, economy, and religion, which the Scriptures state will absolutely come to pass (Rev. 13).

One-Half of the World's Population Dies

Then the sixth angel sounded: And I heard a voice from the four horns of the golden altar which is before God, saying to the sixth angel who had the trumpet, "Release the four angels who are bound at the great river Euphrates." So the four angels, who had been prepared for the hour and day and month and year, were released to kill a third of mankind. Now the number of the army of the horsemen was two hundred million; I heard the number of them. And thus I saw the horses in the vision: those who sat on them had breastplates of fiery red, hyacinth blue, and sulfur yellow; and the heads of the horses were like the heads of lions;

---

[136] Mark Hitchcock, *Corona Crisis*, 89.
[137] World Population Clock, https://www.worldometers.info/world-population/, accessed 10/27/22, 3:30 pm, CST.
[138] How Many People Die a Year, https://www.theworldcounts.com/populations/world/deaths, accessed October 2, 2022, 5:15 PM, CST.

and out of their mouths came fire, smoke, and brimstone. By these three plagues a third of mankind was killed—by the fire and the smoke and the brimstone which came out of their mouths. For their power is in their mouth and in their tails; for their tails are like serpents, having heads; and with them they do harm. But the rest of mankind, who were not killed by these plagues, did not repent of the works of their hands, that they should not worship demons, and idols of gold, silver, brass, stone, and wood, which can neither see nor hear nor walk. And they did not repent of their murders or their sorceries or their sexual immorality or their thefts. (Revelation 9:13–21)

Dr. David Jeremiah, a noted pastor, prolific author, and scholar provides instructional material regarding biblical plagues.

> Exactly what are pandemics, and what does the Bible have to say about them? The word *pandemic* did not show up in our dictionaries until 1853to describe an outbreak of disease that exceeds an epidemic. The Latin prefix *pan* means "all." The root term *demic* comes from the word *demotic* from which we get *democracy.* It means "belonging to the people." A pandemic is something that belongs to the whole population of earth.
>
> By contrast, the prefix *epi* is a Greek term meaning "upon" or "at" or "near." An *epidemic* is an illness that spreads among the people. But a *pandemic* spreads to people everywhere. Since these are modern words, they do not appear in the Bible. But the Scriptures have words that describe the same thing. In fact, there are six ancient words in the original Hebrew and Greek texts of the Bible that describe what we would call a pandemic. The Bible uses those words 127 times.[139]

COVID-19 set the world's response for how people will react to the pestilences and plagues in the future. When the coronavirus pandemic began, people did not run to church to find the Lord. In fact, various local, state, and federal agencies shut down public assemblies for various periods of time. Many Christians were very frustrated with the harsh restrictions the government temporarily placed on church attendance. However, the crucial issue is that the

---

[139] David Jeremiah, *Where Do We Go From Here?* (Nashville, TN.: W. Publishing Group, 2021), 52.

government had the ability to impose the restrictions in the first place. This unprecedented move by government agencies foreshadows the control that the Antichrist will impose upon the world when he demands the worship of all people. The sanction for those who refuse to worship the Antichrist is death (Rev. 13:11-15). Satan's plan is in its beginning stages, as he and the demonic army manipulate those in high places to set the stage for the future worldwide reign of his ultimate pawn, the Antichrist.

The question that all should ask is, have churches across America and the world seen an influx of people who are seeking God, based on the many deaths that resulted from COVID-19? Have people, in general, turned to God, the Bible, or even church to find an answer to the extremely important question, where will they go when they breathe their last breath? Unfortunately, the overall reaction to the pandemic has not been to turn to God, but to generally follow the same path that those living in the horrible seven-year Tribulation will take, even after over 50% of the world's population dies, which is over 4 billion people in a short three to five-year period (Rev. 6-9). The world's reaction to COVID-19 sets the stage for how people, in general, will react to the catastrophic number of deaths that are going to occur during the Tribulation. "But the rest of mankind, who were not killed by these plagues, did not repent of the works of their hands, that they should not worship demons, and idols of gold, silver, brass, stone, and wood, which can neither see nor hear nor walk. And they did not repent of their murders or their sorceries or their sexual immorality or their thefts" (Rev. 9:20–21).

Will Anyone Survive the Wrath of God?
For then there will be great tribulation, such as has not been since the beginning of the world until this time, no, nor ever shall be. And unless those days were shortened, no flesh would be saved; but for the elect's sake those days will be shortened. (Matt. 24:21–22)

COVID-19 proved that a new world order is on the way. The Scriptures prove that the satanic trinity, made up of Satan, Antichrist, and the false prophet will in fact implement the one-world government, economy, and religion. Billions of people will die during the seven-year Tribulation. The unfortunate fact is that the majority of those living during that time will follow the deceptive, satanic leadership, and refuse to repent and receive the forgiveness of the

Lord Jesus (Matt. 24:4, 24; Rev. 9:20, 21; 16:9, 11). How many people will actually survive the catastrophic worldwide judgments?

Several years ago, at a prophecy conference, I heard a speaker make what I thought was a significant mistake. He was speaking about the number of people who would die during the seven-year Tribulation. He stated, at least 90% of the world's population will die during the Tribulation. I knew that according to the fourth seal judgment one-fourth of the world's population will die. I knew the sixth trumpet judgment will result in one-third of the remaining population dying. Combining those two judgments will result in 50% of the world's population dying.

After the speaker finished, I quickly went to his resource table and confronted him on his speculation that over 90% of the world's population will die. He kindly reminded me that there are four sets of seven judgments in the book of Revelation, the seals, trumpets, thunder, and bowl or vial judgments. He asked me the question, based on the extremely deadly nature of the judgments, not just the fourth seal and the sixth trumpet judgments, how many people do you think will die? He then quoted the words of Jesus that He spoke in the Olivet Discourse regarding the impact of the Tribulation judgments, "And unless those days were shortened, no flesh would be saved; but for the elect's sake those days will be shortened" (Matt. 24:22). God will confine the devastating judgments to the seven-year timeframe, for if He did not, every person on earth would die, similar to what took place during the Genesis Flood.

Dr. Mark Hitchcock presents a penetrating question that forces a person to think about the personal impact COVID-19 should have on one's life.

> The question we should be asking, in light of coronavirus, is not *Is this the judgment of God?* The pertinent question is, *Am I right with God?* This means the current crisis affords each of us a unique opportunity. The coronavirus contagion is a wake-up call, a piercing alarm, urging everyone to turn to Jesus and then come clean every day by turning away from anything in our lives that is not pleasing to God. It's an opportunity to make sure we're ready for the any moment coming of Christ, which all signs indicate could be very soon.[140]

---

[140] Mark Hitchcock, *Corona Crisis*, 60.

The question Dr. Hitchcock poses is exactly the issue you should ask yourself when thinking about the pandemic. Are you right with God? Have you ever received the gift of salvation? The apostle Paul provides the path to eternal life with the Lord Jesus.

> But when the kindness and the love of God our Savior toward man appeared not by works of righteousness which we have done, but according to His mercy He saved us, through the washing of regeneration and renewing of the Holy Spirit, whom He poured out on us abundantly through Jesus Christ our Savior, that having been justified by His grace we should become heirs according to the hope of eternal life.
> (Titus 3:4–7)

COVID-19, despite the horrible truth that over 6.5 million people died from the devastating virus, is a preview of what Satan will use to set up the one-world government, economy, and religion. My very good friend, whom I deeply loved, the late Dr. Jimmy DeYoung, many times stated the following, "the stage has been set, all the actors are in place, and the curtain is about to be raised, therefore, keep looking up *until*." Dr. DeYoung knew that we are seeing things in the current generation, such as the dramatic changes in society brought about by the world's reaction to COVID-19, resulting in the very rapid move towards globalism. The one-world order will not come to fulfillment *until* Jesus Christ first comes in the clouds and removes the church, the body of Christ, from this earth (1 Thess. 4:13-18; 1 Cor. 15:50-54). Satan, the great deceiver, and liar is working non-stop to set up his one-world system. COVID-19 is just another piece of the puzzle to bring God's prophetic Word to fulfillment.

CHAPTER FIVE
LAWLESSNESS

For the mystery of lawlessness is already at work; only He who now restrains will do so until He is taken out of the way. And then the lawless one will be revealed, whom the Lord will consume with the breath of His mouth and destroy with the brightness of His coming. The coming of the lawless one is according to the working of Satan, with all power, signs, and lying wonders, and with all unrighteous deception among those who perish, because they did not receive the love of the truth, that they might be saved. (2 Thess. 2:7–10)

I had the privilege of working in law enforcement with the Milwaukee County Sheriff's Office for 32 years, which culminated in serving as the acting Sheriff in Milwaukee County, Wisconsin from September 2017 through January 2019. When I joined the Sheriff's Office, America in general had a totally different attitude towards law enforcement than what currently exists. Most communities across America viewed police in a positive light, and it was a pleasure for officers to serve in the law enforcement profession. Segments of American society have significantly changed their perception of the police. Americans in general did not just decide one day that police were bad. It was the work of certain violent activist groups who took every opportunity to criticize police actions, promote an anti-police agenda, and even call for defunding the police. The mainstream media added fuel to the fire of these activists, who rioted in the streets as they raged against police and police actions--themselves acting out utter lawlessness in the process.

The importance of the cultural shift against law enforcement, which the globalist, social agenda is now promoting, lies in the fact that during the prophetic biblical end-times scenario, lawlessness will be the norm. The agenda of the globalists requires a complete change in the way society functions. Though socialists are actively executing the tactics defined in the first chapters of the socialist playbook against American democracy, there currently remains a significant number of mostly conservative-leaning people who refuse to yield to the socialist agenda. Those embracing the liberal, socialist, Marxist, dictatorial agenda, will do whatever it takes to disrupt the local and state governments who choose to uphold the rule of law.

This chapter summarizes the moves federal, state, and local governments have already made to disrupt adherence to the strict rule of law. The purpose of this information is not to advocate for a political position or for a conservative or liberal perspective on what the country needs for public safety. The specific purpose is to point out the current path of government towards a lawless society, which absolutely will become the norm during the seven-year Tribulation (2 Thess. 2:7-10). Today's criminal activity and the government's response to it are setting the stage for Bible prophecy to be fulfilled. The only positive truth that comes from the information provided in this section, is that the removal of the Church Age saints at the Rapture is getting closer. The worse society gets, the closer the coming of Jesus Christ is to take Christians home to heaven (1 Thess. 4:13-18). The apostle Paul stated that perilous times would characterize the last days, immediately before the return of the Lord Jesus (2 Tim. 3:1). Based on the data presented in this chapter, it certainly can be concluded that the coming of Jesus Christ is imminent.

CRIME STATISTICS

There are many databases that track various types of crime in America. The Gun Violence Archive (GVA) provides current and historical data that is very instructional (see Figures 5.1 and 5.2). There is no denying that America has experienced a significant number of gun violence incidents that resulted in a high number of injuries and deaths. Many social agencies and community groups have valiantly tried over the years to implement social programs, either private or governmental, to stop the out-of-control violence. To date, social engineering and government programs provide very little documented relief from the violence. Scripture provides the only answer regarding what must take place to change the violent culture, as government never had the ability to change a person's heart. Only God can change a sinful human being and provide the means whereby a person chooses to live a law-abiding lifestyle instead of one committed to crime (2 Cor. 5:17).

Figure 5.1 shows the total number of gun violence incidents that occurred in the United States from 2014 through September 2022. A gun violence incident is an incident in which one or more persons are killed or injured as a result of a gun being fired.

Year	Total Number of Gun Violence Incidents
2014	39,516
2015	48,127
2016	54,700
2017	58,108
2018	54,142
2019	39,590
2020	43,688

Figure 5.1[141]

Figure 5.2 shows the number of gun violence incidents, categorized by type, over a seven-year period.

GVA - Seven Year Review	2014	2015	2016	2017	2018	2019	2020
Deaths - Willful, Malicious, Accidental	12,418	13,537	15,112	15,679	14,896	15,448	19,411
Suicides by Gun	21,386	22,018	22,938	23,854	24,432	23,941	Pending
Injuries - Willful, Malicious, Accidental	22,779	27,033	30,666	31,265	28,284	30,186	39,492
Children [aged 0-11] Killed or Injured	603	695	671	733	664	695	999
Teens [aged 12-17] Killed or Injured	2,318	2,695	3,140	3,256	2882	3,122	4,142
Mass Shooting	269	335	382	346	336	417	611
Murder-Suicide	624	530	549	608	623	632	573
Defensive Use [DGU]	1,531	1,393	2,001	2,107	1874	1,597	1,478
Unintentional Shooting	1,605	1,969	2,202	2,039	1691	1,905	2,315

Figure 5.2[142]

The total number of mass shootings in America from January 1, 2022 through October 3, 2022 was 517 incidents, resulting in 2,173 injured and 516 people dead. In 2021 there were 675 incidents, 64 more mass shootings than occurred in 2020 (see Figure 5.2), resulting in 2,777 injured and 676 people dead. The year 2022 is on track to exceed the number of mass shootings that occurred in 2021. The statistics amply document the trend toward increased gun violence in America. This is not shocking, as the Scriptures make it clear that

---

[141] Gun Violence Archive, https://www.gunviolencearchive.org/past-tolls, accessed October 3, 2022, 3:45 PM CST.
[142] Gun Violence Archive, https://www.gunviolencearchive.org/, accessed October 3, 2022, 5 PM cst

violence and perilous times will increase during the last days of the Church Age (2 Tim. 3:1).

Active shooter incidents in the United States have been on a significant rise since 2019 (see Figure 5.3). An active shooter is one or more individuals actively engaged in killing or attempting to kill people in a populated area. Active shooter incidents in 2017, 2018, and 2019 were 30. In 2020, there were 40 active shooter incidents, a 33% increase. In 2021, there were 61 active shooter incidents, an increase of 52.5%. The rise in violent crime rightly concerns the average person as the numbers and associated horrific outcomes continue on an upward trend.

Figure 5.3 shows the trend of active shooter incidents from 2017 through 2021.

Incident Statistics

Active Shooter Incidents 2017–2021

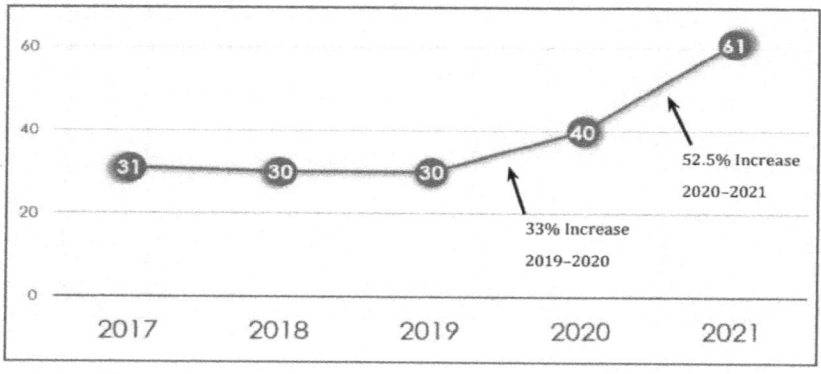

Year	Incidents
2017	31
2018	30
2019	30
2020	40
2021	61

33% Increase 2019–2020
52.5% Increase 2020–2021

Figure 5.3[143]

The American public has a right to know why there is a constant rise in the number of violent crimes. The biblical answer is that humanity is sinful (Rom. 3:10-23). Unless a person realizes their sinful condition and their need to begin a personal relationship with Jesus Christ (John 3:16; Eph. 2:8-9), there is the potential that the person could choose a criminal or violent lifestyle. When a person accepts God's gift of salvation by placing their faith in the death, burial, and resurrection of Jesus Christ as the complete payment for their sins, the wonderful truth is that the Holy Spirit immediately

---

[143] Active Shooter Incidents in the United States, U.S. Department of Justice Federal Bureau of Investigation, 3.

indwells the new believer (1 Cor. 3:16; 6:19 12:13). The Holy Spirit will convict a Christian if they begin to stray from living a lifestyle that is pleasing to the Lord (John 16:8). This is not to say that a Christian will absolutely not commit a criminal act, but the likelihood diminishes if a person chooses to be a God-honoring, law-abiding citizen.

There are many other reasons why violent crime is rising. One of the reasons is that the judicial system has dramatically changed over the years by becoming more interested in alleged criminal rights than victim rights. District attorneys were more likely to hold criminals accountable in the past. One of the reasons district attorneys are more hesitant to prosecute criminals is the high incarceration rate, which not only costs taxpayers billions of dollars every year, but brings associated pressure from politicians, social agencies, and others who want to reduce the number of inmates. According to the Bureau of Justice Statistics, the annual cost of mass incarceration in the United States is $81 billion. But that figure addresses only the cost of operating prisons, jails, parole, and probation — leaving out policing and court costs, and costs paid by families to support incarcerated loved ones.[144] In addition, jails and prisons are overcrowded, resulting in consent decrees, which may mandate the early release of offenders, or finding placement in an alternative facility.

Another factor that places pressure on district attorneys to reduce prosecutions is the rise in claims of social injustice. Groups that promote a reduction in prosecutions claim that law enforcement unfairly targets certain people groups. Many politicians and social groups strongly contend that district attorneys should not charge or prosecute individuals alleged to have committed a crime. The same groups want the offenders to reenter the community, where they allegedly will change their behavior based on the support of their friends, family, and community.

The Sentencing Project, which is attempting to reduce the number of prison inmates, including those with life sentences, made the following three suggestions: abolish life without parole, limit all

---

[144] Mass Incarceration Costs $182 Billion Every Year, Without Adding Much to Public Safety, Equal Justice Initiative, February 6, 2017, https://eji.org/news/mass-incarceration-costs-182-billion-annually/, accessed October 3, 2022, 10:52 PM, CST.

life sentences to 20 years except in rare circumstances, and accelerate and expand release opportunities.[145]

District attorneys across the country must review the cases brought to them mainly by law enforcement agencies, and determine if they will charge an alleged crime. District attorneys have a few options they can consider when reviewing a case. They can choose to criminally charge the case, at which point it goes through the judicial system where either a judge or jury will determine if the person is guilty or innocent. If the jury or judge determines a person to be guilty, the judge determines the punishment. When a judge sentences a criminal, they usually consider the suggested punishment from the district attorney and defense attorney.

A second option a district attorney can employ after reviewing the presented facts of a case is to refuse to issue any charges, resulting in the person going free.

Prosecutors may refuse to press charges because they think it unlikely that a conviction will result. No matter what the prosecutor's personal feelings about the case, the prosecutor needs legally admissible evidence sufficient to prove the defendant's guilt beyond a reasonable doubt. Even if a person is arrested, he might not be charged with a crime. This is because each decision – the decision to arrest and the decision to file charges – is made by a different authority. Police arrest someone when they believe that he has committed a crime. But only the District Attorney's Office can file charges against someone. [146]

A third option a district attorney can use is deferred prosecution. US Legal defines deferred prosecution as follows.

Deferred Prosecutions are basically informal agreements between the defense lawyer, the defendant, and the prosecutor to dismiss a case up front, that is, in advance of the accused agreeing to some concessions. Depending on

---

[145] Ashley Nellis, No End In Sight: America's Enduring Reliance on Life Imprisonment, The Sentencing Project, February *17, 2021, https://www.sentencingproject.org/publications/no-end-in-sight-americas-enduring-reliance-on-life-imprisonment/?gclid=EAIaIQobChMI6KqBmL_F-gIV6BPUAR0WJAgIEAAYASAAEgJsJvD_BwE, accessed October 3, 2022, 10:59 PM, CST.*

[146] Hobart Ledner DVM, Why Will The District Attorney Not Bring Charges, September 2021, Attorney-FAQ.com, https://attorney-faq.com/why-will-the-district-attorney-not-bring-charges, accessed October 3, 2022, 9:45 PM CST.

the circumstances, a misdemeanor prosecutor might choose to offer a deferred prosecution after a case has been filed against the defendant. Some of the circumstances that affect this decision include: difficulty in proving the case, the defendant's lack of criminal history, etc.

With a deferred prosecution agreement, the defendant must admit his/her guilt, waive the same constitutional rights as s/he would if s/he were pleading guilty before a judge, agree to specific written terms of the agreement (including counselling, community service hours, etc.) and promise not to break any law more serious than a speeding ticket. If the defendant breaks this agreement, the County Attorney can refile the original case and already has the defendant's confession in his refiled case. Successfully completed deferred prosecutions are eligible for complete expunctions. Deferred Prosecutions are basically informal agreements between the defense lawyer, the defendant, and the prosecutor to dismiss a case up front, that is, in advance of the accused agreeing to some concessions. Depending on the circumstances, a misdemeanor prosecutor might choose to offer a deferred prosecution after a case has been filed against the defendant. Some of the circumstances that affect this decision include: difficulty in proving the case, the defendant's lack of criminal history, etc.

With a deferred prosecution agreement, the defendant must admit his/her guilt, waive the same constitutional rights as s/he would if s/he were pleading guilty before a judge, agree to specific written terms of the agreement (including counselling, community service hours, etc.) and promise not to break any law more serious than a speeding ticket. If the defendant breaks this agreement, the County Attorney can refile the original case and already has the defendant's confession in his refiled case. Successfully completed deferred prosecutions are eligible for complete expunctions.[147]

---

[147] US Legal, Deferred Prosecution Law and Legal Definition, https://definitions.uslegal.com/d/deferred-prosecution/, accessed October 3, 2022, 9:37 PM CST.

Various agencies put out statistical data on the number of incarcerated people in the United States. However, some agencies may skew the data to promote their own political or social agenda. Therefore, when reviewing statistical data, it is important to consider who compiled the data, and the methodology that was used. One can easily find conflicting data when comparing data from various sources.

The following data comes from the Bureau of Justice Statistics (BJS), which I, having been in the law enforcement field for 32 years, consider to be very reliable data. The data collection for the BJS reports is historically between one and two years old. The following information documents the reduction of prosecutions and incarcerations, which points to the issue that even though violent crimes are increasing, the judicial system holds less people accountable.

- At yearend 2020, an estimated 5,500,600 persons were under the supervision of adult correctional systems in the United States, 11% fewer than at the same time the previous year (adjusted for persons on dual correctional statuses).
- The decline in the correctional population during 2020 was due to decreases in both the community supervision population (down 276,700, or 6.6%) and the incarcerated population (down 294,400, or 18.9%).
- About 7 in 10 persons under correctional supervision were supervised in the community (3,890,400) at yearend 2020, while about 3 in 10 (1,691,600) were incarcerated in a state or federal prison or local jail.
- From 2010 to 2020, the correctional population decreased 22.4% (down 1,588,400 persons).
- From 2010 to 2020, the decrease in the probation population accounted for 63.1% of the total decline in the correctional population.[148]

Lawlessness, or the trend leading to a lawless society, involves the failure of government to enforce the laws that are in place and justly punish evildoers for breaking those laws. After the

---

[148] Rich Kluckow, DSW, and Zhen Zeng, Ph.D., BJS Statisticians, March 2022, Correctional Populations in the United States, 2020 – Statistical Tables, NCJ Number 303184, https://bjs.ojp.gov/library/publications/correctional-populations-united-states-2020-statistical-tables, accessed October 3, 2022, 10:28 PM, CST.

worldwide Flood, and the destruction of all but eight people, God originated human government specifically to protect His people (Gen. 9:6). The legislative branch of the government designs laws to protect individuals and society. However, when law enforcement either fails to enforce the laws, based on political pressure or poor leadership, lawlessness becomes the norm. If law enforcement is active and enforcing the laws, and then the district attorney's office refuses to charge the cases brought before them by law enforcement, or employs deferred prosecution, lawlessness increases. When law enforcement and the district attorney's office work together to prosecute criminals, and a liberal court refuses to impose appropriate punishment after the court or a jury determines the defendant is guilty, lawlessness increases.

CIVIL UNREST

Many urban areas in the recent past experienced riots, looting, businesses burned down, property destroyed, and violent attacks that resulted in injuries and even death. Many people's lives, property, and livelihoods were devastated by the numerous high-profile civil unrest incidents that occurred between 2020 and 2022. Some of the most high-profile incidents included:

- The Breonna Taylor protests, May 26, 2020
- George Floyd protests May 26, 2020
- Kenosha, Wisconsin unrest and shootings, August 23 and 25, 2020
- Minneapolis false rumor riot, August 26–28, 2020
- Red House eviction defense protest, December 8, 2020; and the
- Dolal Idd protests, December 30, 2020–January 4, 2021
- Derek Chauvin protests, March 7, 2021–June 25, 2021
- Atlanta shooting protests, March 16, 2021
- Daunte Wright protests, April 11, 2021–December 23, 2021
- Winston Boogie Smith protests and Uptown unrest, June 3, 2021–November 3, 2021
- Vehicle-ramming attack June 13, 2021
- Kyle Rittenhouse protests in Wisconsin November 1, 2021–November 19, 2021
- Amir Locke protests, February 2, 2022–April 8, 2022
- Portland, Oregon protests, February 20, 2022
- Jayland Walker protests, June 27, 2022–July 17, 2022

- Andrew Tekle Sundberg protests, July 14 and 16, 2022.[149]

Groups such as Black Lives Matter, Voces de la Frontera, Antifa, Proud Boys, and others became high profile during the civil unrest events. Those who actively follow the national news should recognize several of the events just cited.

It is not my intention to report on the nature of these incidents, or the groups and individuals who took part. There is plenty of information readily available on these events and the participants. The issue under examination is the rise of lawlessness in the United States, which is setting the stage for the implementation of God's prophetic seal, trumpet, thunder, and bowl judgments (Rev. 6-16) and the one-world government, economy, and religion (Rev. 13).

Jesus Himself, in the Olivet Discourse, provided a detailed prophecy regarding what will occur in the seven-year Tribulation. One of the horrific things that will take place is the massive increase in lawlessness. Jesus speaks about the unlawful persecution and suffering that God's people will endure during the Tribulation.

> Then they will deliver you up to tribulation and kill you, and you will be hated by all nations for My name's sake. And then many will be offended, will betray one another, and will hate one another. Then many false prophets will rise up and deceive many. And because lawlessness will abound, the love of many will grow cold. (Matt. 24:9–12)

America, and other countries around the world, are in the early stages of what one day will become a catastrophic reality: utter lawlessness. The second seal judgment, which conservative, biblical, dispensational scholars believe will be released at the beginning of the seven-year Tribulation,[150] speaks to horrific violence as the result of the lawless society that will exist. "When He opened the second seal, I heard the second living creature saying, 'Come and see.' Another horse, fiery red, went out. And it was granted to the one who sat on it to take peace from the earth, and that people should kill one another; and there was given to him a great sword" (Rev. 6:3–4).

---

[149] 2020-2022 United States Racial Unrest, https://en.wikipedia.org/wiki/2020%E2%80%932022_United_States_racial_unrest, accessed October 4, 10:20 PM CST.

[150] Ed Hindson and Thomas Ice, Charting the Bible Chronologically (Eugene, OR.: Harvest House Publishers, 2016), 125.

The globalist agenda includes various forms of protest and civil unrest to move their ideology forward. When the satanic one-world system is fully implemented, specifically during the last half of the Tribulation, not even the current globalists can imagine the devastating loss of life that will occur when the Antichrist begins his satanically led rule (Dan. 9:27; 1 John 2:18; Rev. 13:1-10).

BIBLICAL RESPONSE TO LAWLESSNESS

Romans 13:1–7 Biblical Response to Lawbreakers

Let every soul be subject to the governing authorities. For there is no authority except from God, and the authorities that exist are appointed by God. Therefore, whoever resists the authority resists the ordinance of God, and those who resist will bring judgment on themselves. For rulers are not a terror to good works, but to evil. Do you want to be unafraid of the authority? Do what is good, and you will have praise from the same. For he is God's minister to you for good. But if you do evil, be afraid; for he does not bear the sword in vain; for he is God's minister, an avenger to execute wrath on him who practices evil. Therefore you must be subject, not only because of wrath but also for conscience' sake. For because of this you also pay taxes, for they are God's ministers attending continually to this very thing. Render therefore to all their due: taxes to whom taxes are due, customs to whom customs, fear to whom fear, honor to whom honor. (Rom. 13:1–7)

Christians have differing opinions and interpretations of Romans 13. There are Christians who strongly oppose the government and its leaders, and loudly proclaim their resistance. There are others who are silent about governmental issues, rarely engage in politics, and even refuse to vote. The purpose of discussing Romans 13 in relation to lawlessness is that the apostle Paul, who lived under a tyrannical, harsh Roman rule, exhorts God's people to submit to those in authority. Therefore, God's people should be law-abiding people. Paul is clearly talking about secular government, based on the context of Romans 13.

Richard Longenecker provides a scholarly analysis regarding why there are varying interpretations and applications of Romans 13:1-7.

> From the earliest Christian readings of 13:1–7 to readings of the passage today, there have been diverse views regarding

the occasion for and the intended purpose of the exhortations and appeals in this passage. A widespread understanding among the early Church Fathers was (1) that there existed in the Christian congregations at Rome some "overly enthusiastic" or "extremist" believers in Jesus who thought that the gospel message of "new life in Christ" and "God's inauguration of a new age in human history" required a rejection of everything that had to do with "this age" and "the old world," which would have included their rejection of all forms of human government and their refusal to pay taxes and tolls levied by any human authority, and (2) that Paul was in this passage endeavoring to counter such a perversion of the Christian message. This understanding of the occasion and purpose of 13:1–7 has been accepted by a number of interpreters of fairly recent times.

Other interpreters have argued that the edict of Claudius in A.D. 49, which expelled a large number of Jews from Rome "because the Jews constantly made disturbances at the instigation of Chrestus" coupled with a possibly earlier edict of Claudius in 41, which allowed the Jews of Rome to continue their "traditional mode of life" but ordered them "not to hold meetings" was remembered with both anguish and resentment by the Christians at Rome (especially by Jewish believers, but also by many Gentile believers). So it is argued that Paul's exhortations of 13:1–7 were intended to stifle any continuing resentment against Rome and its officials by believers in Jesus, in order to ward off any possible recurrence of official antagonism by the city's authorities that would be prejudicial against the "Christ followers" of the city—who were, in all likelihood, still viewed by the city's officials as a Jewish sect because of their claim to be believers in Jesus of Nazareth, whom they viewed as the Jewish Messiah.[151]

---

[151] Richard N. Longenecker, *The Epistle to the Romans: A Commentary on the Greek Text*, ed. I. Howard Marshall and Donald A. Hagner, New International Greek Testament Commentary (Grand Rapids, MI: William B. Eerdmans Publishing Company, 2016), 949–950.

John MacArthur provides additional exegetical insight into Romans 13 and addresses the issue of when, if ever, a Christian should openly oppose the established government.

> Historically, Christians have been involved, frequently in the name of their faith, in the forceful overthrow of oppressive and sometimes despotic governments. Democracy and political freedom are commonly identified with Christianity. For such reasons it is difficult for many Christians to be clear, or even objective and honest, about a passage so unambiguously restrictive as Romans 13:1–7. Many evangelicals strongly believe that the American Revolution was wholly justified, not only politically but biblically. They believe that the rights to life, liberty, and the pursuit of happiness not only are divinely endowed but that their attainment and defense somehow is Christian and thereby justified at whatever cost, including that of armed rebellion when necessary. Obviously, such action is forbidden by God, and, judged in light of our present text, it is equally obvious that the United States was born out of violation of Scripture.... Because most Jews of that day believed the Messiah would come as a political deliverer, many of Jesus' disciples expected Him to free them from the Roman yoke. But He made no call for political or social reform, even by peaceful means. He never attempted to capture the culture for biblical morality or to gain greater freedom. To the contrary, He declared unambiguously, "Render to Caesar the things that are Caesar's; and to God the things that are God's" (Matt. 22:21). On a later occasion He told His disciples, "The scribes and the Pharisees have seated themselves in the chair of Moses; therefore all that they tell you, do and observe, but do not do according to their deeds; for they say things, and do not do them" (Matt. 23:2–3). Those wicked leaders were not to be emulated, but they were to be obeyed. Changing the form of government or superficially moralizing it were not Jesus' goals. He sought to redeem individual souls. [152]

Are believers in Jesus Christ called to fight corrupt governments, or to evangelize those who have yet to receive the gift

---

[152] John F. MacArthur Jr., *Romans*, vol. 2, MacArthur New Testament Commentary (Chicago: Moody Press, 1991), 206–211.

of eternal life? Christians need not be confused regarding their biblical mandate regarding what God called them to accomplish. John MacArthur rightly, and courageously, pointed out the mission that Jesus Christ gave to His people, which is to propagate the gospel (Luke 19:10; 1 Tim. 1:15; 2 Cor. 5:20). I would challenge Christians who embrace rebellion, and even violence against the government, to go through the New Testament and find even one passage that encourages that type of behavior. The only civil disobedience documented in the New Testament is when religious or government officials demanded God's people to stop preaching the gospel, which was an untenable demand (Acts 4:19-20; 5:17-22).

John MacArthur provides an excellent conclusion on how Christians should act towards the government, even when the government is not supportive of Christians.

> What, then, is the Christian's responsibility to society, and to government in particular, if we are to remain "aliens and strangers" in this world (1 Pet. 2:11) who have a platform to call people to salvation? How are we to live in the world but not be of it (John 17:11, 16)? In the present text, Paul presents the two basic principles that answer those questions. First: Be subject to government (v. 1); and second: Pay taxes (v. 6). Those commands summarize the Christian's civic duty. It is through fulfilling those two obligations that we "render to Caesar the things that are Caesar's; and to God the things that are God's" (Matt. 22:21).[153]

Titus 3:1-2

The apostle Paul instructs Titus on how to guide Christians to a right attitude toward those in authority, including government leaders. "Remind them to be subject to rulers and authorities, to obey, to be ready for every good work, to speak evil of no one, to be peaceable, gentle, showing all humility to all men" (Titus 3:1–2).

Donald Guthrie provides an important analysis of this passage, which once again exhorts God's people to obey those in authority over them.

> Christian behavior in contemporary society was of utmost importance for the furtherance of the gospel. No new advice needs to be given to these Cretan Christians for Titus is to

---

[153] Ibid.

remind the people to be subject. This latter verb, which implies 'loyal' subjection, shows clearly the Christian's duty towards the civil administration. The same descriptive words, *rulers and authorities*, are combined several times in Paul's writings, and generally refer to spiritual agencies. But here the apostle evidently fears that the turbulent Cretans might too readily implicate the church in political agitation which could only bring the gospel under suspicion. The Greek verb *peitharchō* translated *to be obedient* expresses generally conformity to the regulations of the civil authorities.

The Christian should *be ready to do whatever is good*, in the community in which he lives. Where good citizenship demands communal action, he must always be cooperative, provided no question of conscience is involved.[154]

There are Christians who hold a mean-spirited attitude towards government officials with whom they disagree. Social media, personal conversations, and even the classroom and pulpits become someone's bully pulpit to demean others. Leaders, whether secular or Christian, have the right and responsibility to educate and warn their people. However, God qualifies how Christians transmit important information that may be negative in content, which is to speak the truth in love (Eph. 4:15). Paul's admonition to Titus states that God's people should avoid using negative, caustic rhetoric. "Remind them to be subject to rulers and authorities, to obey, to be ready for every good work, to speak evil of no one, to be peaceable, gentle, showing all humility to all men" (Titus 3:1–2).

2 Thessalonians 2:1–4

Now, brethren, concerning the coming of our Lord Jesus Christ and our gathering together to Him, we ask you, not to be soon shaken in mind or troubled, either by spirit or by word or by letter, as if from us, as though the day of Christ had come. Let no one deceive you by any means; for that Day will not come unless the falling away comes first, and the man of sin is revealed, the son of perdition, who opposes and exalts himself

---

[154] Donald Guthrie, *Pastoral Epistles: An Introduction and Commentary*, vol. 14, Tyndale New Testament Commentaries (Downers Grove, IL: InterVarsity Press, 1990), 223–224.

above all that is called God or that is worshiped, so that he sits as God in the temple of God, showing himself that he is God.

The apostle Paul speaks about the first major event that must happen before the Antichrist, also called the lawless one, takes his position as the world leader. The apostle Paul states *a falling away* must precede the introduction of the Antichrist (2 Thess. 2:3). Spiros Zodhiates provides an analysis regarding the meaning of *falling away*.

> *Apostasía* means to depart, or as in Acts 21:21 "forsake" and in 2 Thess. 2:3, "a falling away." In 2 Thess. 2:3 the word *apostasía* does not refer to genuine Christians who depart from the faith, but mere professors who, without divine grace, succumb to the Satanic deception of the Antichrist. If those who are truly Christ's and through the Holy Spirit have become members of His body (1 Cor. 12:13) could be detached, then the assurances Jesus gave that His own will not perish would be made null and void (John 10:28, 29).[155]

John MacArthur agrees with Spiros Zodhiates' conclusion, but adds a crucial comment regarding the Rapture of the Church Age saints and the apostasy or falling away as stated in 2 Thessalonians 2:3.

> The Thessalonians had forgotten that Paul told them when he was there that the Day of the Lord will not come unless the apostasy comes first. Out of all the precursors of the Day of the Lord (Joel 2:31; 3:14; Mal. 4:5), Paul singled out the apostasy. He was not, of course, setting a posttribulational date for the Rapture (he did not tell his readers that they would live to experience the apostasy and the unveiling of the man of lawlessness). Paul's point was merely that the apostasy will precede the Day of the Lord. And since the apostasy has not yet taken place, the Day of the Lord could not have arrived.[156]

Therefore, the man of lawlessness (Antichrist) cannot be revealed until a severe falling away from the truth of God's Word takes place. The next section, which covers 2 Thessalonians 2:6-10, provides the missing information on the chronological order of events leading to

---

[155] Spiros Zodhiates, *The Complete Word Study Dictionary: New Testament* (Chattanooga, TN: AMG Publishers, 2000).

[156] John F. MacArthur Jr., *1 & 2 Thessalonians*, MacArthur New Testament Commentary (Chicago: Moody Press, 2002), 271.

the arrival of the Antichrist, when lawlessness will be at its most caustic and diabolical level.

The Thessalonian Christians who lived during the first century suffered extreme persecution. The apostle Paul explained the Tribulation to them when he started the church in Thessalonica. However, Paul was only in Thessalonica for three weeks, so needless to say, they were not theologically grounded (Acts 17:1-4). Paul wanted the Thessalonians to understand that even though they were suffering unlawful persecution, this was absolutely not the Tribulation. The first proof Paul gave that they were not in the Tribulation period was the fact that the falling away from sound doctrine had yet to occur. The second major event that must occur before the Tribulation, begins is the appearance of the lawless one, the Antichrist (Dan. 9:27). Mark Hitchcock and Jeff Kinley add to this discussion as follows.

> The second event that must occur before the final Tribulation can begin is the revelation or unveiling of the "man of sin." The man of sin is none other than the final Antichrist. "Man of sin" is one of his many aliases recorded in Scripture. The verses that follow describe the outrageous nature of his sin. "(He) opposes and exalts himself against every so-called god or object of worship, so that he takes his seat in the temple of God, proclaiming himself to be God." The Antichrist's outrageous self-deification will be the final step downward in man's rebellion against the true God. The relationship between the apostasy and the Antichrist is clear. The final great falling away will prepare the world for the reception of the final Antichrist. [157]

2 Thessalonians 2:6–10

And now you know what is restraining, that he may be revealed in his own time. For the mystery of lawlessness is already at work; only He who now restrains will do so until He is taken out of the way. And then the lawless one will be revealed, whom the Lord will consume with the breath of His mouth and destroy with the brightness of His coming. The coming of the lawless one is according to the working of Satan, with all power, signs, and lying wonders, and with all

---

[157] Mark Hitchcock & Jeff Kinley, *The Coming Apostasy* (Carol Stream, IL.: Tyndale House Publishers, Inc., 2017), 32.

unrighteous deception among those who perish, because they did not receive the love of the truth, that they might be saved.

America, and other countries around the world, currently endure high crime rates and the associated outcomes. The current increased rise in lawlessness is the precursor to what will take place in the seven-year Tribulation when the rule of law will all but disappear. The satanically empowered Antichrist will inaugurate his one-world, global dictatorship, and lawlessness will abound. However, before the Antichrist starts his satanic reign, the apostle Paul states that "He who now restrains" lawlessness will be taken out of the way. The Greek word *katéchō,* which the NKJV translates as restrains, means to suppress, restrain, hinder, or withhold.[158] The context of the passage points to the ministry of the Holy Spirit as that which is currently restraining the ultimate lawless one from achieving global power. The Holy Spirit currently indwells all those who have placed their faith in the Lord Jesus Christ and received the gift of eternal life (Eph. 2:8-9; Titus 3:5-6; 1 Cor. 3:16; 6:19; 12:13). Christians currently have an important part in controlling lawlessness by living a holy life and allowing the Holy Spirit to work through them. When Jesus Christ removes Christians from this earth, the current work of the Holy Spirit in restraining lawlessness will come to an end (1 Thess. 4:13-18; 1 Cor 15:50-54).

Theologically, it is important to keep in mind that the Holy Spirit's restraining work stops at the end of the Church Age, but His ministry on earth does not stop. John MacArthur adds to this truth.

> The phrase taken out of the way must not be interpreted to mean that the Holy Spirit will be removed from the world. That is impossible, since He is omnipresent. Nor could anyone be saved during the Tribulation (cf. Rev. 7:14) apart from His regenerating work (John 3:3–8; Titus 3:5). The phrase refers not to the removal of the Holy Spirit from the world, but rather to the cessation of His restraining work.[159]

Paul states the mystery of lawlessness is already at work, which is exactly what this chapter supported. Second Timothy 3:1 also states that perilous times will come in the last days of the Church Age. Peter warns the people of God to, "Be sober, be vigilant;

---

[158] Spiros Zodhiates, *The Complete Word Study Dictionary: New Testament* (Chattanooga, TN: AMG Publishers, 2000).

[159] John F. MacArthur Jr., *1 & 2 Thessalonians*, MacArthur New Testament Commentary (Chicago: Moody Press, 2002), 279.

because your adversary the devil walks about like a roaring lion, seeking whom he may devour" (1 Pet. 5:8). Virtually everyone in America is disturbed by the significant increase in lawlessness and the lack of accountability for criminals and those holding roles in the judicial system in many areas of the country. The only good news associated with this reality is that everything is pointing to the imminent return of Jesus Christ in the clouds, to remove one very fortunate generation of believers in Jesus Christ (1 Thess. 4:17). Once that wonderful event takes place, then the Antichrist will rise to power. The lawless Antichrist removes peace, safety, and the rule of law, as he inaugurates his seven-year reign of terror on earth.

CHAPTER SIX
GENDER IDEOLOGY

The material covered in this chapter is difficult for most Christians to read, much less accept as a reality in society. However, gender dysphoria, which in its most simplistic form regards a person of any age questioning if their biological birth sex is actually what they want as their long-term identity, is an international issue. An increasing number of individuals are making the decision to attempt to change their sex, not just verbally, but by undergoing sophisticated drug therapies and surgeries. This stands in complete antithesis to the Scriptures when interpreted literally. However, there are many pastors and theologians who allegorize and spiritualize the Bible to make it support their claims that attempting to changing one's sex is not only allowed but supported by Scripture.

In addition to individuals attempting to change their sex, is the significant number of people engaging in same-sex intimate relationships. One has only to follow the news, television programming, commercials, movies, or any public media source to see and hear material on same-sex intimate relationships. The federal government has been vocal on this issue, and many state and local governments also make strong statements either supporting or decrying same-sex intimate relationships, and the legal ramifications and implications, such as forcing shared bathrooms and establishing same-sex orientation as a protected class. Legislators enacted laws to protect the claimed rights of same-sex couples, and in certain cases provide same-sex couples the same financial benefits as heterosexual couples.

Scripture speaks frankly about same-sex intimate relationships, but the current culture either dismisses the Bible or changes the literal meaning of the forbidding texts to suit their personal desires. The purpose of this chapter is to shed light on another major factor on the globalist agenda that will eventually lead to a one-world government, economy, and religion. The material in this section will shock the conscience of many a reader.

Licensed doctors prescribe drugs and perform surgeries in an attempt to give a person the physical attributes of the opposite sex. Professional counselors provide guidance and support affirming a child's, adolescent's, and adult's desire to abandon their biological sex. The contemporary culture accepts in varying degrees same-sex intimate relationships that in Biblical times, and up until fairly recently in the United States, the law forbade.

A hallmark of the globalist agenda is to dismantle biblical ethics, morality, and the family; and to move society in a direction where eventually the one-world dictator (the Antichrist) will command worship from the entire population of the world, with the penalty of death for those who refuse to worship him (Rev. 13:15). The Christian community that adheres to a literal interpretation of Scripture, opposes same-sex intimate relations based on it being direct disobedience to God's design for the family and intimate relations within the confines of marriage (Rom.1:24-28). In addition, puberty suppression therapies and surgeries done to remove and reconstruct a person's sexual organs interfere with normal human development and mutilate healthy human bodies for the purpose of a desired end that can never be achieved to the fullness of one's birth gender. The government and society are moving the culture in an anti-God direction, which corresponds exactly with what the apostle Paul stated would take place towards the end of the Church Age (2 Tim. 3:1).

There is a very important question that must be addressed before moving forward with this section, which is, "How should we treat those who engage in the activity presented in this chapter?" Ephesians 4:15 admonishes the Christian to always speak the truth in love. I provide the same advice publicly to the church that I pastor. Every person is welcome to attend our church. We welcome every person, regardless of their background, or what they did last night or during their life. We will treat every person with respect and dignity, and provide them with a positive environment. We will not compromise Biblical truth, and we will lovingly preach and teach God's Word to all who desire to listen. Those who choose not to embrace the commandments, principles, and doctrine contained in God's Word have the right to maintain their private beliefs. If a person maintains a cordial attitude, they are most welcome. The truth of God's Word is for everyone. Some people embrace the Scriptures immediately, and for others, it is a long process. Christians should have the attitude that if any person, regardless of their beliefs, is open to hearing what the Lord stated in the Scriptures, they should be given the opportunity to hear the Word of God in a loving environment. Here we stand, we shall not be moved.

PUBERTY SUPPRESSION THERAPIES

Puberty suppression is one of the most disturbing trends to impact children since people cast their children into the fire as a sacrifice to Baal. Society in America and around the world has perpetrated many injustices against youth. However, puberty suppression therapies, along with the political and public pressure placed upon many children to change their sexual identity, results in long-term, and in many cases, permanent life-changing alterations. Puberty suppression may be defined as follows by those who oppose a biblical lifestyle.

> The reversible first step of endocrine medical treatment in transgender youth, which allows for two very important aspects of transgender management. Firstly, it buys the patient, family, and their medical team time to fully evaluate the presence and persistence of gender dysphoria. Secondly, it successfully prevents the development of cis-gender unwanted secondary sexual characteristics.[160]

The definition contains several terms that are foreign to many people including *gender dysphoria* and *cis-gender*. The next section summarily defines several of the acronyms and terms used by the transgender community that will help when reading this material.

Acronyms Associated with Gender Reassignment

The purpose of presenting this list and the associated concepts is to educate those who may not be aware of what is taking place throughout society (public schools, social service agencies, courtrooms, school boards, internet sources, etc.) by those seeking to influence children, teens and other vulnerable people with gender ideology. Knowledge of this material, at least on a basic level, is valuable so that when these concepts do come up with your children, grandchildren, or even in adult conversation, you understand the actual issues and how to respond.

- AIS: Androgen Insensitivity Syndrome
- FSH: Follicle Stimulating Hormone/Gonadotrophins
- FtM: Female to Male
- GD: Gender Dysphoria
- GID: Gender Identity Dysphoria

---

[160] Panagiotakopoulos, L. Transgender medicine - puberty suppression. *Rev Endocr Metab Disord* **19**, 221–225 (2018). https://doi.org/10.1007/s11154-018-9457-0, accessed October 10, 2022.

- GNC: Gender Non-Compliant
- GNRH: Gonadotrophin Releasing Hormones – Puberty Blockers
- GV: Gender Variant, Gender Queer, Gender Diverse
- Luteinizing Hormone / Gonadotrophins
- MtF: Male to Female
- Precocious Puberty – Early onset of puberty
- ROGD: Rapid Onset Gender Dysphoria
- SRS: Sexual Reassignment Surgery
- T: Transgender
- TGNC: Transgender, Gender Non-Conforming
- WPATH: World Professional Association of Transgender Health, Standards of Care for the Health of Transsexual, Transgender, and Gender Nonconforming People[161]

Definitions of Important Terminology

- Birth Gender: Sex at birth
- Binary Gender: Sex at birth
- Biological Gender: Sex at birth
- CIS-Gender: Sex at birth
- Desisters: Stop gender change after started
- Experienced Gender: The subjective or fluid gender expression often associated with social transition.
- Gatekeepers: Those who encourage individuals seeking gender reassignment drugs and surgery to stop before actually starting the transformational process.
- Natal Gender: Sex at birth
- Persisters: Maintain gender transforming protocols
- Puberty Suppressors: Medications that interrupt the puberty process.
- Queer: An umbrella term for gender and sexuality minorities. Also a synonym for multi-sexualities such as bisexuality, pansexuality or polysexuality. Can also be a term for someone that feels no other labels fit them.[162]
- Transphobic: Fear of transsexuality.
- XX Chromosomes: Female genetics

---

[161] Michael S. Dellaperute, *The Danger of Puberty Suppression* (Eugene, OR.: Resource Publications, 2019), 9-29.

[162] Queer-Vocab, https://www.scribd.com/document/99759719/Queer-Vocab, accessed October 10, 2022.

- XY Chromosomes: Male genetics[163]

Political & Social Pressure

Where do children get the idea to reject their biological sex? There are arguments from the secular side that children are not always born with the genetics that match who they really are as a person. This is a significant issue in the current culture, and as the government, schools, and society place more of an emphasis on gender dysphoria, the greater the number of young people who become confused, or discontent with their body. The cultural environment can easily influence children and adolescents, and the more they hear the rhetoric concerning transgenders, sex changes, sex therapy, homosexuality, lesbianism, and the list goes on, the more an impressionable child considers the delusion that they may be in the wrong body.

Everyone, including children, desires to feel loved and happy. When children, teenagers, or adults do not feel accepted by their peers, they will do whatever is within their power to find acceptance and love. A boy who experiences bullying from the more athletic and stronger males may decide the better part of valor is to consider an alleged sex change where he will find more acceptance. A girl who does not like her body, and finds it difficult to find acceptance, may decide it is because she really is a male and needs to have a masculine body. There is a plethora of reasons why a child or adolescent may choose to change who they are.

Christians, and many others whom society classifies as conservatives, hold the perspective that your biological sex (from birth) is not up for debate or change. The only reason a child determines they are not in the right body is based on the influence of the current culture and those who control or have a voice in the person's life. Children who suffer emotional abuse, physical and sexual assaults, hatred from their parents, bullying at school, or poor treatment by teachers, coaches, and peers, desperately want to find love and acceptance. Society provides a rather new alternative for a child to consider in making their life allegedly better, which is that they must be in the wrong body.

---

[163] Ibid.

The internet provides easy access to the proliferation of sexually explicit material for children, teenagers, and adults. Erwin Lutzer, a noted pastor and author, made the following statement.

> The cellphone in a teenager's hand is doing more to shape their worldview than one hour of Sunday school or the admonitions of parents. We are failing to pass our faith on to the next generation because they are captives to the culture, social media, their peers, and the indoctrination of the public schools. Parents clothe their children, feed them, and send them to school, but the hearts of their kids are being stolen and molded by a world that many of us don't understand.[164]

The main point of this section is not to provide a psychological analysis regarding why individuals choose to reject their biological sex. The point is to stress the continual influence of the globalists to discount what God designed and mandated (man, woman, marriage, and the family), for the express purpose of ridding the earth of the Christian and conservative position. Christianity and conservatives stand as a major obstacle for the one-world, self-absorbed, satanically-led future dictator. Keeping this strategic outcome in mind is vitally important.

Portions of the medical community place significant pressure on the families of children struggling with gender dysphoria to start puberty blockers while a child determines if they truly want to be like the opposite sex. The first medical step in halting a child's normal sexual development is for a prescriber to administer GnRH analogues, which are defined as follows.

> GnRH analogues, also known as puberty blockers, are a medical treatment available to support the healthy development of transgender adolescents. By halting puberty, puberty blocking medications have been shown to reduce gender dysphoria, (e.g. discomfort with sex characteristics), and promote mental health. [165]

The Mayo Clinic provides a rather graphic explanation of what puberty blockers actually do to the human body.

---

[164] Erwin Lutzer, *We Will Not be Silenced* (Eugene, OR.: Harvest House Publishers, 2020), 156.

[165] Laura Kuper, Puberty Blocking Medications: Clinical Research Review, IMPACT LGBT Health and Development Program, https://www.scribd.com/document/459868447/Kuper-2014-Puberty-Blockers-Clinical-Research-Review-pdf, accessed October 10, 2022.

Puberty's physical changes can cause intense distress for many gender-nonconforming adolescents. When taken regularly, GnRH analogues suppress the body's release of sex hormones, including testosterone and estrogen, during puberty.

Sex hormones affect:
- **Primary sex characteristics.** These are the sexual organs present at birth, including the penis, scrotum and testicles and the uterus, ovaries, and vagina.
- **Secondary sex characteristics.** These are the physical changes in the body that typically appear during puberty. Examples include breast development and growth of facial hair.

In those identified as male at birth, GnRH analogues decrease the growth of facial and body hair, prevent voice deepening, and limit the growth of genitalia.

In those identified as female at birth, treatment limits or stops breast development and stops menstruation.[166]

So-called clinical research analysts pressure individuals to start GnRH puberty blockers as early as possible to allegedly help young people who struggle with their sexual identity.

Historically, transgender individuals were required to wait until age 18 to receive gender affirming medical care of any kind. Increasingly, transgender individuals are requesting care at earlier ages due to larger social shifts and visibility and acceptance that have resulted in earlier ages of "coming out." As a result, gender clinics specializing in the medical treatment of transgender individuals are offering cross-sex hormone therapy at younger ages (1 to 18 years old). In addition, a number of doctors are now prescribing puberty blockers to adolescents with strong physical dysphoria that persists or emerges with the onset of puberty. Puberty blockers are prescribed after an assessment process with a

---

[166] Mayo Clinic Staff, Puberty Blockers for Transgender and Gender-Diverse Youth, June 18, 2022, https://www.mayoclinic.org/diseases-conditions/gender-dysphoria/in-depth/pubertal-blockers/art-20459075, accessed October 27, 2022, 9:15 pm, CST.

multidisciplinary team and adolescents are tracked over time and provided with support during the transition period.[167]

When reading the clinical research of those who support the use of puberty blockers, one may emotionally sympathize with a child who truly is struggling with their identity. However, the clinical research never discusses or attempts to discover the root issue of the child's struggle, which if uncovered and dealt with, would in all statistical probability, stop the child from pursuing a treatment that will never solve the root issue. Once again, we turn to a clinical research report to understand what puberty blockers literally do to a child's body.

GnRH analogues (puberty blockers) are a synthetic form of the human body's GnRH hormone. These are the two hormones that stimulate the testes to produce testosterone in the ovaries to produce estradiol. Testosterone and estradiol are responsible for the changes that occur during puberty.

GnRH analogues can be taken in the form of injections monthly, or every three months, or small implants that are placed under their skin for up to 12 months. Treatment of transgender adolescents with puberty blockers is fairly recent. As a result they have not been approved by the US Food and Drug Administration (FDA) for use in the population. However, for approximately the past 30 years, the same medications have been successfully used to treat precocious puberty with few side effects identified. A number of studies have been conducted that have tracked these patients over time. Several small studies have also been conducted on transgender adolescents. Together these studies provide information on the impact that puberty blockers have on development.[168]

Those who embrace puberty blockers and the results turn to the next level of treatment, which is reassignment surgery. Keep in mind when reading the following quote that it represents those who support surgical procedures to change the physical characteristics one has at birth.

---

[167] Laura Kuper, Puberty Blocking Medications: Clinical Research Review, IMPACT LGBT Health and Development Program.
[168] Ibid.

Gender affirming medical care is considered medically necessary treatment for transgender individuals who experience physical dysphoria, (i.e. distress associated with physical sex characteristics.) While not all individuals who experience a discrepancy between their gender identity and sex assigned at birth experience physical dysphoria, many do. Forms of gender affirming medical care include use of hormones and gender affirmation surgeries, (e.g., "top" surgeries, "bottom" surgeries, facial feminization, and laser hair removal. [169]

The impact of puberty blockers on the early stages of puberty are profound. Clinical studies show that if the GnRH drugs are administered at the onset of puberty, the changes in muscle tone and genitals may actually be stopped and reversed. However, the further along the child is in puberty, the less likely the changes that already took place in their body can be reversed. Clinical studies point out that females start physical changes as early as 12 years old. The goal of those who support puberty blockers is to start the drugs as close as possible to when puberty is about to begin.

There are conflicting opinions on the long-term effects of GnRH analogues. There are those who state, "GnRH analogues are a fully reversible intervention, because once the medication is stopped, the biological changes of puberty resume as they would have if puberty blockers were not used to delay the process."[170] Taking a different position on the use of puberty blockers, Mary Jackson, a WORLD journalist, provides the following.

> In a Dec. 2 preprint of the study from the Tavistock and Portman National Health Service Foundation Trust, all but one child treated for gender dysphoria with puberty-blocking drugs went on to take cross-sex hormones to alter their sex characteristics permanently. The study also showed that children's bone density and normal growth flatlined with puberty blockers as compared to their peers, and participants reported no improvement in their psychological well-being. The findings support a growing body of evidence showing the

---

[169] Ibid.
[170] Ibid.

harm and irreparable damage of experimental medical treatments for children with gender dysphoria.[171]

There are profound negative effects of puberty blockers in human development, as documented in clinical research. GnRH analogues reportedly stop sudden growth spurts that commonly occur during puberty, and they also prevent the normal increase in bone density. The body continues to grow while on puberty blockers, but the normal growth pattern takes place at a slower pace.[172] Therefore, this very new practice and its long-term repercussions, are at a minimum partially unknown. Yet, many well-meaning parents and guardians, and medical professionals, continue the politically correct process of initiating changes to an innocent child's sex characteristics, which may lead to their assent to life-changing irreversible surgeries. Erwin Lutzer provides a terse analysis of this issue. "Perhaps nowhere do we see the work of Satan in America as clearly as we do in the sexualization of children--destroying their identity, confusing their gender, and creating unresolved guilt and self-hatred."[173]

Clinical research supports the fact that most individuals who submitted to puberty blocker and cross-sex hormone therapies became infertile. However, if the individual stops taking the treatments, there is a possibility that fertility will resume, though the research states that is a small probability.[174] For those who are content with the sex-changing treatments, the next phase is to undergo life-changing surgery, where the anatomical appearance is surgically reconstructed to look like that of the opposite sex. That which started as a child in distress results in a total transformation of the physical characteristics. The original male or female anatomy with which the child was born is removed or reconstructed during radical gender surgeries. The psychological impact on those who engage in such life-altering changes remains as varied as the number of people who engage in the behavior.

---

[171] Mary Jackson, Study: Effects of Puberty-Blockers Can Last A Lifetime, December 18, 2020, WORLD, Study: Effects of puberty-blockers can last a lifetime | WORLD (wng.org), accessed October 27, 2022, 9:50 pm, CST.

[172] Laura Kuper, Puberty Blocking Medications: Clinical Research Review, IMPACT LGBT Health and Development Program.

[173] Lutzer, 156.

[174] Laura Kuper.

Homosexuality and lesbianism are not new issues. The Bible brought this fact to light nearly 2,000 years ago. However, that which was biblically and politically incorrect has taken on a whole new acceptance. Not only are same-sex marriages politically acceptable, but the government also now protects and provides benefits to same-sex couples, which were formerly only available to heterosexual couples. That landscape has not only taken on a new dimension, but now the liberal-leaning society is pushing for the sexuality of children to be the new focus. Why have many governmental leaders, legislators, social engineers, and those who embrace liberalism been so loud and strong in supporting transgender therapy for pre-pubescent children? Why have many public schools started teaching very young students about transgender issues?[175] Why have those who embrace biblical ethics and morals been the subject of disdain by liberals? Once again, it is no surprise regarding what is taking place in a once-conservative Christian nation.

> But know this, that in the last days perilous times will come: For men will be lovers of themselves, lovers of money, boasters, proud, blasphemers, disobedient to parents, unthankful, unholy, unloving, unforgiving, slanderers, without self-control, brutal, despisers of good, traitors, headstrong, haughty, lovers of pleasure rather than lovers of God, having a form of godliness but denying its power. And from such people turn away! (2 Tim. 3:1–5)

Gender Identity Post-Pubescent
Acronyms Associated with Gender Reassignment

The following list of acronyms is provided for the sole intent of educating those who have little to no understanding of the significant changes taking place in society in regard to sexual ideology. Various venues incorporate the terms on a continual basis to influence the young vulnerable population. Parents, grandparents, guardians, teachers, youth leaders, and others who hear such terms,

---

[175] Taylor Penley, Wisconsin parents outraged over inappropriate sex education curriculum for elementary schools: 'Really bad', https://www.foxnews.com/media/wisconsin-parents-outraged-inappropriate-sex-education-curriculum-elementary-schools-really-bad, accessed October 12, 2022, 10:24 am CST.

yet have no idea what they actually mean, could mistakenly support something that they actually oppose on an ethical and moral basis.
LGBTQ2S+

This stands for Lesbian, Gay, Bisexual, Transgender, Queer or Questioning, Two-Spirit, and additional orientations.

- **L: Lesbian**—A woman who is attracted to other women, either sexually, romantically or otherwise.
- **G: Gay**—Someone who is emotionally, sexually, romantically, or otherwise attracted to a person of their own gender. Though the term typically refers to the attraction of a man to another man, it can also be used to describe women or refer to the queer community as a whole.
- **B: Bisexual**—A person who is emotionally, sexually, romantically, or otherwise attracted to more than one gender.
- **T: Transgender**—A person who does not identify with the gender assigned to them at birth, either fully or in part. It's important to note that transgender is not a sexual orientation. Other words commonly used to describe folks who are transgender include gender fluid, non-binary, genderqueer, and gender non-conforming.
- **Q: Queer**—Historically, the term "queer" was used as an insult, but some folks in the LGBTQ2S+ community have reclaimed it as a sign of pride. It's used to encompass a general intersection between all groups, including individuals who don't identify with any other identity in LGBTQ2S+.
- **Q: Questioning**—The Q in LGBTQ2S+ can also stand for "questioning." This term may be used by people who are unsure about their sexual orientation and/or their gender identity.
- **2S: 2-Spirit**—Two-Spirit or 2-Spirit is an important term for some Indigenous people and cultures. Two-spirit honors the diverse and fluid nature of gender and attraction, and spiritual identity.
- **+: Plus**—This term refers to any additional gender and/or sexual orientation that hasn't been defined yet. It's an

acknowledgment that our language may not yet be adequate to describe how someone may possibly identify.[176]

Definitions of Important Terminology

- **AGENDER**: a person with no (or very little) connection to gender, no personal alignment with the concepts of either man or woman, and/or someone who sees themselves as existing without gender.
- **ASEXUAL:** A person who experiences little or no sexual attraction to others and/or a lack of interest in sexual relationships/behaviour. They may or may not experience emotional, physical, or romantic attraction. Asexuality differs from celibacy in that it is a sexual orientation, not a choice. People who are asexual may call themselves ace.
- **AROMANTIC:** A person who experiences little or no romantic attraction to others and/or has a lack of interest in romantic relationships/behaviour.
- **BISEXUAL or BI:** A person who experiences sexual, romantic, physical, and/or spiritual attraction to more than one gender, not necessarily at the same time.
- **CISGENDER:** A person whose sense of personal identity or gender does correspond to the sex they were assigned at birth.
- **GAY:** Used in some cultural settings to represent men who are attracted to men in a romantic, intimate sense.
- **GENDERFLUID**: A person who does not identify with the gender binary and moves within genders and gender stereotypes.
- **GENDERQUEER**: A person who does not identify or express their gender within the gender binary. Those who identify as genderqueer may identify as neither men nor women, may see themselves as outside of or in between the gender binary, or may simply feel restricted by gender labels.
- **HETEROSEXISM:** Prejudice against individuals and groups who display non-heterosexual behaviors or identities, combined with the majority power to impose such prejudice. Usually used to the advantage of the group in power. Any

---

[176] Boomerang, What Does LGBTQ2S+ Stand For and How to Be An Ally?, contact@goboomerang.com, 20 Bay Street, 17th Floor Toronto, Ontario, M5N 2J8, https://www.goboomerang.com/blog/health-wellness/lgbtq2s-ally/, accessed October 12, 2022, 10:58 am CST.

attitude, action, or practice backed by an institutional power that subordinates people because of their sexual orientation.
- **INTERSEX:** An umbrella term that describes people born with any of 30 different variations in sex characteristics including chromosomes, gonads, sex hormones, or genitals.
- **LESBIAN:** Usually refers to a woman who has a romantic and/or sexual orientation toward women.
- **LGBTQ2S+ ALLY:** Someone who confronts heterosexism, anti-LGBTQ2S+ biases, heterosexual and cisgender privilege in themselves and others; believes that heterosexism, homophobia, biphobia, and transphobia are social justice issues.
- **NON-BINARY or ENBY**: A person whose gender identity does not fall within the binary genders of man or woman.
- **PANSEXUAL**: A person who experiences sexual, romantic, physical attraction for members of all gender identities/expressions.
- **QUEER:** a multi-faceted word that is used in different ways and means different things to different people. 1) Attraction to people of many genders. 2) Don't conform to cultural norms around gender and/or sexuality. 3) A general term referring to all non-heterosexual people. Some within the community, however, may feel the word has been hatefully used against them for too long and are reluctant to embrace it.
- **QUESTIONING:** An individual who is unsure of and/or exploring their gender identity and/or sexual orientation.
- **TRANSGENDER:** A person whose sense of personal identity or gender does not correspond to the sex they were assigned at birth, or does not conform to gender stereotypes. [177]

Political & Social Pressure

The globalist's agenda to destroy the family and biblical morality through the propagation of the LGBT agenda came to life in 1969. David Horowitz provides an excellent summary of the event.

In the early morning hours of June 28, 1969, New York City police raided the Stonewall Inn, a gay bar on Christopher

---

[177] Vanderbilt University, https://www.vanderbilt.edu/lgbtqi/resources/definitions, accessed October 12, 2022, 10:40 am CST.

Street and Greenwich Village. Police raids were a common occurrence at the Stonewall Inn, and the bar patrons usually cooperated with police. This night was different.

The patrons threw coins and bottles at the police and refused to disperse. The commotion spilled out onto Christopher Street and attracted a crowd of onlookers. As arrests were made, a crowd of more than 400 people heckled and jeered the police. In minutes the protests escalated into a violent clash in the street. Some protesters taunted the police was shouts of "Gay power!" That night, police arrested 13 people, and dozens more were hospitalized.

The next night, a crowd again gathered in front of the Stonewall Inn. When police arrived, people shouted and chanted in protest. The gatherings clogged Christopher Street for six nights in a row. One of those nights again turned violent, causing numerous injuries. These events became known as the Stonewall Riots and the site of the Stonewall Inn is considered the birthplace of the LGBT rights movement.

The radicals define gay liberation not as the inclusion of gay Americans into the existing social contract, but as the destruction of that construct. As the central symbol of their revolt, gay radicals practiced a defiant promiscuity. It was an in-your-face challenge to what they regarded as a repressive "sex negative" culture. Gay radicals believed that monogamous marriage and the nuclear family were tyrannical structures imposed on them by their heterosexual "oppressors."

Their name for the oppression was "heteronormativity" and they set out to overthrow it.

In the view of gay radicals, existing sexual provisions reflected no lessons drawn from humanity's biological realities and moral experience; they were merely "social constructs" imposed by an oppressive culture. Consequently, gay liberators did not seek civil tolerance, respect, and integration into the public order of "bourgeois" life. On the contrary, they were determined to do away with traditional middle-class standards of morality, sexual restraint, and even public hygiene.[178]

Once again, it is extremely important to consider how a Christian should treat those who embrace a non-biblical lifestyle. Commonly, the Christian community makes the following statement when addressing any behavior that falls outside of the Bible's allowance, which is to hate the sin, but love the sinner. The fact is, all have sinned and come short of the glory of God (Rom. 3:23). There is a multitude of things that are displeasing to God, which by definition is sinful behavior. The wonderful news is that God loves people, despite their sin, and gave His life to pay their sin debt. "But God demonstrates His own love toward us, in that while we were still sinners, Christ died for us" (Rom. 5:8). God calls Christians to be His ambassadors, and lovingly share the greatest news ever given to humankind that Christ Jesus came into the world to save sinners from their sins and the penalty for sin (2 Cor. 5:20; Eph. 4:15; Luke 19:10; 1 Tim. 1:15). Therefore, those who engage in behavior not consistent with God's design for intimacy, which is one man and one woman brought together in marriage (Gen. 1:27-28; 2:24; Matt. 19:4-6; Mark 10:6-8; 1 Cor. 6:16; Eph. 5:31-33), should still be treated with respect and dignity. Christians should never condone anti-biblical behavior. However, Christians should not expect sinful behavior to change until a person first receives the Lord Jesus Christ as their personal Savior. The new Christian is immediately indwelt by the Holy Spirit (1 Cor. 3:16; 6:19; 12:13), and He will bring conviction and help for the person to make the needed lifestyle changes (2 Cor. 5:17).

The Old Testament law discusses multiple sexual sins that specifically the Jewish people, and proselytes to Judaism, were not to violate.

> Moreover, you shall not lie carnally with your neighbor's wife, to defile yourself with her…You shall not lie with a male as with a woman. It is an abomination. Nor shall you mate with any animal, to defile yourself with it. Nor shall any woman stand before an animal to mate with it. It is perversion. (Lev. 18:20–23)

The New Testament also addresses the practice of homosexual and lesbian behavior in several passages. Pastors, Bible

---

[178] David Horowitz, *Dark Agenda, The War to Destroy Christian America* (West Palm Beach, FL.: Humanix Books, 2018), 109-111)

teachers, and students should not consider changing the literal meaning of the Word of God to match their personal beliefs, wants, or desires. God meant what He stated and stated exactly what He meant. The following texts specifically address those living in the Church Age, which includes the current generation.

For this reason God gave them up to vile passions. For even their women exchanged the natural use for what is against nature. Likewise also the men, leaving the natural use of the woman, burned in their lust for one another, men with men committing what is shameful, and receiving in themselves the penalty of their error which was due. (Rom. 1:26–27)

Do you not know that the unrighteous will not inherit the kingdom of God? Do not be deceived. Neither fornicators, nor idolaters, nor adulterers, nor homosexuals, nor sodomites, nor thieves, nor covetous, nor drunkards, nor revilers, nor extortioners will inherit the kingdom of God. (1 Cor. 6:9–10)

As Sodom and Gomorrah, and the cities around them in a similar manner to these, having given themselves over to sexual immorality and gone after strange flesh, are set forth as an example, suffering the vengeance of eternal fire. (Jude 7)

A gallop poll reveals extremely important statistical data regarding those who identify as LGBT in America. The poll reveals an increasing trend in the numbers of those who choose the LGBT lifestyle, and it identifies which age groups are most prone to embrace something other than a heterosexual relationship.

> The percentage of U.S. adults who self-identify as lesbian, gay, bisexual, transgender, or something other than heterosexual has increased to a new high of 7.1%, which is double the percentage from 2012, when Gallup first measured it.
>
> Gallup asks Americans whether they personally identify as straight or heterosexual, lesbian, gay, bisexual, or transgender as part of the demographic information it collects on all U.S. telephone surveys. Respondents can also volunteer any other sexual orientation or gender identity they prefer. In addition to the 7.1% of U.S. adults who consider themselves to be an LGBT identity, 86.3% say they are straight or heterosexual, and 6.6% do not offer an opinion. The results are based on aggregated 2021 data, encompassing interviews with more than 12,000 U.S. adults.

The increase in LGBT identification in recent years largely reflects the higher prevalence of such identities among the youngest U.S. adults compared with the older generations they are replacing in the U.S. adult population.[179]

The following gallop poll statistics show a significant increase in the number of those in the younger generation who reject a heterosexual lifestyle. This should come as no surprise to anyone watching the massive campaign for acceptance and promotion of the LGBTQ lifestyle by the government, many medical professionals, liberal academics, vast portions of the media, and even many in the religious community.

Roughly 21% of Generation Z Americans (born between 1997 and 2003), who have reached adulthood, identify as LGBT. That is nearly double the percentage of Millennials who do so, and the gap widens when compared with earlier generations.

	LGBT %	Straight/Heterosexual %	No response %
Generation Z (born 1997-2003)	20.8	75.7	3.5
Millennials (born 1981-1996)	10.5	82.5	7.1
Generation X (born 1965-1980)	4.2	89.3	6.5
Baby boomers (born 1946-1964)	2.6	90.7	6.8
Traditionalists (born before 1946)	0.8	92.2	7.1

Figure 6.1

Generation Z adults made up 7% of Gallup's 2017 national sample, but in 2021 accounted for 12% as more from that generation reached age 18 over the past four years. In contrast, the proportion of those born before 1946 has fallen from 11% in 2017 to 8%.

Since Gallup began measuring LGBT identification in 2012, the percentage of Traditionalists, Baby Boomers, and Generation X adults who identify as LGBT has held relatively steady. At the same time, there has been a modest uptick

---

[179] Jeffrey M. Jones, LGBT Identification in U.S. Ticks Up to 7.1%, February 17, 2022, https://news.gallup.com/poll/389792/lgbt-identification-ticks-up.aspx, accessed October 12, 2022, 2:50 PM CST.

among Millennials, from 5.8% in 2012 (when some members of the generation had not yet turned 18) to 7.8% in 2017 and 10.5% currently.

The percentage of Generation Z who are LGBT has nearly doubled since 2017, when only the leading edge of that generation (born between 1997 and 1999) had reached adulthood. At that time, 10.5% of the small slice of the generation who were adults identified as LGBT.

More than half of LGBT Americans, 57%, indicate they are bisexual. That percentage translates to 4.0% of all U.S. adults. Meanwhile, 21% of LGBT Americans say they are gay, 14% lesbian, 10% transgender, and 4% something else. Each of these accounts for less than 2% of U.S. adults.[180]

Pew Research conducted a poll in 2020 that documented an increase in the acceptance of homosexuality internationally and domestically. They specifically determined that in the United States 72% of people believe homosexuality is acceptable, compared with just 49% in 2007.[181]

The globalist agenda is loudly proclaiming in real-time the necessity for the entire world to embrace the homosexual, lesbian, gay, bi-sexual, and transgender worldview, and lifestyle. Jeff Kinley, a conservative Bible scholar, states a profound truth regarding the current sexual trends. "We live in a culture that by and large accepts all types of sexual expression. The spirit of the age now demands that heterosexuals accept homosexuality as normal and morally appropriate. And the controversy over gay marriage is not going away. In fact, it will gain momentum in the last days."[182]

Joe Dallas, who had been a practicing homosexual, wrote a compelling book on the transformation God performed in His life. Joe stated that he struggled with the question of whether it was "possible to be actively homosexual, Christian, and confident of a right standing before God. I knew better, of course. I knew the Scriptural condemnations of homosexuality in both the Old and New

---

[180] Jeffrey M. Jones, LGBT Identification in U.S. Ticks Up to 7.1%.

[181] Jacob Poushter and Nicholas Kent, The Global Divide on Homosexuality Persists, Pew Research Center, June 25, 2020, https://www.pewresearch.org/global/2020/06/25/global-divide-on-homosexuality-persists/, accessed October 12, 2022, 2:40 pm CST.

[182] Jeff Kinley, *As it was in the Days of Noah* (Eugene, OR.: Harvest House Publishers, 2014), 99.

Testaments were clear and final, and any attempt to get around them was purely self-serving. But it *was* self, after all, that I was serving in those days. Every major decision I had made that year-- entering the pornographic bookstore, the adultery, the homosexuality--had been based on what I wanted, not on what I knew to be right."[183] Joe Dallas, like many others, who for a season embraced immorality as an acceptable lifestyle, finally decided to follow the biblical Jesus, and a biblical lifestyle. Change is possible through the life transformation that Jesus brings to those who choose to embrace Him.

This chapter brings to light the extreme conditions that Satan and the demonic army are currently using to bring about the catastrophic changes that will eventually set the norm for the Antichrist's one-world religion, government, and economy. Jeff Kinley states the issue in a thought-provoking way. "Tragically, we now live in a world that celebrates same-sex marriages, and shames those who uphold God's design. It is a world that views those who parade their sin like Sodom as being courageous heroes. While it is impossible, irresponsible, and foolish to make predictions regarding the exact timing of the last days, there do appear to be storm clouds gathering on the horizon. A planet that is intoxicated with its own sexual pursuits and perversions is a sure sign we are closer now than ever."[184] God allows the globalist agenda to progress to accomplish His will as outlined in the prophetic Scriptures. Christians should not find the tremendous increase in immorality domestically and internationally to be unusual. The apostle Paul warned that in the last days of the Church Age, dangerous, perilous times would come (2 Tim. 3:1).

Everything discussed to this point is a warning and an invitation, that it is time for all people to realize their desperate need to turn to Jesus Christ and accept the gift of eternal life by placing their faith in the death, burial, and resurrection of Jesus Christ who made the once for all sacrifice to pay for the sins of all who believe on Him. "For by grace you have been saved through faith, and that not of yourselves; it is the gift of God, not of works, lest anyone should boast" (Eph. 2:8–9). There has never been a better time than this very moment for one to realize they are a sinner, in need of

---

[183] Joe Dallas, *The Gay Gospel? How Pro-Gay Advocates Misread the Bible* (Eugene, OR.: Harvest House Publishers, 2007), 13.
[184] Kinley, As it was in the Days of Noah, 107.

forgiveness, which the Lord Jesus Christ, God's Son, provided when He left heaven's glory, and willingly went to the cross to fully pay one's sin debt (1 Cor. 15:3-4; 2 Cor, 6:2).

CHAPTER SEVEN
CLIMATE CHANGE

A NEW DECEPTION

Climate change and global warming stir up a great deal of emotion from Christian and secular audiences. Many times, when someone utters the words "climate change" in a church or conservative group, people will snicker or outright laugh. On the opposite end of the spectrum are those who take very seriously the government and media attention given to global warming and climate change. The research from the biblical and secular perspective may surprise even many in the Christian community. The next statement may appear shocking at first, but as the literal interpretation of Scripture will prove, God Himself brings about global warming on two different occasions in the prophetic Scriptures. This chapter addresses this important biblical truth with biblical support.

The globalists sound the global warming and climate change alarm with great emphasis on the potentially imminent destruction of the earth, if the countries of the world do not hasten to implement extreme measures, specifically in the fossil fuel industry. In fact, this issue may have a much more profound impact on globalism than even COVID-19, which is slowly losing the constant attention of the globalists. However, literally, as I am writing this paragraph, a news bulletin has appeared stating, "Mask Mandate Reinstated on Milwaukee County Buses," referring to Milwaukee County Wisconsin, where I live.[185] So much for the fading impact of COVID-19.

Climate change has profound short-term and long-term potential implications that are a politician's dream come true for manipulating the populace. People, for the most part, do not respond to straightforward facts and data. Many people respond to stories and emotionally charged presentations. Politicians who attempt to win a campaign with honest documented facts, and fail to appeal to the emotional side of the voters, will likely lose the election.

---

[185] Mask Mandate Reinstated On Milwaukee County Buses, WISN-ABC, October 14, 2022, https://wisn.com/article/mask-mandate-reinstated-on-milwaukee-county-buses/41626891, accessed October 14, 2022, 3:30 PM CST.

For those who still allow mainstream television into their home, turn on any station and pay attention to the commercials. How many of the television commercials use a dog, cat, or other appealing animal? What percentage of the remaining commercials use young children or babies? Most of the time, the commercials have nothing to do with babies, children, or animals, but people respond to engaging, emotionally captivating visuals. If the company investing its money in advertising understands what visually appeals to consumers, it can immediately gain their attention. If a company can also brand its product effectively, helping people remember the product, and then combine that brand with an emotionally good feeling, they will sell their product.

How do you sell the public on the necessity for all countries to band together on an issue? Why would America ever consider partnering with a country steeped in socialism, Marxism, Communism, globalism, or totalitarianism that uses an extremely harsh religious or cultural dictatorship to control its citizens? How can Satan himself manipulate the entire world to eventually embrace and worship the Antichrist (Rev. 13:4)? Enter in COVID-19 and the World Health Organization (WHO), which is setting the stage for the global system.

> The World Health Organization leads and champions global efforts to achieve better health for all. By connecting countries, people, and partners, we strive to give everyone, everywhere an equal chance at a safe and healthy life.
>
> From emerging epidemics such as COVID-19 and Zika to the persistent threat of communicable diseases including HIV, malaria and tuberculosis and chronic diseases such as diabetes, heart disease and cancer, we bring together 194 countries and work on the frontlines in 150+ locations to confront the biggest health challenges of our time and measurably advance the well-being of the world's people.[186]

Enter in the World Meteorological Organization (WMO), which declares itself to be "a specialized agency of the United Nations (UN) with 193 Member States and Territories. It is the UN system's authoritative voice on the state and behavior of the Earth's atmosphere, its interaction with the land and oceans, the weather

---

[186] World Health Organization (WHO), https://www.who.int/, accessed October 14, 2022, 3:45PM CST.

and climate it produces and the resulting distribution of water resources."[187]

The adage, "Never let a good crisis, perceived or real, go to waste", characterizes the globalist agenda for putting the one-world system in place. The purpose of this chapter is to summarize the real and perceived issues associated with global warming and climate change. Of utmost importance, is understanding the scriptural chronological timeline, and the exact timing and length of events that must take place before God destroys the world by fire, a minimum of 1,007 years from today, barring that the Rapture has not occurred at the time of the your reading this book. Yes, God will eventually destroy the earth by fire. However, the Scriptures also detail that the world must exist a minimum of 1,007 years after the Rapture of the Church Age saints, which has not taken place as of the writing of this book. These statements of fact are documented in this chapter and should provide a real sense of comfort for those, who up to this point, embrace the false, unbiblical claims that the world faces catastrophic annihilation in the short term.

A major premise of this book is that Satan always has a plan to deceive people regarding the truth of God's Word. Satan is fully aware that he will endure eternal punishment in the lake of fire (Rev. 20:10) unless, in his corrupt mind, he can stop God's prophetic plan (James 2:19). Satan began his catastrophic work in the garden of Eden when he deceived Eve, and subsequently, Eve encouraged Adam to sin against God's commandment not to eat from the forbidden tree. God commanded Adam not to eat of the tree of the knowledge of good and evil before God created Eve (Gen. 2:16-22). When Adam subsequently ate from the forbidden tree, he gained the sinful nature, resulting in that corrupt nature passing from the father to their offspring (Rom. 5:12). The biological fact is that every person has a human father, and thus Scripture states that "all have sinned" (Rom. 3:23). There is one exception to this undeniable truth. Jesus Christ was conceived of the Holy Spirit and born of a virgin (Isa. 7:14; Matt. 1:23; Luke 1:26-33). The virgin birth was an absolute necessity, for if Jesus would have had a human father, He would have inherited the sin nature from His father, thus disqualifying Jesus as the sinless,

---

[187] Who We Are, World Meteorological Organization, https://public.wmo.int/en/about-us/who-we-are#:~:text=WMO%20is%20a%20specialized%20agency,resulting%20distribution%20of%20water%20resources, accessed October 14, 2022, 3:15 PM CST.

perfect Savior, who died, was buried, and rose from the dead three days later to pay the entire price for sin (1 Cor. 15:1-4; John 3:16-17; Eph. 2:8-9; Heb. 7:27; 9:12; 10:10).

The Scriptures, in Genesis 3, record the account of Satan's initial deception of Eve, and Adam's subsequent failure to obey God. Satan, the master liar and deceiver (John 8:44), will not stop his attempt to thwart God's plan until the Lord literally casts him into the lake of fire at the end of the millennial kingdom (Rev. 20:1-10). Until that time, Satan relentlessly engages in deceptive tactics to discount the Word of God and deceive as many people as possible.

The globalists incorporated global warming and climate change into their portfolio of manipulative measures to gain the world's attention, and obtain buy-in and cooperation on solving what they maintain is a massive worldwide crisis. The stated crisis stands in direct contrast and opposition to the Scripture's account of God's prophetic timeline.

David Horowitz provides an analysis of those who reject the reality of God and look to themselves for the answers to the world's problems.

> It is a fantasy in which human beings aspire to act as gods and create new worlds, and it is nothing new. It is the faith of Marxists and Communists who set out to transform the world from the one we know into one that is entirely different, liberated. It is the essence of the original sin recorded in Genesis, when Satan tempted the first man and woman, saying "Then your eyes shall be open and ye shall be gods (Gen. 3:5)."[188]

The natural conclusion from this statement is that the issues the world currently faces, and the globalist agenda, are the direct results of the worldwide movement away from the one true God, who created the universe and everything in it (Ex. 20:11; Col. 1:16). Therefore, those who portend disaster and exaggerate the impact of natural, cyclical climate changes as the basis for a unified global response, are unequivocally manipulating the world's populations with a highly suspect political agenda. The one-world government is Satan's goal (Rev. 13), and the claims of climate change alarmists play

---

[188] David Horowitz, *Dark Agenda, The War to Destroy Christian America* (Palm Beach, FL.: Humanix Books, 2018), 12.

just one more part in assuring that God's perfect, infallible Word will come to fulfillment exactly as stated.

The Scriptures speak to the fact of Satan's deceptive tactics.

> Why do you not understand My speech? Because you are not able to listen to My word. You are of your father the devil, and the desires of your father you want to do. He was a murderer from the beginning, and does not stand in the truth, because there is no truth in him. When he speaks a lie, he speaks from his own resources, for he is a liar and the father of it. (John 8:43-44)

In addition, the Bible warns the reader to constantly be on guard and carefully analyze what others are postulating as truth.

> Beware lest anyone cheat you through philosophy and empty deceit, according to the tradition of men, according to the basic principles of the world, and not according to Christ. For in Him dwells all the fullness of the Godhead bodily; and you are complete in Him, who is the head of all principality and power. (Col. 2:8–10)

AWAKENING OF CLIMATE CHANGE

Position 1: Climate change is destroying the earth!

Climate change activists and organizations provide a great deal of information through open-source materials. One simply has to access the internet, type in the words "climate change," and immediately nearly two-million results appear.

The Suzuki Foundation provides a concise definition of climate change on its website.

> "Climate change" describes a change in the average conditions — such as temperature and rainfall — in a region over a long period of time. Earth's climate is always changing over long periods of time and has been hotter and cooler than it is now, but the pace of change has sped up significantly in recent decades. Scientists are deeply concerned about the changes they've observed since the Industrial Revolution.
>
> Although the terms "climate change" and "global warming" are often used interchangeably, some experts note a difference: global warming is the overall phenomenon whereby global average temperatures are slowly increasing.

Climate change is the result of global warming. That is, as global temperatures increase, climatic conditions change in various ways.

Human-caused climate change is affecting the planet in ways that could alter all life on Earth. It's the biggest, most urgent problem we face. In fact, many — including the David Suzuki Foundation — use stronger terms such as CLIMATE EMERGENCY, CLIMATE CRISIS, CLIMATE DISRUPTION, GLOBAL HEATING and CLIMATE CHAOS to reflect the severity.[189]

The Suzuki Foundation formulated a top-ten list of things one can do to mitigate the impact of climate change.

1. Urge government to take bold, ambitious climate action now
2. Help raise climate ambition by painting your town with climate art
3. Use energy wisely — and save money too!
4. Mobilize for local climate action
5. Green your commute
6. Start a climate conversation
7. Consume less, waste less, enjoy life more
8. Invest in renewables and divest from fossil fuels
9. Eat for a climate-stable planet
10. Get politically active and vote[190]

Nothing on the list appears to have a radical, globalist agenda. The organization presents its material in a kind, matter-of-fact way.

The impact of livestock farming is an extremely interesting subject when analysed from a climate change perspective. Therefore, those who portend disaster and exaggerate the impact of natural, cyclical climate changes as the basis for a unified global response, are unequivocally manipulating the world's populations with a highly suspect political agenda.

According to the UN Food and Agriculture Organization, livestock farming produces 65 percent of human-related nitrous oxide, which has 296 times the global warming potential as CO_2. It

---

[189] What is Climate Change?, David Suzuki Foundation, https://davidsuzuki.org/what-you-can-do/what-is-climate-change/?gclid=EAIaIQobChMIzbuuxuvn-gIVTBTUAR2FWwT9EAAYASAAEgKm6fD_BwE, accessed October 17, 2022, 1:00 PM CST.

[190] Ibid.

also contributes "37 percent of all human-induced methane (23 times as warming as CO_2), which is largely produced by the digestive system of ruminants, and 64 percent of ammonia, which contributes significantly to acid rain." But methane stays in the atmosphere for about 12 years, and nitrous oxide for about 114, while CO_2 remains for thousands of years.[191]

Emissions also vary by livestock. Pigs and poultry contribute about 10 percent of global agricultural emissions[192] but provide three times as much meat as cattle — which are responsible for about 40 percent of emissions — and use less feed. Some plant agriculture also causes global warming. Wetland rice cultivation produces methane and nitrous oxide emissions, the latter because of nitrogen fertilizer use. Different agricultural methods also have varying effects on climate. And some people, such as the Inuit, have adapted to meat-based diets because fresh produce is scarce — and flying it in causes more emissions than hunting and eating game.[193]

Though the statistics are compelling, do they represent a real danger to the environment? The scientific community will no doubt continue to research this highly controversial and politically charged issue. One thing is certain, the Biden administration in the White House has taken a strong position in claiming that global warming and climate change are extreme threats to the country. Besides being very vocal on this issue, the White House is taking significant measures, including investing billions of hard-earned tax-payer money to address what they claim is a worldwide crisis.

The White House provides open-source material through "fact sheets," that express their position on multiple issues, and the solutions they intend to implement. Several fact sheets deal with

---

[191] Chris Mooney, The Hidden Driver of Climate Change That We Too Often Ignore, The Washington Post,
March 9, 2016 at 1:29 p.m. EST, https://www.washingtonpost.com/news/energy-environment/wp/2016/03/09/the-hidden-driver-of-climate-change-that-we-too-often-ignore/, accessed October 17, 2022, 1:35 PM CST.

[192] Brian Walsh, The Triple Whopper Environmental Impact of Global Meat Production, TIME.com, Ecocentric, October 16, 2013,
https://science.time.com/2013/12/16/the-triple-whopper-environmental-impact-of-global-meat-production/, accessed October 17, 2022, 1:27 PM, CST.

[193] David Suzuki, Eating Less Meat Will Reduce Earth's Heat, David Suzuki Foundation, May 19, 2016,
https://davidsuzuki.org/story/eating-less-meat-will-reduce-earths-heat/, accessed October 17, 2022, 1:40 PM CST.

climate change and global warming, such as this one published on July 20, 2022, titled *President Biden's Executive Actions on Climate to Address Extreme Heat and Boost Offshore Wind*. The fact sheet begins with, "Today, President Biden will reiterate that climate change is a clear and present danger to the United States. Since Congress is not acting on this emergency, in the coming weeks, President Biden will announce additional executive actions to combat this emergency." The President is quoted as wanting to change the crisis "into an opportunity by creating good-paying jobs in clean energy and lowering costs for families." The Federal Emergency Management Agency (FEMA) announced "2.3 billion dollars in funding for its Building Resilient Infrastructure and Communities (BRIC) program for Fiscal Year 2022—the largest BRIC investment in history, boosted by the President's Bipartisan Infrastructure Law." The funding will, according to the government's perspective, "help communities increase resilience to heat waves, drought, wildfires, flood, hurricanes, and other hazards by preparing before disaster strikes."[194]

The second major initiative in the fact sheet is to lower cooling costs for communities suffering from extreme heat. How will the federal government accomplish this objective? "In April, the Biden-Harris Administration released $385 million through LIHEAP to help families with their household energy costs, including summer cooling—part of a record $8 billion that the Administration has provided, boosted by the President's Bipartisan Infrastructure Law."[195] Those who embrace socialism, and using taxpayer money to accomplish it should be encouraged.

---

[194] The White House, Fact Sheet: Biden-Harris Administration Launches New Climate Portal to Help Communities Navigate Climate Change Impacts - The White House, September 8, 2022, https://www.whitehouse.gov/briefing-room/statements-releases/2022/09/08/fact-sheet-biden-harris-administration-launches-new-climate-portal-to-help-communities-navigate-climate-change-impacts/, accessed October 17, 2022, 2:35PM CST.

[195] Ibid.

[195] David Suzuki, Eating Less Meat Will Reduce Earth's Heat, David Suzuki Foundation, May 19, 2016, https://davidsuzuki.org/story/eating-less-meat-will-reduce-earths-heat/, accessed October 17, 2022, 1:40 PM CST.

[195] The White House, Fact Sheet: Biden-Harris Administration Launches New Climate Portal to Help Communities Navigate Climate Change Impacts - The White House, September 8, 2022, https://www.whitehouse.gov/briefing-room/statements-releases/2022/09/08/fact-sheet-biden-harris-administration-

The fact sheet goes on to tout billions of more dollars the Federal Government is spending to provide "record funding to increase community resilience." Those who embrace liberal, social outcomes, and have little concern for the national debt, long-term inflation, and the financial impact on generations to come, should find the next announcement encouraging. "Last year, President Biden doubled the funding available through FEMA's Building Resilient Infrastructure and Communities (BRIC) program. This year, he is doubling it again, to a historic level of $2.3 billion available for states, local communities, Tribes, and territories to proactively reduce their vulnerability to heat waves, drought, wildfires, flood, hurricanes, and other hazards boosted by the President's Bipartisan Infrastructure Law."[196]

A White House fact sheet from September 8, 2022, titled *Biden-Harris Administration Launches New Climate Portal to Help Communities Navigate Climate Change Impacts*, introduces a new internet portal to keep Americans informed on significant weather conditions.

> Americans are feeling the intensifying impacts of the climate crisis—from extreme heat across the country, including the dangerous "heat dome" gripping California this week; record-breaking floods across the South and Midwest; Western drought straining the water supplies that millions depend on; and more wildfires threatening communities. Last year, the 20 largest climate-related disasters alone took hundreds of lives, caused untold hardships, and racked up more than $150 billion in damages.
>
> In addition to providing more detailed, location-specific data about climate threats, the new portal also brings together multiple federal information sources and funding opportunities to help communities better prepare for and respond to climate impacts—including historic resilience funding from the President's Bipartisan Infrastructure Law for states and communities around the country. Together with the Inflation Reduction Act, the Biden-Harris Administration is providing historic levels of support to expand resilience

---

launches-new-climate-portal-to-help-communities-navigate-climate-change-impacts/, accessed October 17, 2022, 2:35PM CST.
[195] Ibid.
[196] Ibid.

programs, protect U.S. communities, economies, and infrastructure from the worsening impacts of climate change, and improve the nation's climate mapping and data capabilities.[197]

The portal should provide excellent information regarding weather conditions and patterns, and it appears to be an excellent way for Americans and others to access important data. The challenging piece of this initiative is for the government to prove that climate change and global warming are actually the documented, confirmed reasons for the weather patterns and conditions, as there is only speculative conclusions made that lack empirical, scientific data. The alleged crisis is also highly suspect in light of the 100% accuracy of Bible prophecy, which mandates a minimum of 1,007 more years for this earth to exist (Dan. 9:27; Rev. 20:1-7).

A White House fact sheet from September 16, 2022, titled *ICYMI: Week of Climate Action from the Biden-Harris Administration*, discusses multiple major actions for dealing with the "climate crisis." The initiatives include electric vehicles. The fact sheet states, "President Biden highlighted the $85 billion invested since he took office to make electric vehicles, batteries, and chargers in America. He also announced the Administration's approval of the first 35 state plans for EV charging made possible by the President's Bipartisan Infrastructure Law."[198] The second cited initiative is the offshore wind project, to make offshore wind platforms along the West Coast, Gulf of Mexico, and other areas. The Administration set a new deployment goal of 15 gigawatts of floating offshore wind by 2035.[199]

The third White House initiative cited is the cleaner industry and construction materials project "to prioritize purchase of lower-carbon steel, concrete, asphalt, and flat glass—materials that account for nearly half of all U.S. manufacturing greenhouse gas emissions." The fourth initiative is for climate-smart agriculture "to support a first round of 70 projects—reaching more than 50,000

---

[197] Ibid.
[198] The White House, ICYMI: Week of Climate Action from the Biden-Harris Administration - The White House, September 16, 2022, https://www.whitehouse.gov/briefing-room/statements-releases/2022/09/16/icymi-week-of-climate-action-from-the-biden-harris-administration/, accessed October 17, 2022, 3:45 PM CST.
[199] Ibid.

farms and sequestering over 50 million metric tons of greenhouse gas emissions."[200]

The initiatives carry an extremely large price tag, and the actual ability to implement the projects is suspect, based on the availability of materials needed, especially when producing the massive number of rechargeable batteries needed for electric cars. Once again, all of the initiatives, according to the White House, are in response to climate change. Conservatives and liberals can find common ground on not wasting resources and caring for the world's resources in a responsible manner. However, are the initiatives and plans scheduled for implementation in America and other countries the best response to a climate crisis, or simply a political response to a perceived crisis? One fact is for sure: The infallible Bible documents that there will be a future one-world government, economy, and religion. Two of the defining subjects that are fomenting the need for a global response are climate change and global warming. The crucial issue is not whether the government's response to climate change is appropriate. The root issue is whether the current alleged climate crisis is the mechanism, or one piece of a larger puzzle, for the Antichrist to one day implement his one-world dictatorship.

Position 2:
Climate Change is Occurring, but Will Not Destroy the Earth

Searching the internet via Google, using the following phrase, "conservative documentation against climate change," results in about 71.5 million hits, a massive number, but a fraction of what is available on the subject of climate change through the internet. When defending the conservative viewpoint on climate change, a balanced, factual response is appropriate. Therefore, the following summary avoids sensational rhetoric and meanspirited criticism. The most reasonable and balanced sources highlight the real issues associated with climate change, and then provide a reasonable analysis of those facts.

Lee Lane, a writer for *The New Atlantis*, an online journal provides a balanced overview on the topics of climate change and global warming. The report states, "While climate science faces daunting epistemological problems, a sober reading of its findings implies that while climate change is not an imminent crisis, it is a real

---

[200] Ibid.

phenomenon worthy of attention."[201] In addition, the report states that conservatives that have objected to the agenda of the climate change proponents have saved the country large amounts of money that were slated for the government to spend without producing the intended results. In contrast, the report also criticizes conservatives for their failure to establish scientific evidence that clearly and convincingly supports their position. "By dogmatically asserting that no serious threat is on the horizon, too many conservatives have removed themselves from the debate about how to hedge our bets sensibly by finding ways of reducing the risks climate change poses while minimizing the economic impact."[202]

The following is a well-balanced introduction to climate change from a non-partisan viewpoint.

> Climate change — or global warming, as it was once more commonly known — is an extremely complex phenomenon influenced by both human activity and natural processes. Agriculture, the burning of fossil fuels, and many other human activities release "greenhouse gases" — so called because they absorb energy in a way that allows sunlight to warm the atmosphere. Carbon dioxide is the most important of the greenhouse gases influenced by human activity, but methane and a number of others are also important. Once these gases enter the atmosphere, natural processes withdraw them into various "sinks," such as the oceans, vegetation, and soil. But human activity is releasing these greenhouse gases into the atmosphere at higher rates than they're being drawn out through the natural cycles, so their concentrations in the atmosphere are rising — particularly that of carbon dioxide. Atmospheric carbon dioxide measured at the Mauna Lea observatory in Hawaii increased from 315 parts per million in 1959 to 396 parts per million in 2013. Concentrations of carbon dioxide have not been that high during the entire history of human civilization, and

---

[201] Lee Lane, Toward a Conservative Policy on Climate Change, Clashing worldviews, green politics, and a path forward, *The New Atlantis*, Number 41, Winter 2014, pp. 19-37, https://www.thenewatlantis.com/publications/toward-a-conservative-policy-on-climate-change, accessed October 17, 2022, 4:30 PM CST.

[202] Ibid.

perhaps even in the entire time that our species has walked the earth.

As greenhouse gas concentrations continue to rise, the average global temperature is expected to rise as well. As it does, it will affect the world's climate in myriad ways. Some of the changes will be harmful, others may be beneficial. At present, it is far from clear exactly what all those changes will be, where they will occur, or when we can expect them to take place, much less just who will benefit or suffer from them.[203]

The following is a list of the 15 counties that produce the highest amounts of carbon dioxide from fossil fuels per person. The United States ranks number 13 based on emissions per capita. However, when listing the countries by the actual amount of CO_2 emissions from fossil fuels, the United States moves to the top of the list. The data from one report can prove two different points based on how one interprets and arranges the data.

For each country, the value represents the amount of carbon dioxide emission from fossil fuel in 2019:

1. United States: 5.1 Billion Metric Tons[204]
2. Saudi Arabis: 614.607 Million Metris Tonnes
3. Canada: 584.846 Million Metris Tonnes
4. Australia: 433.379 Million Metris Tonnes
5. Kazakhstan: 277.365 Million Metris Tonnes
6. United Arab Emirates: 222.612 Million Metris Tonnes
7. Qatar: 106.528 Million Metris Tonnes
8. Kuwait: 98.953 Million Metris Tonnes
9. Oman: 92.953 Million Metris Tonnes
10. Turkmenistan: 90.523 Million Metris Tonnes
11. Bahrain: 438 Million Metris Tonnes
12. Trinidad and Tobago: 32.744 Million Metris Tonnes
13. Luxembourg: 740 Million Metris Tonnes
14. Brunei: 7.020 Million Metris Tonnes
15. Palau: 1.330 Million Metris Tonnes[205]

---

[203] Ibid.

[204] One metric tonne (ton) is equal to approximately 2,205 pounds.

[205] Trish Novicio, 15 Countries With The Highest Average Carbon Dioxide Emissions Per Person, March 15, 2021, https://finance.yahoo.com/news/15-countries-highest-average-carbon-161359972.html, accessed October 17, 2022, 5:20 PM CST.

The following statistics show the top ten producers of CO_2 emissions as measured in 2021, without taking into account their emissions per capita.

1. China: 14.1%
2. United States: 5.7%
3. India 3.4%
4. United Kingdom: 3.3%
5. Indonesia: 1.8%
6. Russia: 1.6%
7. Brazil: 1.5%
8. Japan: 1.1%
9. Iran: 0.9%
10. Saudi Arabia: 0.7%[206]

The reason for presenting two different reports is to show that an analyst can select the data that tells the story they want to be told. Using the first set of data points, an analyst ranked countries based on the the highest average emissions per person. However, that list did not include China, which literally produces well over twice the CO_2 emissions than the United States. In fact, according to the second data set, the top nine countries listed as the largest emission offenders are conspicuously missing from the first data set. The top ten offenders include China, the United States, India, the United Kingdom, Indonesia, Russia, Brazil, Japan and Iran, yet only the United States appears in the first report, which covered the "15 Countries with the Highest Average Carbon Dioxide Emissions Per Person."

In the United States, cars are one of the highest producers of CO_2 emissions (see Figure 7.1). There are nearly 300 million registered cars in the United States.[207] The government and green energy proponents highly recommend moving from gas-powered vehicles to vehicles that run on battery power and are charged at

---

[206] Helen Regan and Carlotta Dotto, US vs. China: How the world's two biggest emitters stack up on climate, CNN, Updated 2:29 AM EDT, Wed November 3, 2021, https://www.cnn.com/2021/10/28/world/china-us-climate-cop26-intl-hnk/index.html, accessed October 17, 2022, 8:40 PM CST.

[207] US VIO (Vehicles in Operation) Vehicle Registration Statistics: See How Many Cars in The US, Hedges & Company, https://hedgescompany.com/automotive-market-research-statistics/auto-mailing-lists-and-marketing/, accessed October 17, 2022, 10:30 PM CST.

home, or at public stations. The government plans to install the necessary infrastructure across the country to charge electric vehicles.[208]

CO2 emissions by fuel type, United States
Annual carbon dioxide (CO₂) emissions from different fuel types, measured in tonnes per year.

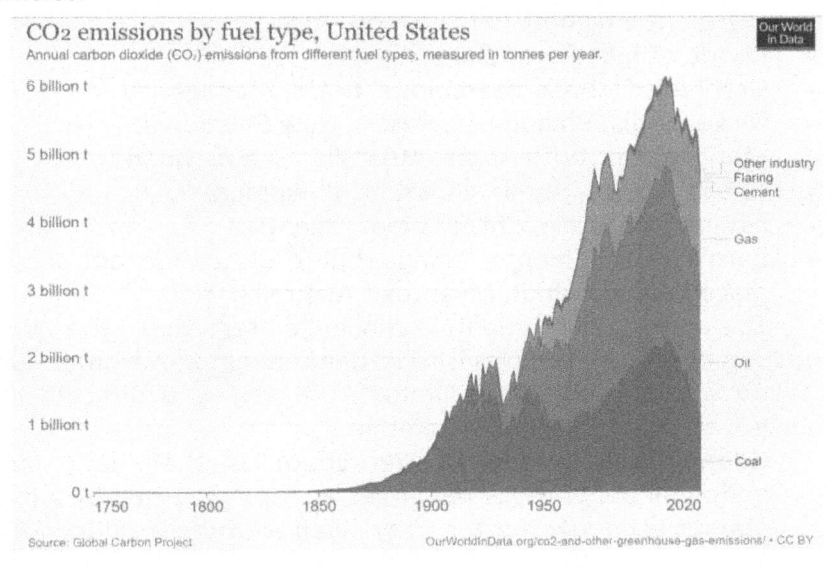

(Chart showing emissions from 1750 to 2020, with categories: Other industry, Flaring, Cement, Gas, Oil, Coal. Y-axis ranges from 0 to 6 billion t.)

Source: Global Carbon Project
OurWorldInData.org/co2-and-other-greenhouse-gas-emissions/ • CC BY

Figure 7.1[209]

One of the key challenges to the mass production of electric-powered vehicles is supplying the minerals necessary to produce the batteries. The typical electric vehicle requires 441 pounds of mineral resources per vehicle, which is six times more than what a gas-powered vehicle requires. The following is the list of minerals needed per vehicle.

- Graphite – 146 lbs.
- Copper – 117 lbs.
- Nickel – 74 lbs.
- Manganese – 54 lbs.
- Cobalt – 29 lbs.

---

[208] The White House, Fact Sheet: The Biden-Harris Electric Vehicle Charging Action Plan, - The White House, DECEMBER 13, 2021, https://www.whitehouse.gov/briefing-room/statements-releases/2021/12/13/fact-sheet-the-biden-harris-electric-vehicle-charging-action-plan/, accessed October 17, 2022, 11:25 PM, CST.

[209] Hannah Ritchie and Max Roser, United States: CO₂ Country Profile, CO2-by-source.svg, https://ourworldindata.org/co2/country/united-states, accessed October 17, 2022, 10:55 PM CST.

- Lithium – 20 lbs.
- Rare Earth Elements – 1.1 lbs.[210]

The required minerals are mined in the following countries (countries are listed from the highest to lowest producers).
- Copper: Chile, Peru, China, Congo
- Graphite: China, Mozambique, Brazil, Madagascar
- Nickel: India, Philippines, Russia, New Caledonia
- Manganese: South Africa, Australia, Gabon, Ghana
- Cobalt: Congo, Russia, Australia, Philippines
- Lithium: Australia, Chile, China, Argentina
- Rare Earth Elements: China, United States (distant second place behind China), Myanmar, Australia[211]

The next governmental challenge regarding the mass production of electric vehicles is to obtain the minerals from around the world where supplies are limited, the mining is difficult, and certain governments are uncooperative.

> Geopolitically, many of the countries that have large endowments of these resources are not governed by a free-market economy nor are they allied with those nations that are. Russia, China, and Myanmar come to mind. The first two of those countries particularly may wish to keep these resources for their own supply.

> Even in more stable jurisdictions, some of these deposits are quite remote, and require tremendous logistics and up-front capital to produce. Furthermore, there are long lead times in many metal and mineral project developments, raising questions about the ability to ramp up supply.[212]

Therefore, the United States faces a significant challenge in producing electric vehicles across the country. Getting the infrastructure to the level that quickly charges electric vehicles in every urban and rural area of the United States is also a massive challenge.

---

[210] Michael DiMarco, Natural Resources Needed for Electric Cars: An Opportunity for Investors?, Last Updated March 25, 2022, Ask Money, https://www.askmoney.com/investing/natural-resources-needed-for-electric-cars-an-opportunity-for-investors?utm_content=params%3Ao%3D1465803%26ad%3DdirN%26qo%3DserpIndex&ueid=81d9a186-1cef-412e-90d6-b89230027182, accessed October 17, 2022, 10:15 PM CST.

[211] Ibid.

[212] Ibid.

PEW Research provides the following summary of the Biden Administration's approval rating regarding the issue of climate change.

> Large majorities of Americans remain broadly supportive of several policies to address climate change. Majorities of Americans say the federal government is doing too little to protect water and air quality, and address climate change. About seven-in-ten Americans say their local community has experienced extreme weather in the past year. Fifty-five% of U.S. adults oppose phasing out gasoline cars by 2035. Younger Republicans are more open to federal action and policy proposals to address climate change than older Republicans."[213]

The report also found a significant difference between Republicans and Democrats regarding their approval of President Biden's work on climate change. "Ratings of Biden's approach to climate change – and the federal government's role dealing with the issue – are deeply partisan. A majority of Republicans and independents who lean to the GOP (82%) say Biden's climate policies are taking the country in the wrong direction. Among Democrats and Democratic leaners, most say Biden is moving the country in the right direction on climate policy (79%)."[214] Therefore, there remains a significant division between conservatives and liberals regarding their perspectives and conclusions about climate change, and a plethora of other issues. The division should come as no surprise, based on the extreme political and ideological divide that currently exists in America. Climate change is simply one more divisive issue

The globalists must keep climate change and global warming as major agenda items on the world stage. The fear of the end of the world and imminent death is not a heartwarming scenario, but it gets the attention of the global population. The strongest drive of any human being, who is not suffering from depression, is survival. Therefore, the globalists must keep this issue, along with other emotionally charged subjects, such as pandemics, economics, and

---

[213] Brian Kennedy, Alec Tyson and Cary Funk, Americans Divided Over Direction of Biden's Climate Change Policies, July 14, 2022, https://www.pewresearch.org/science/2022/07/14/americans-divided-over-direction-of-bidens-climate-change-policies/, accessed October 17, 2022, 10:40 pm CST.
[214] Ibid.

public safety in the news to usher in the one-world system. The satanically led agenda is well underway to fulfill biblical prophecy exactly as stated.

ABSOLUTE PROPHETIC CLIMATE CHANGE

The Bible emphatically states that there will be massive global warming that takes place at the end of the yet future seven-year Tribulation period. God will pour out His wrath upon a world that embraces Satan, the Antichrist, and the false prophet. Revelation 6-16 describes in detail three main sets of judgments--the seal, trumpet, and bowl judgments.

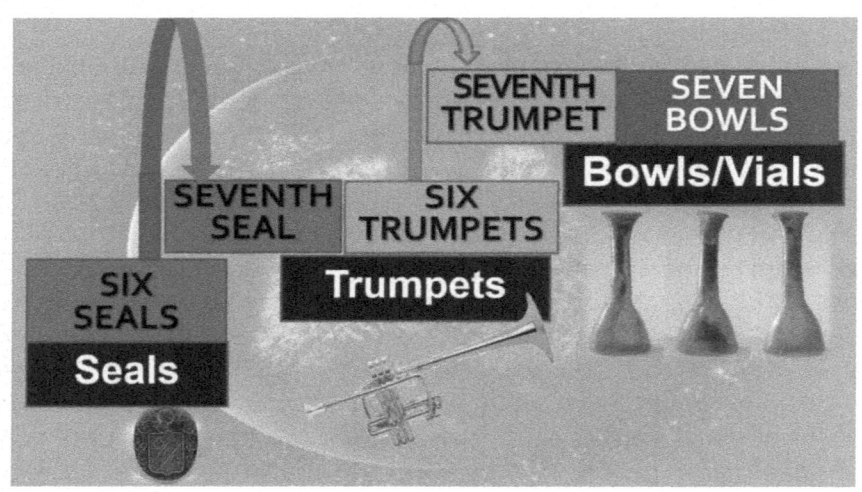

Figure 7.2

In addition, the apostle John states God will pour out His wrath on the earth with seven undisclosed *thunder* judgments (Rev. 10), which occur after the seven trumpet judgments. God designed the judgments to call all of those living during that future seven-year period to repent and prepare for the second coming of Jesus Christ to earth (Matt. 24-25; Rev. 4:2-19:10). Jesus Christ returns to the earth to end the seven catastrophic years of the Tribulation, and to inaugurate His theocratic millennial kingdom (Rev. 19:11-20:7).

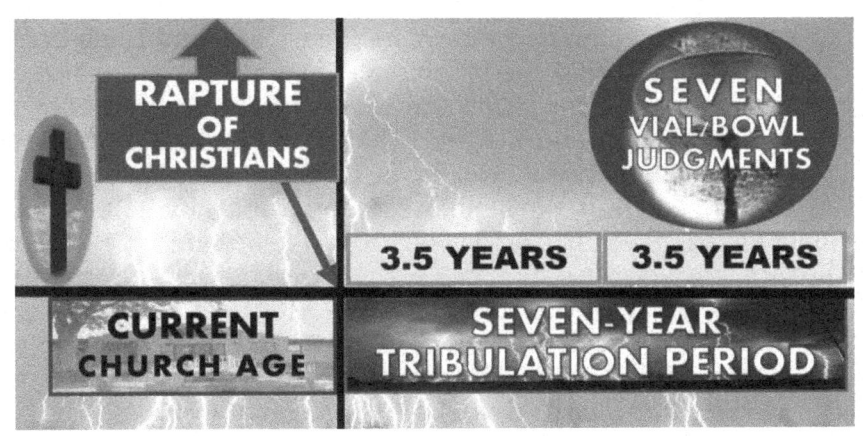

Figure 7.3

The seven bowl judgments occur very shortly before the second advent of Jesus Christ. The judgments are so incredibly powerful and catastrophic that if they were prolonged no one would survive (Matt. 24:22). The fourth bowl judgment is the first time God will literally cause a worldwide global warming. "Then the fourth angel poured out his bowl on the sun, and power was given to him to scorch men with fire. And men were scorched with great heat, and they blasphemed the name of God who has power over these plagues; and they did not repent and give Him glory" (Rev. 16:8–9). *Scorched* is the translation of the Greek word *kaumatizō*, which means to harm by heat, scorch, burn, to be scorched, or seared (Matt. 13:6; Mark 4:6; Rev. 16:9).[215] The Scripture does not reveal the exact temperature and impact of the extreme heat. However, what the text does describe is such an unbearable heat that people will scream out at God and blaspheme Him, instead of repenting of their evil ways and turning to the Lord for deliverance and salvation. God will bring the extreme heat to an end before He returns to the earth. The Lord will change the earth back to Edenic conditions during His kingdom on earth (Isa. 11:6-9; 51:3).

> 'Thus says the Lord GOD: "On the day that I cleanse you from all your iniquities, I will also enable you to dwell in the cities, and the ruins shall be rebuilt. The desolate land shall be tilled instead of lying desolate in the sight of all who pass by. So they will say, 'This land that was desolate has become like the

---

[215] James Swanson, *Dictionary of Biblical Languages with Semantic Domains: Greek.*

garden of Eden; and the wasted, desolate, and ruined cities are now fortified and inhabited.' Then the nations which are left all around you shall know that I, the LORD, have rebuilt the ruined places and planted what was desolate. I, the LORD, have spoken it, and I will do it." (Ezek. 36:33–36)

At the end of the millennial kingdom, which is 1,000 years of virtual heaven on earth, God will destroy the earth and the heavens by fire.

But the day of the Lord will come as a thief in the night, in which the heavens will pass away with a great noise, and the elements will melt with fervent heat; both the earth and the works that are in it will be burned up. Therefore, since all these things will be dissolved, what manner of persons ought you to be in holy conduct and godliness, looking for and hastening the coming of the day of God, because of which the heavens will be dissolved, being on fire, and the elements will melt with fervent heat? Nevertheless we, according to His promise, look for new heavens and a new earth in which righteousness dwells. (2 Pet. 3:10–13)

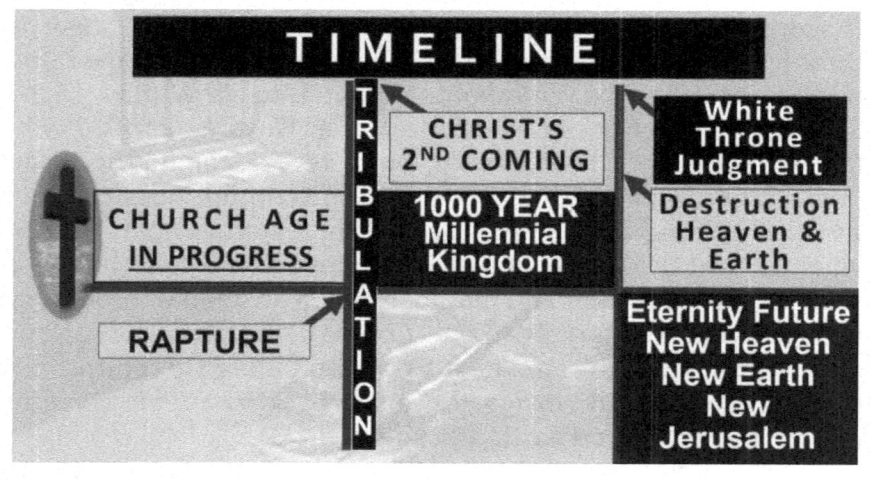

Figure 7.4

God will destroy the heavens and the earth based on Satan and sinful humankind corrupting that which God created perfect (Gen. 3:17-19). The Lord subsequently creates a new heaven, new earth, and New Jerusalem. God ushers in the eternal state, where all believers who embraced Him will live for eternity in His presence.

Now I saw a new heaven and a new earth, for the first heaven and the first earth had passed away. Also there was no more sea. Then I, John, saw the holy city, New Jerusalem, coming down out of heaven from God, prepared as a bride adorned for her husband. And I heard a loud voice from heaven saying, "Behold, the tabernacle of God is with men, and He will dwell with them, and they shall be His people. God Himself will be with them and be their God. And God will wipe away every tear from their eyes; there shall be no more death, nor sorrow, nor crying. There shall be no more pain, for the former things have passed away." (Rev. 21:1–4)

The globalist latches on to a false, satanically directed narrative, to accomplish their ultimate goal of a one-world government, economy, and religion, and the annihilation of Christianity. The Christian community must constantly keep in mind that when something contradicts the Scriptures and gains significant support from the secular world, there just might be a satanic deception that is setting the stage for Bible prophecy to be fulfilled. Climate change and global warming are simply more stage-setting issues in Satan's deceptive toolbox, to bring about his goal of worldwide domination, which he will obtain for a seven-year period.

SECTION FIVE: ONE-WORLD ECONOMY
CHAPTER EIGHT

The concept of a one-world economy can no longer be dismissed as a delusion of conspiracy theorists and doomsday preachers. Governments, economists, global organizations, bankers, investors, and many other entities are now actively researching the possibility of a one-world digital currency and banking system. The international rise of bitcoin[216] and other digital currencies, which many people have yet to fully understand, is rapidly gaining ground. As a result, the U.S. government is examining the potential for fraud, criminal activity, and foreign interference related to digital currencies, all of which could cause untold damage to businesses, individuals, and national interests.[217] These developments set the stage for the fulfillment of the apostle John's prophecy, made nearly two thousand years ago under the inspiration of the Holy Spirit, that a one-world economy would be a means by which the Antichrist would execute control over the people of the world.

Since the use of digital currencies is a newer concept, the following definitions should provide insight. Ivy Wigmore, who worked with TechTarget, defines digital currency as a "medium of exchange that is generated, stored and transferred electronically. Digital currencies are not typically associated with any country's government or represented in physical forms like the coins and notes of traditional currencies."[218] The current lack of government involvement makes digital currency very attractive on their finances, but also because the value digital currency is not determined by

---

[216] Ben Hernandez, Bitcoin's Use in International Transactions Should Continue Increasing, VettaFi, September 23, 2022, https://www.etftrends.com/crypto-channel/bitcoins-use-in-international-transactions-should-continue-increasing/, accessed October 24, 2022, 9:15 am cast.

[217] White House, White House Releases First-Ever Comprehensive Framework for Responsible Development of Digital Assets - The White House, September 16, 2022, https://www.whitehouse.gov/briefing-room/statements-releases/2022/09/16/fact-sheet-white-house-releases-first-ever-comprehensive-framework-for-responsible-development-of-digital-assets/, accessed October 24, 2022, 9:25 am, CST.

[218] Ivy Wigmore, Definition Digital Currency, TechTarget, WhatIs.com, 2022, https://www.techtarget.com/whatis/definition/digital-currency, accessed October 29, 2022, 9:10 am, CST.

government economies. One significant issue that is covered in this chapter regards the government's increasing interest in digital currency, and how to implement regulations.

Cryptocurrencies, the most common category of digital currency, are the type that comes to mind for most people when they hear the term. Cryptocurrencies rely on encryption to secure the processes involved in generating units and conducting transactions. They are used similarly to conventional money for purchases online and in person and are accepted by an increasing number of sellers... Virtual currencies, another subset of digital currencies, are mediums of monetary exchange that are confined to particular software-based environments. David Chaum, an American computer scientist and cryptologist, first introduced the idea of digital currencies in his 1983 research paper, "Blind signatures for untraceable payments."[219]

THE GREAT RESET

Then I saw another beast *[the false prophet, the third member of the false satanic trinity]* coming up out of the earth, and he had two horns like a lamb and spoke like a dragon. And he exercises all the authority of the first beast in his presence, and causes the earth and those who dwell in it to worship the first beast *[Antichrist]*, whose deadly wound was healed. He performs great signs, so that he even makes fire come down from heaven on the earth in the sight of men. And he deceives those who dwell on the earth—by those signs which he was granted to do in the sight of the beast, telling those who dwell on the earth to make an image to the beast who was wounded by the sword and lived. He wasgranted power to give breath to the image of the beast, that the image of the beast should both speak and cause as many as would not worship the image of the beast to be killed.

He *(false prophet)* causes all, both small and great, rich and poor, free and slave, to receive a mark on their right hand or on their foreheads, and that no one may buy or sell except one who has the mark or the name of the beast, or the number of his name. Here is wisdom. Let him who has understanding calculate the

---

[219] Ibid.

number of the beast, for it is the number of a man: His number is 666. (Rev. 13:11–18)

The World Economic Forum (WEF) is an organization which states it is dedicated to the advancement of global economics. The WEF comprises a consortium of elitists who want to have a dominant role in the formation of the global system, which could in theory result in the dissolution of the United States as a global power. In addition, the WEF, or the results of their supporters, could eventually have dominion over the global economic system. Their mission statement provides an excellent overview of their intent.

The World Economic Forum is the International Organization for Public-Private Cooperation.

The Forum engages the foremost political, business, cultural and other leaders of society to shape global, regional and industry agendas.

It was established in 1971 as a not-for-profit foundation and is headquartered in Geneva, Switzerland. It is independent, impartial and not tied to any special interests. The Forum strives in all its efforts to demonstrate entrepreneurship in the global public interest while upholding the highest standards of governance. Moral and intellectual integrity is at the heart of everything it does.

Our activities are shaped by a unique institutional culture founded on the stakeholder theory, which asserts that an organization is accountable to all parts of society. The institution carefully blends and balances the best of many kinds of organizations, from both the public and private sectors, international organizations and academic institutions.

We believe that progress happens by bringing together people from all walks of life who have the drive and the influence to make positive change.[220]

The WEF moved to the forefront of the globalist movement during the COVID-19 pandemic in 2020, when the organization unveiled the concept of the *Great Reset*. The *Great Reset* gained worldwide attention, and piqued the interest of governments and media regarding steps that world leaders should consider to recover

---

[220] Klaus Schwab, Now is the Time for a Great Reset, World Economic Forum, June 23, 2020, https://www.weforum.org/agenda/2020/06/now-is-the-time-for-a-great-reset/, accessed October 26, 2022, 8:15 am, CST.

and move forward from the effects of governments' response to the pandemic.

In September 2020, the WEF posted the following statements, among others, regarding the Great Reset.

> COVID-19 lockdowns may be gradually easing, but anxiety about the world's social and economic prospects is only intensifying. There is good reason to worry: a sharp economic downturn has already begun, and we could be facing the worst depression since the 1930s. But, while this outcome is likely, it is not unavoidable.
>
> To achieve a better outcome, the world must act jointly and swiftly to revamp all aspects of our societies and economies, from education to social contracts and working conditions. Every country, from the United States to China, must participate, and every industry, from oil and gas to tech, must be transformed. In short, we need a "Great Reset" of capitalism.[221]

Do not underestimate the influence of the WEF on global economics. The citizens of every country look to their government to provide a stable economy. However, the idea of a stable economy is an elusive dream in many places around the world, including America at the present time. As has been stated many a time, by many a politician and businessperson, never let a good crisis go to waste.

On January 24, 2020, the WEF made the following announcement in an attempt to provide guidance on the implementation of digital currencies.

- Today, the World Economic Forum announces the first global consortium focused on designing a framework for the governance of digital currencies, including stablecoins
- The Global Consortium for Digital Currency Governance will aim to increase access to the financial system through innovative policy solutions that are inclusive and interoperable

---

[221] Ibid.

- Opportunities for financial inclusion will be only unlocked if the space is regulated properly and includes public-private cooperation across developed and high-growth markets.[222]

The operative word in the announcement is *global*. Once again, the purpose of this book is not to proclaim the benefits or drawbacks of digital currencies. The purpose is to clearly reveal that digital currency is one more tool in the globalist's toolbox leading to the formation of the one-world economic system. God's prophetic Word mandates that a one-world economy must be operational by the mid-point of the seven-year Tribulation (Rev. 13:16-17). What we are observing is the stage being set for the fulfillment of God's Word.

Furthermore, the WEF realized that digital currency would become a major factor in the economies of the world, and they were ready to do the research, and make recommendations on how the process should look to get to the global currency outcome. Reading the entirety of the WEF material, it becomes apparent that they are interested in placing their focus on the governance of the global economy. Whether the WEF is the organization that will implement and have any control over the global economy remains a mystery. God's prophetic Word states that the Antichrist and the false prophet will ultimately enforce the global economic system, but the system could certainly be set in motion by the WEF or another organization that has global intentions

Reading the following statement from the World Economic Forum makes their goals and beginning methodology for implementing the global economic system known.

> Davos, Switzerland 24 January 2020 – Following extensive consultation with the global community, the World Economic Forum announced today the Global Consortium for Digital Currency Governance. Digital currencies are often cited as a tool for financial inclusion, but this opportunity can be realized only when paired with good governance.
>
> This is the first initiative to bring together leading companies, financial institutions, government representatives, technical experts, academics, international organizations, NGOs and

---

[222] Amanda Russo, Governing the Coin: World Economic Forum Announces Global Consortium for Digital Currency Governance, World Economic Forum, January 24, 2020, https://www.weforum.org/press/2020/01/governing-the-coin-world-economic-forum-announces-global-consortium-for-digital-currency-governance/, accessed October 24, 2022, 10:00 am, CST.

members of the Forum's communities on a global level. To tackle the challenge ahead, an international, multistakeholder approach with the public and private sectors working alongside civil society is needed.

This consortium will focus on solutions for a fragmented regulatory system. Efficiency, speed, inter-operability, inclusivity and transparency will be at the heart of this initiative. It will call for innovative regulatory approaches to achieve these goals and build trust. A set of guiding principles will be co-designed to support public and private actors exploring the opportunities that digital currencies present.

"Digital currency, a cross-cutting topic that requires input across sectors, functions, and geographies, is a key area of interest for the Forum," said Klaus Schwab, Founder and Executive Chairman of the World Economic Forum. "Building on our long history of public-private cooperation, we hope that hosting this consortium will catalyse the conversations necessary to inform a robust framework of governance for global digital currencies."[223]

America, and many other countries are open to moving to a cashless society through the complete implementation of a digital currency. Credit and debit cards are already accepted on a global scale, and the next step towards a global digital currency is feasible if governments around the world will embrace it willingly, or be forced to embrace it to stay competitive on the world stage. Domestic and international digital currencies are no longer science fiction, but a very present reality. The challenge is now for the government to move the populace towards acceptance and implementation of a completely digital system, and its governance.

Erwin Lutzer, who has written several books dealing with current events from a biblical perspective, provides the following excellent analysis of these developments.

> Because predicted events sometimes cast their shadow before they arrive, it might be instructive to ask: What do we see happening today that gives us insight into the future? Each generation has pondered this question, and we do so today with renewed interest because the shadows of events that will take place during the tribulation seem to be

---

[223] Ibid.

developing before our eyes. We don't have to agree about whether Christ is coming before or after the tribulation to realize the stage is being set for a one-world government, a one-world currency and worldwide manipulation with universal control, submission, and even worship. [224]

COVID-19 resulted in many people losing their jobs due to governmental restrictions on travel and the size of gatherings. Some businesses were forced to shut down because they were deemed non-essential or because so many employees became sick with COVID and were literally unable to work. Other employees, who refused to comply with vaccine mandates imposed by their employers, were laid off or terminated for non-compliance. In addition, for countries that were already experiencing severe economic downturns due to other fiscal challenges, the COVID-19 pandemic greatly exacerbated their problems.

The pandemic opened the door for the expansion of a clean, no-contact, digital, stable currency. Erwin Lutzer provided good insight on this issue. "Nothing could serve the globalist better than a worldwide economic meltdown that will give the World Bank the opportunity to assert the wealth of nations and begin to control the economy of the world. In accordance with socialist principles, your money would no longer belong to you, but would be portioned out by some 'world bank.'"[225] Dr. Lutzer rightly points out that the World Bank is the intended solution to some of the major economic issues in various countries.

Eventually, according to the prophetic Word, a one-world economy will be implemented. COVID-19 set the stage for governments around the world to control their populace. Government control, and the pressure from certain groups within society, forced the practices of social distancing, wearing masks, closing businesses and churches, and determining which businesses and employees were essential. Many businesses refused cash transactions to avoid the transmission of germs, and accepted only credit cards, which the customer usually placed in a card reader to avoid physical contact with the business associate.

The COVID-19 pandemic provided a major opportunity for the implementation of strong controls by government agencies. Wilfred

---

[224] Erwin Lutzer, *No Reason to Hide*, (Eugene, OR.: Harvest House Publishers, 2022), 234.

[225] Erwin Lutzer, *No Reason to Hide*, 243.

Hahn, a serious student of the Bible, who also worked for three decades on the front lines of the global economy, was a chief investment officer overseeing billions of dollars in capital, and served as the director of research for a major Wall Street firm, speaks from his eclectic background on global economic conditions from a Christian perspective.

> We now recognize that current economic and financial conditions have reached the point that man-made events can impact the sentiment of the entire world almost instantaneously. This is new. It would be one thing if the mood of mankind were to suddenly change in response to a new nuclear winter or something universally cataclysmic such as the blotting out of the sun. However, a massive global response to an economically related occurrence is of a different order in several ways. For one, it is generated by the non-physical actions of humanity itself. It is largely an emotional event, not a physically induced impulse. Secondly, it reveals a common set of affections... a universal reliance upon the prosperity of mankind's global commercial systems.[226]

The WEF saw the opportunity to step in and provide potential solutions on a global level, regarding the economic impact the response to the virus had on various countries. The WEF made it clear that they intended to pursue a global currency and banking system. COVID-19 provided the perfect economic storm for them to advance their agenda. In 2022, the WEF issued a statement regarding the world's uncertain economic situation.

> The May 2022 edition of the Chief Economists Outlook comes out amid extremely high uncertainty about geopolitical developments, the trajectory of the global economy and the next steps for economic policy. Instead of entering a post-COVID recovery phase, economies are experiencing additional shocks, first and foremost from the war in Ukraine and associated geopolitical repercussions, but

---

[226] Wilfred J. Hahn, *Global Financial Apocalypse Prophesied* (Crane, MO.: Defender, 2009), 231.

also from new outbreaks of COVID-19 and lockdowns in major industrial centres.[227]

The WEF advanced its efforts to see the implementation of digital currencies. The WEF completed phase one of its plan by creating the Digital Currency Governance Consortium (DCGC), which held a series of virtual workshops and roundtables to address key questions and governance gaps in digital currency. The subjects of discussion included global frameworks for digital currency governance that would benefit from multi-sector input and co-design. The DCGC is now actively engaged in phase two of its plan, which includes responsible entry of digital currencies into the global monetary system, as central banks continue to adopt cryptocurrencies and privately issued stablecoins. In addition, the DCGC will continue to examine the macroeconomic impacts of digital currencies and provide informed approaches for digital currency regulation. Of utmost importance, especially for those who are convinced that the government will never have the ability to infiltrate their digital currencies and control their use, the DCGC is interested in addressing regulatory learnings and best practices from around the world with respect to stablecoins and cryptocurrency.[228] In reality and function, nothing is beyond the reach of a totalitarian society, especially one that is controlled by Satan.

In 2022, the WEF cited two major issues impacting the economy on a massive scale: COVID-19 and the Russian invasion of Ukraine. Governments' responses to both events have had adverse economic impacts. The WEF issued its projections for the future of the global economy.

Six expectations for the future of the economy:
- Higher inflation alongside lower real wages globally
- Food insecurity in developing economies
- More localization, diversification and politicization of supply chain
- Greater rollback of globalization in goods, labour and technology than services

---

[227] Chief Economists Outlook: May 2022, https://www.weforum.org/reports/chief-economists-outlook-may-2022, World Economic Forum, May 23, 2022, accessed October 24, 2022, 10:27 am, CST.

[228] Digital Currency Governance Consortium, World Economic Forum, https://www.weforum.org/communities/digital-currency-governance-consortium, accessed October 25, 2022, 4:30 pm, CST.

- Sanctions effective in dampening the economic outlook for Russia
- Continued dominance of the US dollar as a global reserve currency[229]

From a global perspective, the WEF is making the case that something drastic must take place as governments around the world face catastrophic challenges.

- Where is food going to come from?
- Can a global stable currency be implemented?
- How will people facing extreme inflation pay their bills?
- How can products that only come from other countries be imported when transportation costs are increasing and workers are at an insufficient level?
- How can countries facing severe economic sanctions survive?
- Will the US dollar remain a significant part of the global reserve currency?

These questions, and so many more disturbing problems, are moving nations on a global level to find alternative solutions to devastating challenges.

The international import and export business provides ample opportunities for criminal activity. The globalist agenda includes mitigating and even silencing the conservative and Christian voices, which tend to follow a law-abiding objective. Oliver North expands on the current corruption that is bound to take place when people reject God, and the results of that rejection in financial dealings.

> The corruption from rejecting God but accepting sin reveals itself in a number of ways including corporate ethics scandals, fraudulent transactions, income-tax evasion, identity theft, influence peddling, money laundering, embezzlement extortion, nepotism, theft, robbery, burglary, bribery, scandals, and cheating to name just a few. When individuals or a nation reject God, they also reject His Word. In fact, anyone who rejects the Bible rejects God because He reveals Himself to us through His Word. This results in predictable but

---

[229] Chief Economists Outlook Centre for the New Economy and Society, World Economic Forum, May 2022, https://www3.weforum.org/docs/WEF_Chief_Economists_Outlook_May_2022.pdf, accessed October 24, 2022, 10:40 am, CST.

tragic consequences, one of which is widespread corruption.[230]

Why are the globalists promoting a global currency? Erwin Lutzer explains. "With a fully digitized currency, wealth could then be more "equitably" distributed, monitored, and weaponized against those who don't play by the rules. All our wealth would ultimately belong to the world bureaucracy that could adjust the economy to maintain "equity." Everyone could be given "their fair share," because technology will have displaced so many jobs, each person could be given a guaranteed basic income. Massively needed wealth would be created digitally."[231]

Erwin Lutzer commentated on the move towards globalism, "Call it the New World Order or the Green New Deal or the Great COVID-19 Reset, or the Fourth Industrial Revolution- we are talking about a world controlled from the top down with a single government, a unified banking system, and one global ruler.[232] The Scriptures provide the exact scenario that the one-world ruler, the Antichrist, will force on all nations, tribes, and people. The Antichrist will control the world's government, economy, and religion. The stage is absolutely being set for Bible prophecy to be fulfilled.

A video attributed to the World Economic Forum reveals eight predictions they anticipate coming to fruition by 2030.
1. You'll own nothing, and you'll be happy. Whatever you want you'll rent and it'll be delivered by drone.
2. The US won't be the world's leading superpower. A handful of countries will dominate.
3. You won't die waiting for an organ donor. We won't transplant organs, we'll "print" them instead. (This is the idea of a 3D printer.)
4. You'll eat much less meat. An occasional treat, not a staple; for the good of the environment and our health.
5. A billion people will be displaced by climate change. We'll have to do a better job of welcoming and integrating refugees.

---

[230] Oliver L. North, *Tragic Consequences* (Nashville, TN.: Fidelis Publishing, 2022), 111.
[231] Erwin Lutzer, *No Reason to Hide*, 244.
[232] Lutzer, No Reason to Hide, 235.

6. Polluters will have to pay to emit carbon dioxide. There will be a global price on carbon. This will help make fossil fuels history.
7. You could be preparing to go to Mars. Scientists will have worked out how to make you healthy in space. The start of a journey to find alien life?
8. Western values will have been tested to the breaking point. Checks and balances that underpin our democracies must not be forgotten.[233]

The predictions might in fact become reality, even though some predictions may seem improbable at the current time. The world, and specifically America, have seen substantial changes in the last few years in the way pandemics, economics, public safety, immigration, energy, "reproductive health" and abortion, the climate, and many more high-profile issues are handled. Now, more than ever, it is imperative that everyone take a very strong look at the Scripture's prophetic warnings regarding exactly what will take place on a global scale, and consider the absolute necessity of receiving Jesus Christ as one's personal Savior to avoid the great global deceptions, and to assure one's eternal destiny.

GOVERNMENT CONTROL IMPLEMENTED

Canada's Trucker Boycott

Legislators throughout history have made laws that provide penalties for those who commit criminal and civil violations. Most people, when they are driving a vehicle and see a police vehicle, they almost instinctively slow down to avoid the potential costly mistake of speeding. When someone violates a civil liberty, the jury or judge may grant the plaintiff a significant monetary award to mitigate the damages. Judges and juries have the authority to impose financial penalties and require restitution within the confines of the law against criminal violators. The ability, however, of a government leader to impose sanctions on individuals reached a new level recently when a large convoy of truckers in Canada initiated a

---

[233] 8 Predictions for the World in 2030, DailyMotion, https://www.dailymotion.com/video/x7y4pxt, accessed October 29, 2022, 11:55 am, CST. The DailyMotion website includes the video under the heading "2 years ago You'll own nothing and you'll be happy (Original Twitter video)."

protest. The truck drivers lined up their trucks and refused to move. Erwin Lutzer comments on the government's tactic.

> If we want to know how a government can use economic control to punish those who disagree with its policies, look no further than to what happened during the massive freedom convoy truckers' protest in Canada in February 2022. The Canadian Prime Minister suspended debate on his decision to exercise emergency powers, and banks were told to freeze the accounts of leaders of the convoy whose names were given to them by the *Royal Canadian Mounted Police* (RCMP). An online account of $10 million in donations raised for the truckers was frozen. After much criticism, the website with the funds announced they would refund the money to the donors. And when the names of those who contributed to the truckers' cause were exposed, some were vilified. He who controls the economy controls the world.[234]

The story highlights the ability of governments to implement economic sanctions on those who refuse to comply with their laws and mandates. The Canadian government's reaction to the protesters to force compliance, simply illustrates what will in fact take place on a global scale when the Antichrist imposes financial sanctions on those who refuse to submit to the one-world economic standards. The Antichrist's satanically empowered world economic system will require every person who desires to buy or sell to receive a mark on their forehead or right hand (Rev. 13:16-17). Those who refuse to follow the government's demands will have to figure out how to survive because they will face the penalty of death for non-compliance. "Jesus Himself addressed the intensity of the seven-year Tribulation when stating "unless those days had been shortened [referring to the seven-year allotment of time], no one would survive" (Matt. 24:22).

China's Social Credit Scores

China represents one of the most controlling governments on the planet when it comes to economic sanctions on its citizens. Communist China commands its people to follow and support their government, and anyone who opposes it will face sanctions. Erwin

---

[234] Erwin Lutzer, *No Reason to Hide*, 244.

Lutzer provides an excellent summary of the *social credit scores* that accompany the citizens of China.

> As you may know, China has been in the process of assigning every person in the country a social credit score. People are rewarded when they comply with government and community expectations and penalized when they don't. What lowers your score? Saying something unfavorable about the ruling authorities, or doing things considered socially detrimental. Even merely associating with someone who is viewed as a negative influence will adjust your score downward. What happens if you have a lower score? You can't borrow money, you can't rent from someone, you can't travel, you might not be allowed on trains, and you certainly are not allowed outside of the country. We can expect that as time goes on, Chinese students who want to study in US colleges and universities will be required to have a high social credit score.[235]

China provides the perfect example of what will take place during the Tribulation. The apostle John states the following regarding the future economic system that will come to fulfillment under the rule of the Antichrist. "He *(false prophet)* causes all, both small and great, rich and poor, free and slave, to receive a mark on their right hand or on their foreheads, and that no one may buy or sell except one who has the mark or the name of the beast *(Antichrist)*, or the number of his name" (Rev. 13:16–17). There should be no doubt in anyone's mind that what God stated in the Scriptures will come to pass exactly as stated. China has already set the stage logistically for the dictatorial global control the Antichrist will implement.

Lutzer makes another important point regarding how China controls the finances of their country. "China has developed a new form of capitalism that can thrive even while the population is manipulated and controlled. You do not need to have state ownership of all businesses and industries as long as you have state control of all transactions. If you can control the people, you don't have to confiscate their businesses and homes-at least not yet."[236] Dictators' self-absorbed agendas are designed to make them

---

[235] Erwin Lutzer, *No Reason to Hide*, 247.
[236] Erwin Lutzer, *No Reason to Hide*, 248.

personally powerful, feared, and obeyed. Satan, the ultimate prideful narcissist, who absolutely hates God, will do everything possible during the Tribulation to bring the world to its knees and to worship him or die (Rev. 13:4, 15).

THE FEDERAL GOVERNMENT'S APPROACH TO DIGITAL CURRENCY

The United States Federal Government responded to the subject of digital currencies in March 2022, when President Biden issued executive order 14067 regarding "Ensuring Responsible Development of Digital Assets." The President ordered that his administration research the status of digital currency, and report back to him with conclusions and potential recommendations. The White House identified what they considered the significant increase in digital currencies, and the potential for fraud, criminal activity, foreign interference, and other important issues.

> Digital assets, including cryptocurrencies, have seen explosive growth in recent years, surpassing a $3 trillion market cap last November and up from $14 billion just five years prior. Surveys suggest that around 16 percent of adult Americans – approximately 40 million people – have invested in, traded, or used cryptocurrencies. Over 100 countries are exploring or piloting Central Bank Digital Currencies (CBDCs), a digital form of a country's sovereign currency.
>
> The rise in digital assets creates an opportunity to reinforce American leadership in the global financial system and at the technological frontier, but also has substantial implications for consumer protection, financial stability, national security, and climate risk. The United States must maintain technological leadership in this rapidly growing space, supporting innovation while mitigating the risks for consumers, businesses, the broader financial system, and the climate. And, it must play a leading role in international engagement and global governance of digital assets consistent with democratic values and U.S. global competitiveness.[237]

---

[237] Legal Alert | US DOJ Responds to Biden Executive Order on Digital Assets | Husch Blackwell, July 1, 2022,

The United States Attorney General responded with a 58-page report titled, *The Report of the Attorney General Pursuant to Section 8(b)(iv) of Executive Order 14067: How To Strengthen International Law Enforcement Cooperation For Detecting, Investigating, And Prosecuting Criminal Activity Related To Digital Assets*. The law offices of Hush Blackwell, a national prestigious firm, provided a summary of the Attorney General's report which included the following.

> The President's Executive Order and the Attorney General's report make clear that not only is the United States pursuing a whole-of-government approach to regulating and policing the cryptocurrency space, but also that it intends to exert its substantial international influence to build the capacity of and promote cooperation between other nations to address perceived threats. Companies operating in the digital currency milieu, including those who rely on or utilize cryptocurrency for any part of their business, should expect a steady increase in inquiries from both U.S. and foreign law enforcement authorities.[238]

On September 16, 2022, the White House issued a fact sheet titled, *Technical Possibilities for a U.S. Central Bank Digital Currency*.

> A United States central bank digital currency (CBDC) would be a digital form of the U.S. dollar. While the U.S. has not yet decided whether it will pursue a CBDC, the U.S. has been closely examining the implications of, and options for, issuing a CBDC. If the U.S. pursued a CBDC, there could be many possible benefits, such as facilitating efficient and low-cost transactions, fostering greater access to the financial system, boosting economic growth, and supporting the continued centrality of the U.S. within the international financial system. However, a U.S. CBDC could also introduce a variety of risks, as it might affect everything ranging from the stability of the financial system to the protection of sensitive data.
> Notably, these benefits and risks might vary significantly based on how the CBDC system is designed and deployed. That is why Executive Order 14067, Ensuring Responsible Development of Digital Assets, placed the highest urgency on

---

https://www.huschblackwell.com/newsandinsights/us-doj-responds-to-biden-executive-order-on-digital-assets, accessed October 25, 2022, 5:34 pm, CST.
[238] Ibid.

research and development efforts into the potential design and deployment options of a U.S. CBDC. The Executive Order directed the Office of Science and Technology Policy (OSTP), in consultation with other Federal departments and agencies, to submit to the President a technical evaluation for a potential U.S. CBDC system.[239]

The White House, Office of Science and Technology Policy, issued a report titled *Technical Evaluation for a U.S. Central Bank Digital Currency System*, in September 2022.

A Central Bank Digital Currency (CBDC) is a digital form of a country's sovereign currency.[240] If the United States issued a CBDC, this new type of central bank money may provide a range of benefits for American consumers, investors, and businesses. For example, a U.S. CBDC might enable transactions that are more efficient and less expensive, particularly for cross-border funds transfers. However, there are also potential risks to consider. A U.S. CBDC might affect everything ranging from the stability of the financial system to the protection of sensitive data. Recognizing these potential upsides and downsides, the Biden-Harris Administration is committed to further exploring the implications of, and options for, issuing a CBDC.[241]

The information regarding the movement towards digital currencies in the U.S., provides a very exciting scenario for the Christian, and one that should get the attention of those wondering if the Bible is truly God's Word. Christians should be thrilled that the prophecies regarding the one-world economy are starting to come together. This points to the fact that the next major event on God's

---

[239] Alondra Nelson, Alexander Macgillivray, and Nik Marda , Technical Possibilities for a U.S. Central Bank Digital Currency, The White House, September 16, 2022, https://www.whitehouse.gov/ostp/news-updates/2022/09/16/technical-possibilities-for-a-u-s-central-bank-digital-currency/, accessed October 25, 2022, 8:21 pm, CST.

[240] Other U.S. Government reports explain CBDCs in greater depth. See, e.g., The Future of Money and Payments. (Sep. 2022). Department of the Treasury; and Money and Payments: The US Dollar in the Age of Digital Transformation. (Jan. 2022). The Federal Reserve.

[241] The White House, Technical Evaluation For A U.S. Central Bank Digital Currency System, Office of Science and Technology Policy, September 2022, https://www.whitehouse.gov/wp-content/uploads/2022/09/09-2022-Technical-Evaluation-US-CBDC-System.pdf, accessed October 25, 2022, 8:35 pm, CST.

prophetic calendar, the snatching or catching away of the body of Christ, referred to by many Christians as the Rapture, is drawing closer every second (1 Thess. 4:13-18; 1 Cor. 15:50-54). Those searching to determine if the Bible is truly God's Word are encouraged to consider the facts presented, not just regarding the formation of the one-world economy, but the many other subjects addressed in this book and supported by Scripture. The Bible truly is the awesome, authoritative, inspired Word of God. 1,000 prophecies in the Bible have come to fulfillment exactly as written. Based on God's perfect record of fulfilling prophecy, the remaining 500 prophecies will also come to fulfillment exactly as stated.

CONCLUSION

The world continues moving in the direction the apostle Paul stated it would during the last days of the Church Age. "But know this, that in the last days perilous times will come" (2 Tim. 3:1). Lawlessness, pandemics, hatred, economic perils, gender dysphoria, promiscuity, pornography, climate hysteria, and racial division top the list of the current trends in America and internationally. Cancelling the culture of conservative Bible-believing Christians, apostasy in the church, terrorism, antisemitism, energy crisis, wars, socialism, Marxism, communism, suicide, substance abuse, vigilantism, and many other issues are loudly proclaiming that domestically and internationally the world has moved away from their Creator, and has embraced the deception promoted by the one who will one day control the ultimate dictator on earth, the Antichrist. Jeff Kinley adds, "Our money still declares 'In God We Trust,' but our actions argue to the contrary. A corrupted government and a morally bankrupt population have joined together in removing much of God."[242]

Isaiah documented Satan's desires. "For you [Satan] have said in your heart: 'I will ascend into heaven, I will exalt my throne above the stars of God; I will also sit on the mount of the congregation On the farthest sides of the north; I will ascend above the heights of the clouds, I will be like the Most High'" (Isa. 14:13–14). Satan knows that he is doomed to an eternity in the lake of fire unless he can somehow stop the Lord Jesus Christ from fulfilling His prophetic plan; however, the Bible states, "The devil, who deceived them, was cast into the

---

[242] Kinley, The End of America, 29.

lake of fire and brimstone where the beast *(Antichrist)* and the false prophet are. And they will be tormented day and night forever and ever."(Rev. 20:10)

Dr. Jimmy DeYoung, a wonderful mentor and friend, who is now in heaven, often made the following statement. "The stage is set, all the actors are in place, and the curtain is about to be raised, and we need to keep looking up, until." The first time I heard those words I wondered what Dr. DeYoung meant when he ended the sentence with *until*. The grammar and sentence structure did not make any sense to me. However, when I became his friend, and understood his passion for the yet future event of the rapture of the Church Age saints, I then comprehended his passion for the fact that we must keep pressing on for the sake of the Gospel *until* Jesus Christ comes in the clouds to take His children home to heaven.

> But I do not want you to be ignorant, brethren, concerning those who have fallen asleep *(died)*, lest you sorrow as others who have no hope. For if we believe that Jesus died and rose again, even so God will bring with Him those who sleep *(have died)* in Jesus. For this we say to you by the word of the Lord, that we who are alive and remain until the coming of the Lord will by no means precede those who are asleep *(believers in Jesus who have died)*. For the Lord Himself will descend from heaven with a shout, with the voice of an archangel, and with the trumpet of God. And the dead in Christ will rise first. Then we who are alive and remain shall be caught up *(Latin word rapturo-rapture)* together with them in the clouds to meet the Lord in the air. And thus we shall always be with the Lord. Therefore comfort one another with these words. (1 Thess. 4:13–18)

The fulfillment of God's prophetic Word documents repeatedly the accuracy of the infallible Word of God, the Bible. Several of the most important passages in Scripture regard the coming of the Lord Jesus Christ to earth some 2,000 years ago to pay the complete debt of sin for all who will place their faith in what He alone accomplished through His death, burial, and resurrection (Isa. 53; 1 Cor. 15:1-4). What a tragedy it would be to understand God's prophetic calendar, and yet fail to receive the free gift of eternal life. God's gift enables one to avoid the horrific events that will in fact take place during the seven-year Tribulation, and the eternal lake of fire that awaits those who fail to receive by faith God's gift of eternal life (Rev. 21:8).

The Scripture states that all people have sinned (Rom. 3:23) and that because of sin, not one person deserves to go to heaven (Rom. 6:23). But the wonderful news is that Jesus, God's very Son, left heaven's glory, was born of a virgin (Isa. 7:14), and lived a sinless perfect life (Heb. 4:15). Jesus Christ willingly went to the cross, where He suffered and paid the sin debt for all who would place their faith in His death, burial, and resurrection (John 3:16; 1 Cor. 15:3-4). God's gift is waiting for you. Carefully read the following:

> For by grace *(God's free unmerited gift)* you have been saved *(saved from your sins and their penalty, which is the eternal lake of fire)* through faith, and that not of yourselves; it is the gift of God, not of works, lest anyone should boast. (Ephesians 2:8–9)

If you have never by faith alone received the gift of eternal life, would you take that gift at this very moment? Receiving a gift means you simply reach out and take what is offered. The Lord Jesus has the gift and is holding it out in front of you to take by faith alone. If you are willing to take God's gift of eternal life by faith, you may want to thank Him. The following simple prayer is a good way to thank the Lord for what you just received by faith alone.

> Dear Lord, I realize that I am a sinner and that I do not deserve to go to heaven. I believe that Jesus Christ came down from heaven, took on the form of a human being, went to the cross to pay for my sins, was buried, and rose from the dead three days later. I am receiving the gift of eternal life by faith, realizing there is nothing I can do to earn my way to heaven. Thank you for saving me from my sins and promising to take me to heaven when I die.

APPENDIX A Genesis 5 and 11 Genealogies

HEBREW

Gen. 5	Antediluvian Patriarchs	1 Birth A.M.	2 First- Born	3 Rest	4 Total	5 Death A.M.
1	Adam	0	130	800	930	930
2	Seth	130	105	807	912	1042
3	Enosh	235	90	815	905	1140
4	Kenan	325	70	840	910	1235
5	Mahalaleel	395	65	830	895	1290
6	Jared	460	162	800	962	1422
7	Enoch	622	65	300	365	---
8	Methuselah	687	187	782	969	1656
9	Lamech	874	182	595	777	1651
10	Noah	1056	600	---	950	2006
	Date of Flood		1656			
Gen. 11	Postdiluvian Patriarchs		2			
1	Shem	1556		500	600	2156
2	Arpachshad	1658	35	403	438	2096
	Kenan (LXX)	---	---	---	---	---
3	Shelah	1693	30	403	433	2126
4	Eber	1723	34	430	464	2187
5	Peleg	1757	30	209	239	1996
6	Reu	1787	32	207	239	2026
7	Serug	1819	30	200	230	2049
8	Nahor	1849	29	119	148	1997
9	Terah	1878	70	135	205	2083
	Flood to Abra(ha)m	1948	292			
	Creation to Flood		1656			
	Total to Abra(ha)m		1948			

Gerhard F. Hasel, Genesis 5 and 11: Chronogenealogies In The Biblical History Of Beginnings, January 1, 1980, https://www.grisda.org/origins-07023, accessed October 31, 2022.

BIBLE TIMELINE

Chronological Index of the Years and Times from Adam unto Christ
From Adam unto Noah's flood are years 1656.
From the said flood of Noah, unto <u>Abraham</u>'s departing from Chaldea, were 422 years
From Abraham's departing from Ur in Chaldea unto the departing of the children of Israel, are 430 years, cited as follows:
Abraham was in Charran five years, and departed in the 75th year:
Begat Isaac when 100 years old, in the 25th year of his departing.
Isaac begat Jacob, when 60 years old.
Israel was in Egypt 220 years.
Then deduct 80 years from this: for so old was Moses when he

conducted the Israelites from Egy
So the rest of the years, that is to say, 130, are divided between Amram and Kohath.
The Kohath begat Amram at the age of 67 years.
Amram, being 65 years, begat Moses, who in the 80th year of his age, departed with the Israelites from Egypt.

So this chronology is the 430 years mentioned in the 12th chap. of Exodus and the 3d chap. to the Galatians.

From the going of the Israelites from Egypt, unto the first building of the temple, are 480 years, after this chronology and account.

Moses remained in the desert or wilderness 40 years.
Joshua and Othniel ruled 40 years; Ehud, 80 years; Deborah, 40 years.
Gideon, 40 years; Abimelech, 3 years; Tola, 23 years; Jair, 22 years;
Then they were without a captain, until the 18th year of Jephthah;
Jephthah, 6 years; Ibzan, 7 years; Elon, 10 years; Abdon, 8 years;
Sampson, 20 years; Heli, judge and priest, 4 years; Samuel and Saul reigned 40 years; David was king 40 years.
Solomon, in the 4th year of his reign, began the building of the temple.

These are the 480 years mentioned in the first book of Kings, chap.vi.

From the first building of the temple, unto the captivity of Babylon, are 419 years and an half.

Solomon reigned yet 36 years; Rehoboam, 17 years; Abija, 3 years.Asa, 41 years; Jehoshaphat, 25 years; Jehoram, 8 years; Ahaziah, 1 year; Athaliah, the queen, 7 years; Joash, 40 years; Amaziah, 29 years; Uzziah, 52 years.
Jehoahaz, 16 years; Ahaz, 16 years; Hezekiah, 29 years; Manasses, 55 years; Amon, 2 years; Josiah, 31 years; Jeoaz, 3 months; Eliakim, 11 years.
Jehoiachin, Jechonias, 3 months; And here begins the captivity of Babylon.

The sum of these years are 419.

Jerusalem was re-edified and built again after the captivity of Babylon, 70 years.

The captivity continued 70 years. The children of Israel were delivered the first year of Cyrus. The temple was begun to be built in the second year of the said Cyrus, and finished in the 46th year, which was the 6th year of Darius. After that Darius had reigned 20

years, Nehemiah was restored to liberty, and went to build the city, which was finished in the 32nd year of the said Darius. All the years from the building of the temple again, are 26 years.
The whole sum of years amount to 70
From the re-edifying of the city, unto the coming of Christ, are 483 years, after this chronology.
It is mentioned in the 9th chap. of Daniel that Jerusalem should be built up again, and that from that time, unto the coming of Christ, are 69 weeks, and every week is reckoned for 7 years. So 69 weeks amount to 483 years; for, from the said year of Darius, unto the 42nd year of Augustus, in which year our Saviour Christ was born, are just and complete so many years, whereupon we reckon, that from Adam unto Christ, are 3974 years, six months, and ten days; and from the birth of Christ, unto this present year, is 1801.
Then the whole sum and number of years from the beginning of the world unto the present year of our Lord God *AD* 1801[243]

---

[243] Chronological Index of the Years and Times from Adam unto Christ, Houston Baptist University, https://hbu.edu/museums/dunham-bible-museum/tour-of-the-museum/bible-in-america/bibles-for-a-young-republic/chronological-index-of-the-years-and-times-from-adam-unto-christ/

Table 1. A comparison of the main text-critical, numerical divergences in Genesis 5 and 11 in the Masoretic Text (MT), the Septuagint (LXX), and the Samaritan Pentateuch (SP). Copyright ABR 2017.

Person	References	MT Age at son	MT Remainder	MT Age at death	LXX Age at son	LXX Remainder	LXX Age at death	SP Age at son	SP Remainder	SP Age at death
Adam	Gen 5:3-5	130	800	930	230	700	930	130	800	930
Seth	Gen 5:6-8	105	807	912	205	707	912	105	807	912
Enosh	Gen 5:9-11	90	815	905	190	715	905	90	815	905
Kenan	Gen 5:12-14	70	840	910	170	740	910	70	840	910
Mahalalel	Gen 5:15-17	65	830	895	165	730	895	65	830	895
Jared	Gen 5:18-20	162	800	962	162	800	962	62[1]	785[1]	847[1]
Enoch	Gen 5:21-23	65	300	365	165	200	365	65	300	365
Methuselah	Gen 5:25-27	187	782	969	187	782	969	67[1]	653[1]	720[1]
Lamech	Gen 5:28-31	182	595	777	188	565	753	53[1]	600[1]	653[1]
Noah	Gen 5:32; 7:11; 8:13-14; 9:28-29; 10:21; 11:10	500/(502)	After the Flood 350	950	500/(502)	After the Flood 350	950	500/(502)	After the Flood 350	950
Shem	Gen 11:10-11	100	500		100	500		100	500	600[2]
Arpachshad	Gen 11:12-13	35	403		135	430/330[3]		135	303	438
Cainan	Gen 11:13b-14b				130	330				
Shelah	Gen 11:14-15	30	403		130	330/403[4]		130	303	433
Eber	Gen 11:16-17	34	430[5]		134	370/270[5]		134	270	404
Peleg	Gen 11:18-19	30	209		130	209		130	109	239
Reu	Gen 11:20-21	32	207		132	207		132	107	239
Serug	Gen 11:22-23	30	200		130	200		130	100	230
Nahor	Gen 11:24-25	29	119[6]		79	129[6]		79	69	148
Terah	Gen 11:26,32; Acts 7:2-4	70/(130)	(75)	205	70/(130)	(75)	205	70	(75)	145[7]
Abraham	Gen 11:26,32; 12:1-4; 21:5; 25:7	100	(75)	175	100	(75)	175	100	(75)[8]	175

---

[1] The numbers in the SP of Genesis 5 for Jared, Methuselah and Lamech were deliberately reduced, matching the chronology of the *Book of Jubilees*. All three die in the year of the Flood. There is no way to explain these figures in the SP except that they were altered to mimic *Jubilees*' unique chronological reductions. Jerome stated that he had manuscripts of the SP that matched the LXX/MT figures for Jared and Methuselah and the MT's figures for Lamech.
[2] The lifespan figures from Shem to Nahor in Gen 11 SP are secondary harmonizations designed to mimic Gen 5, and are not original, inspired texts. They should not be used as a basis for textual reconstruction.
[3] Arpachshad's remaining years were most likely 430. If so, 403 in the MT and 330 in some LXX manuscripts are basic scribal errors.
[4] Shelah's remaining years could be 403 or 330. Text critical arguments have been made for both readings. This will be explored further in *FATA*.
[5] Eber's 430 in the MT is incorrect. Some LXX manuscripts retain the correct figure of 370.
[6] Nahor's remaining year figure of 119 in the MT may be a minor scribal error from 129. The LXX reading of 129 could also be a minor error from 119. Both are plausible.
[7] Terah's lifespan has been deliberately reduced to 145 in the SP to "correct" the chronological matrix for the year of Abraham's birth. LXX/MT retain the correct figure of 205.
[8] All numbers in brackets are based on calculations from other figures, and are not explicitly stated in the biblical text.

244

---

[244] https://biblearchaeology.org/research/biblical-chronologies/2530-from-adam-to-abraham-an-update-on-the-genesis-5-and-11-research-project.

APPENDIX B Worst Pandemics Since the 1st Century

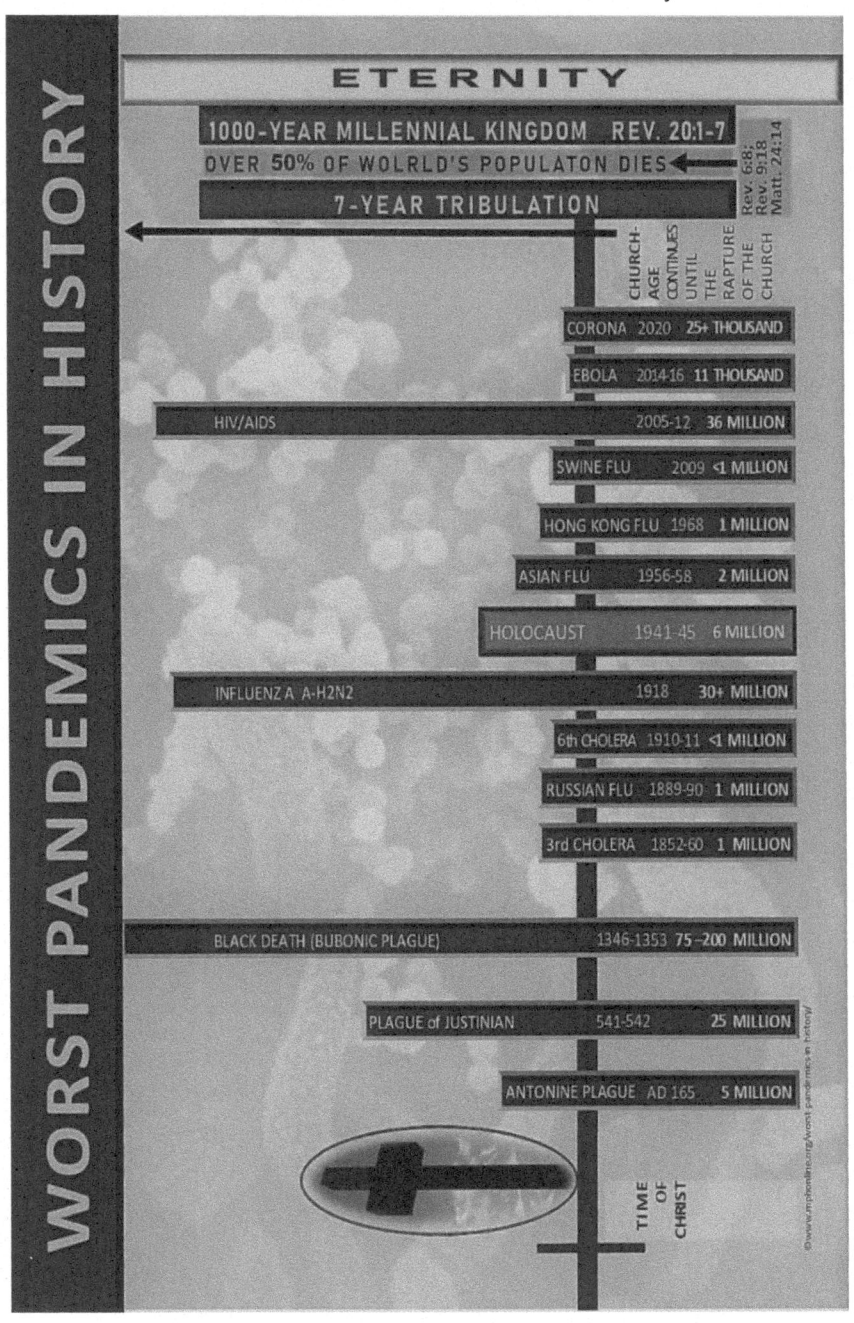

WORST PANDEMICS IN HISTORY

ETERNITY

1000-YEAR MILLENNIAL KINGDOM REV. 20:1-7

OVER 50% OF WOLRLD'S POPULATON DIES ← Rev. 6:8; Rev. 9:18; Matt. 24:14

7-YEAR TRIBULATION

CHURCH-AGE CONTINUES UNTIL THE RAPTURE OF THE CHURCH

Pandemic	Years	Deaths
CORONA	2020	25+ THOUSAND
EBOLA	2014-16	11 THOUSAND
HIV/AIDS	2005-12	36 MILLION
SWINE FLU	2009	<1 MILLION
HONG KONG FLU	1968	1 MILLION
ASIAN FLU	1956-58	2 MILLION
HOLOCAUST	1941-45	6 MILLION
INFLUENZA A-H2N2	1918	30+ MILLION
6th CHOLERA	1910-11	<1 MILLION
RUSSIAN FLU	1889-90	1 MILLION
3rd CHOLERA	1852-60	1 MILLION
BLACK DEATH (BUBONIC PLAGUE)	1346-1353	75-200 MILLION
PLAGUE of JUSTINIAN	541-542	25 MILLION
ANTONINE PLAGUE	AD 165	5 MILLION

TIME OF CHRIST

BIBLIOGRAPHY

Adams, Jay E. *I Timothy, II Timothy, and Titus*, The Christian Counselor's Commentary. Cordova, TN: Institute for Nouthetic Studies, 2020.

Arndt, William. et al., *A Greek-English Lexicon of the New Testament and Other Early Christian Literature*. Chicago: University of Chicago Press, 2000.

Aubuchon, Vaughn. World Population Growth History, Vaughn's Summaries, History Summaries Human Population https://www.vaughns-1-pagers.com/history/world-population-growth.htm, accessed April 17, 2020.

Aune, David E. "Revelation 6-16" in Word Biblical Commentary, general ed. Bruce M. Metzger, OT ed. John D. W. Watts, James W/ Watts, (Nashville, TN.: Thomas Nelson Publishers, 1998), 736.

Barna, George. Release #5: Shocking Results Concerning the Worldview of Christian Pastors, May 10, 2022, https://www.arizonachristian.edu/wp-content/uploads/2022/05/AWVI2022_Release05_Digital.pdf, accessed September 7, 2022, 7:26 PM CST.

Blaising, Craig A. "Malachi," in *The Bible Knowledge Commentary: An Exposition of the Scriptures*, ed. J. F. Walvoord and R. B. Zuck, vol. 1. Wheaton, IL: Victor Books, 1985.

Balz, Horst Robert and Gerhard Schneider. *Exegetical Dictionary of the New Testament*. Grand Rapids, Mich.: Eerdmans, 1990.

Barton, Bruce B., David Veerman, and Neil S. Wilson. *1 Timothy, 2 Timothy, Titus*, Life Application Bible Commentary. Wheaton, IL: Tyndale House Publishers, 1993.

Boring, Ed and John T. Carroll. *The New Testament Library*. Louisville, KY: Westminster John Knox Press, 2012.

Boserup, Brad, Mark McKenney, Adel Elkbuli, Alarming Trends in US Domestic Violence During The COVID-19 Pandemic, The American Journal of Emergency Medicine, Volume 38, Issue 12, December 2020, Pages 2753-2755, https://www.sciencedirect.com/science/article/pii/S07356757 20303077, accessed October 31, 2022, 9:20 am, CST.

Collins, Raymond F. *1 & 2 Timothy and Titus: A Commentary*, ed. C. Clifton Black, M. Eugene Boring, and John T. Carroll, The New Testament Library. Louisville, KY: Westminster John Knox Press, 2012.

Dallas, Joe. *The Gay Gospel? How Pro-Gay Advocates Misread the Bible*. Eugene, OR.: Harvest House Publishers, 2007.

Dellaperute, Michael S. *The Danger of Puberty Suppression*. Eugene, OR.: Resource Publications, 2019.

DiMarco, Michael. Natural Resources Needed for Electric Cars: An Opportunity for Investors?, Last Updated March 25, 2022, Ask Money, https://www.askmoney.com/investing/natural-resources-needed-for-electric-cars-an-opportunity-for-investors?utm_content=params%3Ao%3D1465803%26ad%3DdirN%26qo%3DserpIndex&ueid=81d9a186-1cef-412e-90d6-b89230027182, accessed October 17, 2022, 10:15 PM CST.

Guthrie, Donald. *Pastoral Epistles: An Introduction and Commentary*, vol. 14, Tyndale New Testament Commentaries. Downers Grove, IL: InterVarsity Press, 1990.

Hahn, Wilfred J. *Global Financial Apocalypse Prophesied*. Crane, MO.: Defender, 2009.

Hernandez, Ben. Bitcoin's Use in International Transactions Should Continue Increasing, VettaFi, September 23, 2022, https://www.etftrends.com/crypto-channel/bitcoins-use-in-international-transactions-should-continue-increasing/, accessed October 24, 2022, 9:15 am cast.

Hitchcock, Mark & Jeff Kinley, *The Coming Apostasy*. Carol Stream, IL.: Tyndale House Publishers, Inc., 2017.

Hindson, Mark and Thomas Ice. *Charting the Bible Chronologically*. Eugene, OR.: Harvest House Publishing, 2016.

Hitchcock, Mark. *Corona Crisis*. Nashville, TN.: W Publishing Group, 2020.

Horowitz, David. *Dark Agenda, The War to Destroy Christian America* (West Palm Beach, FL.: Humanix Books, 2018

Jackson, Mary. Study: Effects of Puberty-Blockers Can Last A Lifetime, December 18, 2020, WORLD, Study: Effects of puberty-blockers can last a lifetime | WORLD (wng.org), accessed October 27, 2022, 9:50 pm, CST.

Jeremiah, David. *Where Do We Go From Here?* Nashville, TN.: W. Publishing Group, 2021.

Johnson, Alan F. *Revelation*, in vol. 12. of *The Expositors Bible Commentary*, ed. Frank E. Gaebelein. Grand Rapids: Zondervan, 1981.

Jones, Floyd Nolan. *The Chronology of the Old Testament*. Green Forest, AR.: Master Books, 2004.

Jones, Jeffrey M. LGBT Identification in U.S. Ticks Up to 7.1%, February 17, 2022, https://news.gallup.com/poll/389792/lgbt-identification-ticks-up.aspx, accessed October 12, 2022, 2:50 PM CST.

Kennedy, Brian. Alec Tyson and Cary Funk, Americans Divided Over Direction of Biden's Climate Change Policies, July 14, 2022, https://www.pewresearch.org/science/2022/07/14/americans-divided-over-direction-of-bidens-climate-change-policies/, accessed October 17, 2022, 10:40 pm CST.

Kinley, Jeff. *As it was in the Days of Noah* (Eugene, OR.: Harvest House Publishers, 2014

_____. *After Shocks*. Eugene, OR.: Harvest House Publishers, 2021.

Kluckow, Rich. DSW, and Zhen Zeng, Ph.D., BJS Statisticians, March 2022, Correctional Populations in the United States, 2020 – Statistical Tables, NCJ Number 303184, https://bjs.ojp.gov/library/publications/correctional-populations-united-states-2020-statistical-tables, accessed October 3, 2022, 10:28 PM, CST.

Kuper, Laura. Puberty Blocking Medications: Clinical Research Review, IMPACT LGBT Health and Development Program, https://www.scribd.com/document/459868447/Kuper-2014-Puberty-Blockers-Clinical-Research-Review-pdf, accessed October 10, 2022.

Lane, Lee. Toward a Conservative Policy on Climate Change, Clashing worldviews, green politics, and a path forward, *The New Atlantis*, Number 41, Winter 2014, pp. 19-37, https://www.thenewatlantis.com/publications/toward-a-conservative-policy-on-climate-change, accessed October 17, 2022, 4:30 PM CST.

Lea, Thomas D. and Hayne P. Griffin. *1, 2 Timothy, Titus*, vol. 34, The New American Commentary. Nashville: Broadman & Holman Publishers, 1992.

Ledner, Hobart. DVM, Why Will The District Attorney Not Bring Charges, September 2021, Attorney-FAQ.com, https://attorney-faq.com/why-will-the-district-attorney-not-bring-charges, accessed October 3, 2022, 9:45 PM CST.

LePan, Nicholas. "Visualizing the History of Pandemics," Visual Capitalist, March 14, 2020, https://www.visualcapitalist.com/history-of-pandemics-deadliest/, accessed April 29, 2020.

Levy, David M. *Revelation, Hearing the Last Word*. Bellmawr, NJ.: The Friends of Israel Gospel Ministry, 1999.

Lock, Walter. *A Critical and Exegetical Commentary on the Pastoral Epistles (I & II Timothy and Titus)*, International Critical Commentary. Edinburgh: T&T Clark, 1924.

Longenecker, Richard N. *The Epistle to the Romans: A Commentary on the Greek Text*, ed. I.

Lutzer, Erwin. *No Reason to Hide*. Eugene, OR.: Harvest House Publishers, 2022.

_____. *We Will Not Be Silenced*. Eugene, OR.: Harvest House Publishers, 2020.

MacArthur Jr., John F. *1 & 2 Thessalonians*. MacArthur New Testament Commentary, Chicago: Moody Press, 2002.

_____. *Romans, vol. 2, MacArthur New Testament Commentary*. Chicago: Moody Press, 1991.

_____. *2 Timothy*, MacArthur New Testament Commentary. Chicago: Moody Press, 1995.

Marshall, Howard and Donald A. Hagner, New International Greek Testament Commentary. Grand Rapids, MI: William B. Eerdmans Publishing Company, 2016.

Mercola, Joseph and Ronnie Cummins, *The Truth About COVID-19*. White River Junction, VT.: Chelsea Green Publishing, 2021.

Miller, Steve. *Foreshadows*. Eugene, OR.: Harvest House Publishing, 2022.

Mineo, Liz. The Harvard Gazette, Shadow Pandemic of Domestic Violence, June 29, 2022, https://news.harvard.edu/gazette/story/2022/06/shadow-pandemic-of-domestic-violence/, accessed October 2, 2022, 7:50 PM, CST.

Minor, Eugene. *An Exegetical Summary of 2 Timothy*, 2nd ed. Dallas, TX: SIL International, 2008.

Nellis, Ashley. No End In Sight: America's Enduring Reliance on Life Imprisonment, The Sentencing Project, February *17, 2021,* https://www.sentencingproject.org/publications/no-end-in-sight-americas-enduring-reliance-on-life-imprisonment/?gclid=EAIaIQobChMI6KqBmL_F-gIV6BPUAR0WJAgIEAAYASAAEgJsJvD_BwE,accessed October 3, 2022, 10:59 PM, CST.

Nelson, Alondra, Alexander Macgillivray, and Nik Marda , Technical Possibilities for a U.S. Central Bank Digital Currency, The White House, September 16, 2022, https://www.whitehouse.gov/ostp/news-updates/2022/09/16/technical-possibilities-for-a-u-s-central-bank-digital-currency/, accessed October 25, 2022, 8:21 pm, CST.

Newman Jr., Barclay M. *A Concise Greek-English Dictionary of the New Testament.* Stuttgart, Germany: Deutsche Bibelgesellschaft; United Bible Societies, 1993.

North, Oliver L. *Tragic Consequences.* Nashville, TN.: Fidelis Publishing, 2022

Osborne, Grant R. *Revelation* in *Baker Exegetical Commentary on the New Testament.* Grand Rapids, MI.: Baker Academic, 2006.

Panagiotakopoulos, L. Transgender medicine - puberty suppression. *Rev Endocr Metab Disord* **19**, 221–225 (2018). https://doi.org/10.1007/s11154-018-9457-0, accessed October 10, 2022.

Poushter, Jacob and Nicholas Kent, The Global Divide on Homosexuality Persists, Pew Research Center, June 25, 2020, https://www.pewresearch.org/global/2020/06/25/global-divide-on-homosexuality-persists/, accessed October 12, 2022, 2:40 pm CST.

Regan, Helen and Carlotta Dotto, US vs. China: How the world's two biggest emitters stack up on climate, CNN, Updated 2:29 AM EDT, Wed November 3, 2021, https://www.cnn.com/2021/10/28/world/china-us-climate-cop26-intl-hnk/index.html, accessed October 17, 2022, 8:40 PM CST.

Ritchie, Hannah and Max Roser, United States: CO_2 Country Profile, CO2-by-source.svg, https://ourworldindata.org/co2/country/united-states, accessed October 17, 2022, 10:55 PM CST.

Russo, Amanda. Governing the Coin: World Economic Forum Announces Global Consortium for Digital Currency Governance, World Economic Forum, January 24, 2020, https://www.weforum.org/press/2020/01/governing-the-coin-world-economic-forum-announces-global-consortium-for-digital-currency-governance/, accessed October 24, 2022, 10:00 am, CST.

Schmidt, Richard R. *Daniel's Gap Paul's Mystery, What Paused the Prophetic Calendar.* Hales Corners, WI. Prophecy Focus Ministries, 2016.

_____. *Tribulation to Triumph,* Hales Corners, WI. Prophecy Focus Ministries, 2019

Schwab, Klaus. Now is the Time for a Great Reset, World Economic Forum, June 3, 2020, https://www.weforum.org/agenda/2020/06/now-is-the-time-for-a-great-reset/, accessed October 29, 2022, 9:25 am, CST.

Swanson, James. *Dictionary of Biblical Languages with Semantic Domains: Greek (New Testament)*. Oak Harbor: Logos Research Systems, Inc., 1997.

Suzuki, David. Eating Less Meat Will Reduce Earth's Heat, David Suzuki Foundation, May 19, 2016, https://davidsuzuki.org/story/eating-less-meat-will-reduce-earths-heat/, accessed October 17, 2022, 1:40 PM CST.

Thayer, Joseph H. *Thayer's Greek-English Lexicon of the New Testament*. Peabody, MA.: Hendrickson Publishers, 1896-2002.

Varner, William. "Apocalyptic Literature," in Dictionary of Premillennial Theology A Practical Guide to the People, Viewpoints, and History of the Prophetic Studies, ed. Mal Couch. Grand Rapids: Kregel Publications, 1996.

Walsh, Brian. The Triple Whopper Environmental Impact of Global Meat Production, TIME.com, Ecocentric, October 16, 2013, https://science.time.com/2013/12/16/the-triple-whopper-environmental-impact-of-global-meat-production/, accessed October 17, 2022, 1:27 PM, CST.

Walvoord, John F. *Every Prophecy of the Bible*. Colorado Springs, CO; Chariot Victor Publishing, 1999.

Wigmore, Ivy. Definition Digital Currency, TechTarget, WhatIs.com, 2022, https://www.techtarget.com/whatis/definition/digital-currency, accessed October 29, 2022, 9:10 am, CST.

Woods, Andy, 2 Timothy 021, The De-evolution of Man Part I, 2 Tim 3:1-2a: Sermon at Sugarland Bible Church, February 14, 2016, https://slbc.org/sermon/2-timothy-021-the-de-evolution-of-man-part-1/, Accessed: Tuesday, August 16, 2022, 8:04 AM.

_____. The Call to Persevere, February 28, 2016, 2 Timothy 3:4-9 Lesson 23 2-28-16, De-evolution of Man, Part 3, https://slbc.org/sermon/2-timothy-023-the-de-evolution-of-man-part-3/ , accessed September 7, 2022, 12:15PM.

_____. 2 Timothy 030 – Why Preach The Bible? – Part 5, 2 Timothy - The Call To Persevere, May 8, 2016, Sermon, Sugarland Bible Church, Sugarland Texas, https://slbc.org/sermon/2-timothy-030-why-preach-the-bible-part-5/, accessed September 14, 2022, 9:00 am CST.

_____. 2 Timothy - The Call To Persevere, May 22, 2016, Sermon, Sugarland Bible Church, Sugarland Texas, https://slbc.org/sermon/2-timothy-031-itching-ears-of-the-last-days/accessed September 14, 2022, 9:52 am CST.

_____. 2 Timothy 032 – No Regrets, 2 Timothy 4:5-7, Lesson 33, June 5, 2016, Sermon, Sugarland Bible Church, Sugarland Texas, https://slbc.org/sermon/2-timothy-032-no-regrets/, accessed September 14, 2022, 10:45 am CST.

Yarbrough, Robert W. *The Letters to Timothy and Titus*, ed. D. A. Carson, Pillar New Testament Commentary. Grand Rapids, MI; London: William B. Eerdmans Publishing Company; Apollos, 2018.

Zodhiates, Spiros. *The Complete Word Study Dictionary: New Testament*. Chattanooga, TN: AMG Publishers, 2000.

INTERNET SOURCES AUTHORS NOT IDENTIFIED

2020-2022 United States Racial Unrest, https://en.wikipedia.org/wiki/2020%E2%80%932022_United_States_racial_unrest, accessed October 4, 10:20 PM CST.

2020-2022 United States Racial Unrest, https://en.wikipedia.org/wiki/2020%E2%80%932022_United_States_racial_unrest, accessed October 4, 10:20 PM CST.

2022 World Watch List Booklet, Open Doors, https://www.opendoorsusa.org/2022-world-watch-list-report/, accessed September 20, 2022, found on page 2 of the downloaded booklet.

8 Predictions for the World in 2030, DailyMotion, https://www.dailymotion.com/video/x7y4pxt, accessed October 29, 2022, 11:55 am, CST. The DailyMotion website includes the video under the heading "2 years ago You'll own nothing and you'll be happy (Original Twitter video)."

Active Shooter Incidents in the United States, U.S. Department of Justice Federal Bureau of Investigation.

Boomerang, What Does LGBTQ2S+ Stand For and How to Be An Ally?, contact@goboomerang.com, 20 Bay Street, 17th Floor Toronto, Ontario, M5N 2J8, https://www.goboomerang.com/blog/health-wellness/lgbtq2s-ally/, accessed October 12, 2022, 10:58 am CST.

Business Insider, "Thousands of People in Sweden are Embedding Microchips Under Their Skin to Replace ID Cards," Alexandra MA, May 14, 2018, 8:09 AM ET, https://amp.businesinsider.com/swedish-people-embed-microchips-under-skin-to-replace-id-cards-2018-5, accessed January 16, 2019.

Chief Economists Outlook Centre for the New Economy and Society, World Economic Forum, May 2022, https://www3.weforum.org/docs/WEF_Chief_Economists_Outlook_May_2022.pdf, accessed October 24, 2022, 10:40 am, CST.

Chief Economists Outlook: May 2022, https://www.weforum.org/reports/chief-economists-outlook-may-2022, World Economic Forum, May 23, 2022, accessed October 24, 2022, 10:27 am, CST.

Council of Economic Advisors, U.S. Unemployment Rates Falls to 50-Year Low, October 4, 2019, https://www.whitehouse.gov/articles/u-s-unemployment-rate-falls-50-year-low/, accessed April 29, 2020.

Digital Currency Governance Consortium, World Economic Forum, https://www.weforum.org/communities/digital-currency-governance-consortium, accessed October 25, 2022, 4:30 pm, CST.

Editors of Encyclopedia Britannica, Black Death Pandemic, Medieval Europe (Encyclopedia Britannica, Updated April 15,2020) https://www.britannica.com/event/Black-Death/Cause-and-outbreak, accessed April 17, 2020.

Gun Violence Archive, https://www.gunviolencearchive.org/past-tolls, accessed October 3, 2022, 3:45 PM CST.

How Many People Die a Year, https://www.theworldcounts.com/populations/world/deaths, accessed October 2, 2022, 5:15 PM, CST.

Legal Alert | US DOJ Responds to Biden Executive Order on Digital Assets | Husch Blackwell, July 1, 2022, https://www.huschblackwell.com/newsandinsights/us-doj-responds-to-biden-executive-order-on-digital-assets, accessed October 25, 2022, 5:34 pm, CST.

Mask Mandate Reinstated On Milwaukee County Buses, WISN-ABC, October 14, 2022, https://wisn.com/article/mask-mandate-reinstated-on-milwaukee-county-buses/41626891, accessed October 14, 2022, 3:30 PM CST.

Mass Incarceration Costs $182 Billion Every Year, Without Adding Much to Public Safety, Equal Justice Initiative, February 6, 2017, https://eji.org/news/mass-incarceration-costs-182-billion-annually/, accessed October 3, 2022, 10:52 PM, CST.

Mayo Clinic Staff, Puberty Blockers for Transgender and Gender-Diverse Youth, June 18, 2022, https://www.mayoclinic.org/diseases-conditions/gender-dysphoria/in-depth/pubertal-blockers/art-20459075, accessed October 27, 2022, 9:15 pm, CST.

Measuring Shadow Pandemic, Violence Against Women During COVID-19, https://data.unwomen.org/sites/default/files/documents/Publ

ications/Measuring-shadow-pandemic.pdf, accessed October 29, 2022, 3:10 pm, CST.

Mooney, Chris. The Hidden Driver of Climate Change That We Too Often Ignore, The Washington Post, March 9, 2016 at 1:29 p.m. EST, https://www.washingtonpost.com/news/energy-environment/wp/2016/03/09/the-hidden-driver-of-climate-change-that-we-too-often-ignore/, accessed October 17, 2022, 1:35 PM CST.

Novicio, Trish. 15 Countries With The Highest Average Carbon Dioxide Emissions Per Person, March 15, 2021, https://finance.yahoo.com/news/15-countries-highest-average-carbon-161359972.html, accessed October 17, 2022, 5:20 PM CST.

Other U.S. Government reports explain CBDCs in greater depth. See, e.g., The Future of Money and Payments. (Sep. 2022). Department of the Treasury; and Money and Payments: The US Dollar in the Age of Digital Transformation. (Jan. 2022). The Federal Reserve.

Penley, Taylor. Wisconsin parents outraged over inappropriate sex education curriculum for elementary schools: 'Really bad', https://www.foxnews.com/media/wisconsin-parents-outraged-inappropriate-sex-education-curriculum-elementary-schools-really-bad, accessed October 12, 2022, 10:24 am CST.

Queer-Vocab, https://www.scribd.com/document/99759719/Queer-Vocab, accessed October 10, 2022.

US Legal, Deferred Prosecution Law and Legal Definition, https://definitions.uslegal.com/d/deferred-prosecution/, accessed October 3, 2022, 9:37 PM CST.

US VIO (Vehicles in Operation) Vehicle Registration Statistics: See How Many Cars in The US, Hedges & Company, https://hedgescompany.com/automotive-market-research-statistics/auto-mailing-lists-and-marketing/, accessed October 17, 2022, 10:30 PM CST.

Vanderbilt University, https://www.vanderbilt.edu/lgbtqi/resources/definitions, accessed October 12, 2022, 10:40 am CST.

What is Climate Change? David Suzuki Foundation, https://davidsuzuki.org/what-you-can-do/what-is-climate-change/?gclid=EAIaIQobChMIzbuuxuvn-gIVTBTUAR2FWwT9EAAYASAAEgKm6fD_BwE, accessed October 17, 2022, 1:00 PM CST.

White House, White House Releases First-Ever Comprehensive Framework for Responsible Development of Digital Assets - The White House, September 16, 2022, https://www.whitehouse.gov/briefing-room/statements-releases/2022/09/16/fact-sheet-white-house-releases-first-ever-comprehensive-framework-for-responsible-development-of-digital-assets/, accessed October 24, 2022, 9:25 am, CST.

The White House, Fact Sheet: The Biden-Harris Electric Vehicle Charging Action Plan, - The White House, DECEMBER 13, 2021, https://www.whitehouse.gov/briefing-room/statements-releases/2021/12/13/fact-sheet-the-biden-harris-electric-vehicle-charging-action-plan/, accessed October 17, 2022, 11:25 PM, CST.

The White House, ICYMI: Week of Climate Action from the Biden-Harris Administration - The White House, September 16, 2022, https://www.whitehouse.gov/briefing-room/statements-releases/2022/09/16/icymi-week-of-climate-action-from-the-biden-harris-administration/, accessed October 17, 2022, 3:45 PM CST.

The White House, Fact Sheet: Biden-Harris Administration Launches New Climate Portal to Help Communities Navigate Climate Change Impacts - The White House, September 8, 2022, https://www.whitehouse.gov/briefing-room/statements-releases/2022/09/08/fact-sheet-biden-harris-administration-launches-new-climate-portal-to-help-communities-navigate-climate-change-impacts/, accessed October 17, 2022, 2:35PM CST.

The White House, *Technical Evaluation For A U.S. Central Bank Digital Currency System*, Office of Science and Technology Policy, September 2022, https://www.whitehouse.gov/wp-content/uploads/2022/09/09-2022-Technical-Evaluation-US-CBDC-System.pdf, accessed October 25, 2022, 8:35 pm, CST.

World Health Organization (WHO), https://www.who.int/, accessed October 14, 2022, 3:45PM CST.

WHO Coronavirus (COVID-19) Dashboard, World Health Organization, https://covid19.who.int/, accessed October 1, 2022, 7:19 PM, CST.

Who We Are, World Meteorological Organization, https://public.wmo.int/en/about-us/who-we-are#:~:text=WMO%20is%20a%20specialized%20agency,resulting%20distribution%20of%20water%20resources, accessed October 14, 2022, 3:15 PM CST.

World Population Clock, https://www.worldometers.info/world-population/, accessed 10/27/22, 3:30 pm, CST.